FROM ABANDONMENT TO HOPE

COLUMBIA HISTORY OF URBAN LIFE
Kenneth T. Jackson, GENERAL EDITOR

THE COLUMBIA HISTORY OF URBAN LIFE
Kenneth T. Jackson, GENERAL EDITOR

From Abandonment To Hope

Community-Households in Harlem

JACQUELINE LEAVITT
SUSAN SAEGERT

COLUMBIA UNIVERSITY PRESS
New York

Columbia University Press
New York   Oxford
Copyright © 1990 Columbia University Press
All rights reserved

Library of Congress Cataloging-in-Publication Data

Leavitt, Jacqueline.
From abandonment to hope : community-households in Harlem /
Jacqueline Leavitt, Susan Saegert.
p.   cm. — (Columbia history of urban life)
Bibliography: p.
Includes index.
ISBN 0-231-06846-8
1. Housing—New York (N.Y.)—Abandonment.
2. Housing rehabilitation—New York (N.Y.)
3. Housing, Cooperative—New York (N.Y.)
4. Rental housing—New York (N.Y.)
5. Harlem (New York, N.Y.)
I. Saegert, Susan. II. Title. III. Series.
HD7304.N5L37   1989
334'.1'097471—dc19
89-812
CIP

*Casebound editions of Columbia University Press books are Smyth-sewn
and printed on permanent and durable acid-free paper*

Printed in the United States of America
C 10 9 8 7 6 5 4 3 2 1

CONTENTS

Photographic insert follows p. 152

ACKNOWLEDGMENTS

MANY DIFFERENT people and organizations contributed to our writing. Without assistance from the Urban Homesteading Assistance Board (UHAB) and New York City's Housing Preservation and Development (HPD) Agency, especially those in the Division of Alternative Management (DAMP), we could not have completed this work. Theresa Kilbane and Ed Moses of UHAB deserve particular thanks for sharing their knowledge about how tenant co-ops worked as well as providing introductions to co-op residents. Theresa's knowledge of Spanish permitted us to interview Spanish-speaking tenants as well.

Joan Wallstein, Bruce Dale, Richard Heitler, Eileen White, Steve Kotick, Bill Smith, Michael Simon, and Kevin White of the Division of Alternative Management shared information and discussed their accumulated years of experience with programs for city-owned properties. Bruce Dale deserves special acknowledgment for his continuous multifaceted help and support as well as his important critical insights. Joan Wallstein also deserves recognition for her support of the project and her questioning and challenging of our ideas, based on her knowledge of city policies over the last two decades. We appreciate the work on the surveys of buildings sold by DAMP that Brooks Biderman and Emily Marks did as DAMP interns. Michael Conn, of The City University Graduate Center, also provided invaluable statistical assistance in the analysis of the survey data.

During the course of the research, Michelle Neuguebauer of Columbia University and Ruth Rae and Lynne Manzo of The City University of New York Graduate School and University Center (CUNY GSUC) served as research assistants and we thank them for their contributions. Nicholas Nelson, also of CUNY GSUC, made the final stages of the work possible through his interviewing. The School of Architecture, Urban Planning and Historic Preservation at Columbia University, the Environmental Psychology Sub-Program at CUNY GSUC, and The Graduate School of Architecture and Urban Planning (GSAUP) at the University of California at Los Angeles (UCLA), provided support for the project and preparation of the manuscript. Funding from the National Institute of Mental Health #5T32MH16911-02, the National Institute of Aging #IR03AG05024-01, and the Society for the Psychological Study of Social Issues, as well as from UCLA Academic Senate and Career Development Grants, were crucial to the conduct of the research and the preparation of the manuscript.

Dolores Hayden and Peter Marris were unstinting in the time they devoted to reading drafts, making helpful comments and allowing us to gain a fresh perspective on our research. Others at UCLA also generously read and critiqued this work, including John Friedmann, Margaret FitzSimmons, Allan David Heskin, Leonie Sandercock, and Martin Wachs. Mary Beth Welch, Gail Dubrow, and Susie Wirka worked closely with us on the ideas of the book. Nina Brown and Elissa Dennis were research assistants who searched hard for relevant materials and obscure articles. At Columbia, CUNY GSUC, and UCLA, students who participated in seminars with the authors offered insight, clarification, and challenge that informed this research.

At CUNY, GSUC, Alan Gartner, Delmos Jones, Susan Zalk, Dalton Miller Jones, and David Chapin read drafts and contributed special insights and encouragement. In addition to students already mentioned, Heléne Clark and Eric Glunt entered into the successful completion of the work both through numerous types of concrete assistance and by sharing ideas and comments on drafts with the authors.

At Columbia, Peter Marcuse and Elliott Sclar were instrumental in our reformulation of housing policy. Herbert J. Gans also contributed much through his written publications, his development of ideas, and his personal encouragement at a significant juncture. Susan Reynolds encouraged this work during her time as a student and in her role as an advocate and technical assistant for grassroots women's organizations and housing groups.

Others who read drafts and made important contributions include Sharon Sutton, Stephanie Riger, Charles Hoch, and Ruth Heifetz. We owe much to scores of women's groups and women activists. Many of the members of the National Congress of Neighborhood Women (NCNW) taught us important lessons about women's connections to the community. Jan Peterson, Linda Gray, Lisel Burns, and Ethel Velaz each made unique contributions to our learning. Bertha Gilkey and Rosemary Jackson showed us what a difference a determined woman can make when she joins with others and provides leadership. Charlotte Bunch offered an example of concerned feminism and a breadth of vision that we often appreciated.

Each of us has people to thank who contributed to our lives as well as our work.

For Susan Saegert, Gary Winkel and Laura Saegert-Winkel have been a daily and sustaining part of both. Gary has listened to the story of the research, provided intellectual challenge and at the same time done much of the domestic work which this book attempts to give its due. Laura provided a wonderful, demanding distraction to the completion of the work while also giving inspiration and appreciation when they were much needed. Susan's parents, Joe and Patricia Saegert, her sister Pamela, niece Eleanor and brother-in-law Andrew Ruth also helped keep the world of research and writing and that of family and domestic activity together during this time. Maureen Corbett filled many of the gaps in Laura's life that working parents cannot, and deserves a debt of gratitude. Joan Kelly, who died as this work began, contributed her vitality, intellectual strength, and spirit to it nonetheless.

For Jackie Leavitt, a number of people provided particular encouragement. Frances and Peter Marcuse and Nancy Aeries and Elliott Sclar shared their family life as well as their intellectual stimulation, sense of humor, and great joy of life. Bruce Dale, Tony Schuman, and Joan Wallstein provided important continuity with events in New York that extends over ten years of friendship. In Los Angeles, Irene Wolt, Margaret FitzSimmons, Penny Nanopoulos, Edward Soja, and Benedicte Dousset were unflagging in their support. Elsa Leviseur, Ruth Heifetz, Roslyn Siembieda, and John Siembieda, were reassuring on the many different levels it takes to write a book. From her own parents, Paula and Irving Leavitt, Jackie gained a sense of understanding about how people survive and can thrive.

We owe a special expression of gratitude to Kate Wittenberg, our editor at Columbia University Press. She had faith in our work since she first learned of it and has been steadfast in helping us bring it to fruition. In addition, Marsha Brown, Deborah Jolly, and especially Erika Roos at UCLA GSAUP and D'Alborn Slater and Judith Kubran at CUNY GSUC were always available and gracious in their back-up support. We appreciate the work of Susan Swider for the photography and Li You for his work on the maps.

We also thank the people who let us come into their homes and talked with us about their experiences.

Jacqueline Leavitt   *Susan Saegert*

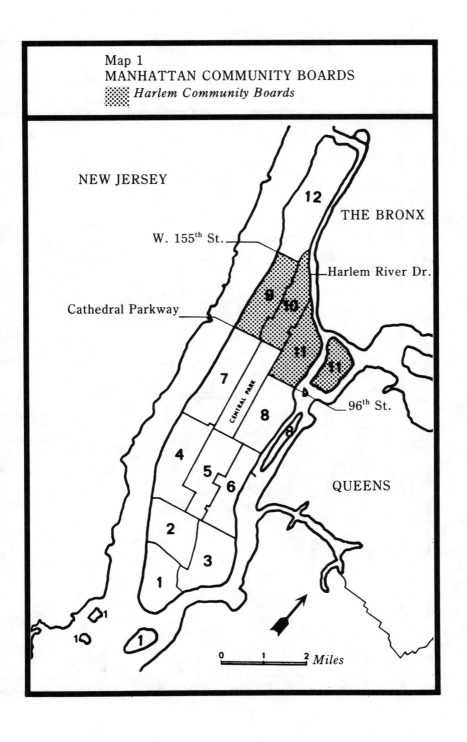

Map 1
MANHATTAN COMMUNITY BOARDS
░░░ *Harlem Community Boards*

NEW JERSEY

12

THE BRONX

W. 155th St.

Harlem River Dr.

Cathedral Parkway

9 10

11

11

7

CENTRAL PARK

8

8

96th St.

4

5

6

QUEENS

2

3

1

1

1

1

0   1   2 *Miles*

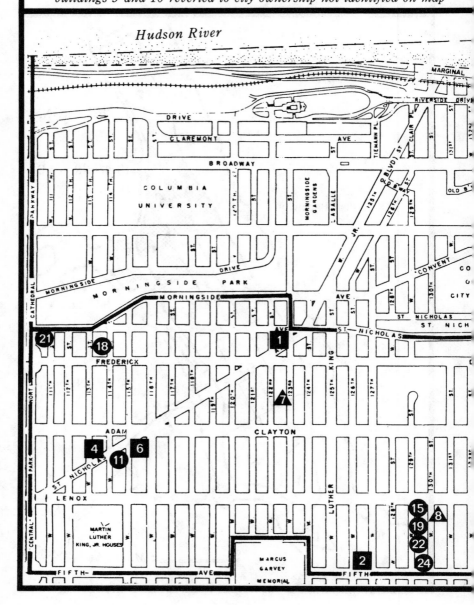

Map 2

BOARDS 9 AND 10, LOCATION OF INTERVIEWS BY BUILDING
* buildings 9 and 10 reverted to city ownership not identified on map

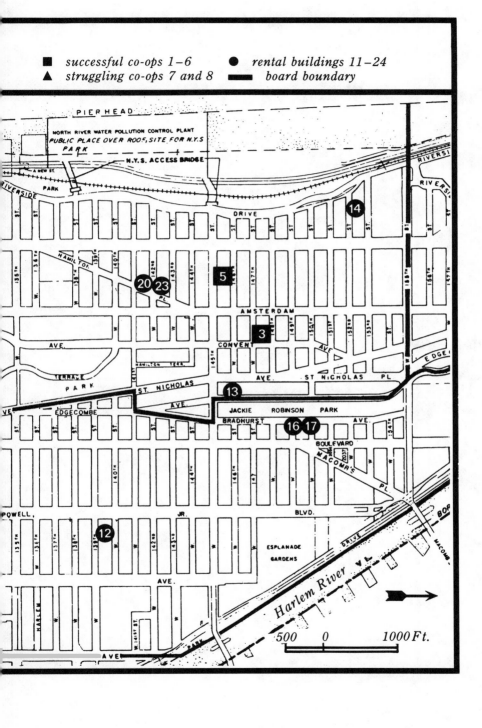

■ *successful co-ops 1–6*   ● *rental buildings 11–24*
▲ *struggling co-ops 7 and 8* ▬ *board boundary*

FROM ABANDONMENT TO HOPE

I

THE PROBLEM: HOUSING ABANDONMENT IN HARLEM

ONE

Housing Abandonment:
A Crisis for Communities
and Households

FOR TWENTY years, from the late 1960s through the early
1980s, parts of New York City experienced a progressive "de-
housing" as landlords abandoned scores of rental property.
Whole sections of the Bronx, Manhattan and Brooklyn were
devastated. The private real estate market was so weak in
some areas that owners preferred to walk away from their buildings rather
than attempt to sell them or continue to operate them at a loss. Thus the
city became the landlord of last resort for at least 100,000 residents. By
1984, New York City managed 26,000 residential units in 4,000 landlord-
abandoned buildings. In some of these buildings, tenants organized to fight
for their homes, first against landlord neglect and abandonment, and then
against the city's inability to cope with its role as largest slum landlord.
Through their unwillingness to follow landlords in the abandonment of their
homes and communities, low-income tenants resisted and reversed a tide
of abandonment so strong as to leave whole neighborhoods of one of the
capital cities of the world reduced to rubble. New York City responded to
the demands of these tenants as well as the need to relieve itself of the
burden of managing these properties by pioneering an unusual set of own-

ership transfer programs. The City's Housing Preservation and Develop-ment Agency (HPD) inaugurated the Division of Alternative Management Programs (DAMP) in 1978. Through these programs, tenants' associa-tions, community groups, and landlords with proven records of providing good low-income housing could buy city-owned buildings. Thus by 1979, the first buildings returned to the market. This book looks at what hap-pened to the people during this transition. It is widely recognized that with-out the actions of tenants and community activists, many of these buildings would be barely habitable and some neighborhoods would have become ghost towns. The city programs were necessary to provide the resources and legitimacy that tenant actions required for success, but programs alone could not have supplied the primary ingredient required to prevent the spread of devastation: people's care and commitment to place and community.

In 219 interviews, 88 that we conducted in Harlem and another 131 we analyzed (conducted by New York City staff and interns throughout the city), tenants who lived through landlord abandonment described their ex-periences and responses.[1] Harlem has been perceived as a black capital since the 1920s. As abandonment spread in New York City in the 1970s, Harlem offered a particularly graphic example of its effects. Sixty percent of the land there came to be owned by the city. The choices facing Harlem's poor black residents were restricted to a narrow, and not very elastic, band. They could have chosen to move to the suburbs, emulating the white flight of the fifties. They could move nearby, within the same area, or they could remain in the landlord-abandoned buildings. Although the number of black suburbanites has increased, the percentage remains low and the at-traction of less built-up suburban areas may not be sufficient to offset the familiar, easily accessible conveniences of urban neighborhoods. Addition-ally, many of the elderly people we interviewed who did have the option to move to the suburbs feared the isolation and disliked the way of life. Nor would rents be competitive with those in abandoned communities. As Alvin L. Schorr has pointed out,[2] low-income people living in slum condi-tions are least able to move away from those communities. They suffer serious dislocation because of the lack of money and influential geograph-ically dispersed networks that successful relocation requires. Within these low-income communities, the younger, more skilled people with fewer fam-ily obligations can move more easily.

The choice to move within the area or to a nearby block does appear in the stories of many of the people we interviewed. This choice is be-tween the relative improvement of one neighborhood over another, al-though still within the larger context of an abandoned community. Our respondents did not have enough money to move into the more gentrifying edges of their community and would perhaps be forced to leave their own neighborhood if and when gentrification expands in their direction.[3]

Confronted with these choices, many tenants stayed in their communities, some seizing the opportunity of landlord disinvestment to take control of their own housing and others struggling to survive in the communities they know and feel attached to.

The following chapters examine the consequences of people choosing to stay in an abandoned community but resisting for the most part life in a landlord-abandoned building. Most of the tenants shared a somewhat similar story of how they came to be in such circumstances. The original landlords from whom they rented have long since been replaced, initially by sons and daughters, then by a succession of seasoned and amateur speculators.[4] A building may have changed hands or "flipped" several times, with each landlord providing fewer services than the one before. Under these circumstances, profits have been known to reach 3,000 percent; for example, a building bought at $6,000 may have sold at over $190,000. What follows may be a dance of destruction with speculators negotiating mortgages with banks or a quick resale.[5] Landlords' expenditures may be reduced further by their not paying city taxes. Where there is any sign of an owner or bank, the city may be providing a subsidy by accepting a de facto installment plan on owed property taxes or providing emergency fuel in winter months. Thus buyers can purchase a building to collect a few months' rent, invest no money, withhold tax payments, and then walk away from their tenants. But the economic transactions fail to convey the impact they have on a community. Beneath the economically dry history of landlord abandonment of low-income housing lies another story of dauntless community homemaking. When the power of this resource is unleashed from the economic and legal systems that constrain it, dilapidated housing units cast off as a landlord's investment can become secure, proudly maintained tenant-owned homes. Even where tenants do not move all the way to ownership of their building, their efforts to make and maintain homes give rise to collective efforts to reverse the abandonment process.

PATTERNS OF TENANTS' RESPONSES

AS NEW York City failed to successfully manage the large volume of housing abandoned in the mid-1970s,[6] the media carried frequent stories of tenants dying from lack of heat in abandoned buildings.

Housing activists militated for more humane conditions for tenants and proposed alternative programs. In response, New York City initiated a number of programs to stabilize and reclaim still inhabited landlord-abandoned buildings.[7] Two of the programs were in direct response to tenants and community groups who were attempting to improve their deteriorated housing conditions. In these programs, ownership was transferred from the city to a tenants' association (Tenant Interim Lease, TIL), who formed a limited equity co-op or to a nonprofit community based organization, which would train tenants to co-op their buildings (Community Management Program, CMP). A third program was the city's response to private landlords who were managing distressed properties, wanted to manage more, and passed the city's screening of their management practices (Private Ownership and Management Program, POMP). (See exhibit A in appendix for a description of programs.) At the time of our study, these three programs had the highest volume of sales. (See exhibit B in appendix for sales by program.)

Tenants responded differently to their initial awareness of landlord abandonment and to the programs initiated by the city to stabilize and reclaim buildings. Some had already begun to take control of their buildings prior to city ownership. Others used their energies to cope with the daily problems of abandonment. For a few, city ownership came as a surprise preceded by little deterioration of services. These different experiences led to varied housing goals, differential involvement with city programs, and ultimately to alternative dispositions of the buildings. Patterns in tenant responses and experiences led us to categorize the buildings studied according to the type of tenure and management during the study period: cooperative tenant ownership; continued city ownership with tenant management aimed at eventual co-op ownership or rental buildings owned by community groups or screened private landlords.

The tenants' stories we tell are unromanticized accounts of self-help and sweat equity, of tiring days and unrelieved nights where people took up hammers and nails and repieced their buildings. Individual experiences of living through landlord abandonment differed remarkably depending on whether or not a building became or was attempting to become a co-op. In these circumstances, tenants exhibited a sense of empowerment that contrasted strongly with the psychological sense of abandonment conveyed by many, especially of the elderly tenants, in buildings brought back from abandonment by community or private landlords.

The survey data from interviews with 131 people supported and extended these findings. Tenants in co-ops rated their housing as physically better, better managed and more satisfactory. They reported more attachment to their homes and more cooperative relationships among tenants. They participated more in the upkeep of the buildings. While many demographic variables such as ethnicity, household type, and length of residence did not affect differential ratings of co-ops and rental buildings, retired people and unemployed residents expressed greater positive evaluations in the co-ops. These groups also viewed their neighborhoods more positively when they lived in co-ops.

Our qualitative data indicated a different pattern of response among residents of co-ops already bought by the tenants and those in tenant-managed buildings still owned by the city. While no study that we know of has looked carefully at how tenants experience and respond to landlord abandonment and co-op development, other studies suggest that different patterns are rather general. Robert Kolodny studied some of the first examples of self-management and low-income cooperatives in New York City.[8] He found higher satisfaction on many dimensions among completed as compared to prospective co-op residents, although the latter had higher expectations that living in a co-op would change their lives. In a second study of early efforts by tenants to control their housing, Ronald Lawson also found high satisfaction among low-income co-op residents, especially when they compared their situations to living in rental buildings.[9] Turnover was low, vacancies were easily filled, and service and maintenance problems werc minor in most buildings. Residents particularly valued controlling their housing situations in both studies. However, Lawson also distinguished among more and less successful attempts at tenant control. Less successful buildings had weaker organizational structures, higher tenant turnover, and more problems with leadership succession. More successful co-ops in both studies had histories of more technical assistance. Neither of these studies investigated the social and psychological dynamics in actual versus prospective, or in more versus less successful, co-ops. The three chapters devoted here to describing successful co-ops, prospective co-ops, and rental buildings include both building histories, resident evaluations, and analysis of the social psychological dynamics underlying and accompanying these situations.

In the case of successful co-ops, some tenant leaders emerged. They organized other tenants to take advantage of the city program to reclaim landlord-abandoned buildings by forming limited equity cooperatives, where each tenant paid $250 for a share in the building.[10] In each of these buildings, their success reflected the ability of the leadership structure to involve a great many of the tenants, identify technical assistance, and by the

extension of their visions and efforts, provide more than shelter. They had
set up "club rooms" where people dropped in to socialize; in a couple of
cases the leaders were exploring the idea of a day-care center. More than
in any of the other buildings, the social life of the tenants was connected
through the co-oping of the building.

In the second scenario, tenants faced more struggles in co-oping, some
finally becoming a cooperative with the aid of technical assistance from
outside groups, others reverting back to the central housing inventory
managed by the city. In these buildings, tenant financial and human resources were often more limited, leadership and organizational development was more difficult, and the community offered fewer supports for
tenant activism.

In the third scenario, tenants were renters whose owners were either
nonprofit community groups or private landlords. Sometimes tenants had
made efforts to take control but problems of conflict, lack of leadership
sophistication, and isolation from technical assistance and community support derailed their attempts. In other buildings where abandonment was
almost unnoticed as the owners changed hands from private landlords to
city-ownership to other more benign private landlords, tenant responses
were more reactive and passive. Many simply experienced a continuation
of life in rental buildings, not very satisfactory, certainly not empowering,
but not desperate either.

TECHNICAL ASSISTANCE AND GOVERNMENT
PROGRAMS: THE ESSENTIAL FACTORS

C OMPARISONS OF the scenarios highlight the importance of
technical assistance and government programs, particularly in the
formation of limited equity cooperatives where there were conflicts and struggles. In comparison, tenants in buildings owned by community groups observed gains in physical conditions but the interviews show
there was an absence of either strong leadership or tenant support for co-
oping. There were some signs of neighboring. In buildings where the bail-
out program was replacing private landlords with private landlords, there
were even fewer indications of tenants knowing each other or that cooperatives could ever work.

The toll abandonment exacts on human life is strongly determined by
how the government responds to who is housed and how communities are

organized. Government funds affect how much technical assistance is available, either directly through its own bureaucracies or through subsidizing nonprofit groups. The halcyon days of technical assistance to grassroots groups were the 1960s' War on Poverty which segued into the 1970s' funding for local development corporations. The War on Poverty was initially directed to the unrepresented poor, and it resulted in marginal improvements for some part of the minority community. A few of the tenant leaders we interviewed drew on their experiences with anti-poverty agencies to assemble resources to fight abandonment. Subsequent legislation attempted to build self-sufficiency into nonprofit local community groups, some of which survived to become stronger through the city's programs. The amount of funding is also tied to requirements for eligibility, for example, mandates for including certain groups or covering a wider territory. This has repercussions on organizational structure, different types having the effect of encouraging or discouraging different participants. Cooperative organizations, for example, have been found to encourage female leadership. Being able to obtain funding also influences the ways in which tenants and community based groups are perceived by foundations, private individuals, and governmental agencies, and this influences further funding.

Funding also reflects how a governing body is viewed by the wider society. Had the city done nothing to save landlord-abandoned buildings, the homelessness problem so visible in the 1980s would have occurred much earlier. Had the city only promoted low-income limited equity cooperatives, the private sector would have objected, alleging socialism and giveaways, particularly about buildings in the better-located, hot real estate markets. When the government steps in to abandoned communities, as it has here, a standoff is at least possible. Some buildings will be saved, perhaps entire parts of neighborhoods, and subsidies and restrictions on speculation will ensure security for some low-income households.

While those who participated in our research survived and sometimes transformed the circumstances of landlord abandonment, their successes and failures began and ended with the limits of government assistance. The combination of landlord abandonment and support from local and federal programs formed a crack in the system of housing provision. From the mid-1970s to the mid-1980s, when the city used federal dollars to repair and rehabilitate buildings, an average of $30,000,000 a year was spent on transfer of ownership programs. Each program sets limits on the extent of repairing or rehabilitating an apartment. During the time of our study, tenant-initiated cooperatives received the least amount of funds for each apartment, ranging from $3,000 to $5,000. In comparison, private landlords received $5,000 to $7,000 for each apartment and community groups about $25,000 per apartment.[11]

GENDER, RACE, AND AGE

THE INTERVIEWS highlight the tenants' patterns of response, and in particular the ways in which women emerged as leaders and nurturers of cooperatives. We had begun the research intending to explore issues about women, poverty, and housing. City-owned housing whose households are predominantly poor, almost 60 percent female-headed, and primarily black and of Hispanic origin presented the opportunity we were looking for.[12] Serendipitously we found that older people, women but also men, were involved in the re-creation of a suitable living environment. Their color was also not incidental to the stories we tell. Race was a constraint, a visible reminder to our respondents about the limitations to their moving. But race also emerged as a source of strength drawn from a collective history. These findings are presented in later chapters.

Having found most housing evaluations one-dimensional, we had hoped to look beyond the issue of just shelter. We were concerned also about peoples' perceptions of themselves and their environments. In our research the incredible strengths and unacknowledged resources of people in conditions brought on by landlord abandonment constantly asserted themselves. Most of the people we spoke with were women. They were left in this scene of abandonment, as they were left out of the housing market, to make homes as best they could without access to sufficient money or other resources that count in the larger society. Their experience of reclaiming abandoned buildings clashed with their standing in the larger society. Many saw in these buildings that could no longer be profitable for a landlord the potential for remaking their community.

The interviews reveal that people were empowered through fighting landlord abandonment. This was clearest among the tenants in the successful cooperatives. Their empowerment was linked to gender. Women were responsible for the daily acts of taking care of their households. Their domestic responsibilities within individual households spilled over into homemaking on a building-wide scale. They took care of physical conditions within the building, and through the social life of the building, organized other tenants and took control over their living environment. Empowerment also grew out of place attachment to particular buildings and to Harlem. Race and age were intertwined with place attachment. The leaders had memories of what life was like in Harlem; this acted as a point of departure in staking a claim to their buildings.

These findings lead us to propose what we call the community-household model, a guideline for developing low-income housing policy issues by juxtaposing the actions taken by people themselves with the resources of the community.[13] Household activities reflected in domestic tasks and social life, both identified primarily with women, do not stop at individual doors. The skills needed and the values attached to households when applied to a building have the potential to effect changes in the larger community. The community, in turn, can act as a resource base for collective households, offering support from churches, schools, other nonprofit organizations, and businesses, to stem abandonment.

In the final chapters we suggest ways in which training, planning, and design, as well as national and more local housing policies, can encourage the development of community-households. The city programs then become the backdrop for understanding tenants' responses to landlord abandonment. That people were able to do much more with these programs is testimony to the leadership exerted by those who society thinks are least able to possess those qualities. That poor black older women and men were in the forefront, that they even have the potential to be leaders, is generally ignored in the development of most low-income housing policy.

TWO

The Setting and the People

WHILE HOUSING abandonment occurred throughout the low-income communities of New York City, the place we studied is a very specific one: Harlem. The word is so connected with black life that it can unleash a torrent of thoughts that go flickering across the mind. If white, there may be a mixture of fear and anxiousness that reveals the racism that has suddenly recaptured the media's attention, dispelling the illusion that all race relations were resolved with JFK's death and Johnson's War on Poverty programs, Martin Luther King's death, and Jesse Jackson's candidacy for president. It did not take the Howard Beach murder in Queens to announce that animosity not only lingers but festers. It is reflected in the racial composition at a music festival during Harlem Week when the only whites are people hawking political pamphlets or an avid jazz fan or foreigner, and in the welter of statistics that show the growing economic gap between whites and nonwhites.

If black, Harlem can be a whole other world of comfort, a cultural spiritual home. It provides a collective history for blacks. Some still see it as a place to get better jobs and a better life. Many have ambivalent feelings, particularly about raising children in a community where there is widespread crime, drugs, rotting houses, rotten education, and the unemployment that plagues their race. The mix of emotions about Harlem goes back to its earliest days when Harlem in space became instrumental in the creation of Harlem of the mind. Historians date the identification of a black community in Harlem either to the period between 1890 and 1914,[1] or to that between 1905 and 1925.[2] Black Harlem was more concentrated then. It ran from about 130th to 145th streets, from Madison Avenue on the east to Seventh Avenue on the west. The hub was not 125th but 135th Street between Fifth and Seventh Avenues (see map 1). A white enclave was as close as 130th Street between Lenox and Fifth Avenues.[3]

Harlem did not become "a Negro world unto itself"[4] until the pressure of more blacks moving into New York, the leaving of the white population, and the tactics of black real estate entrepreneurs renting units in buildings originally intended for whites occurred. Margaret Perry wrote that "it seemed inevitable by 1915 that Harlem would become a black community,"[5] "'a place' as well as a state of mind."[6] Tenants who came to New York City during this time told us of their experiences of being the first blacks to rent apartments in their buildings. They spoke of a physical world of attractive lobbies and doormen, intermingled with remembered excitement about their opportunities for the future.

The Harlem Renaissance period focused world attention on its poets, writers and other artists. The period flourished from about 1919 to 1932, and crystalized the Harlem of the mind which was to endure long after. Nathan Irvin Huggins described the legacy of Renaissance Harlem.

> Of course the place remained—a part of a city—but it was still more than that. The very name continued to connote a special spirit, new vitality, black urbanity, and black militancy. Through the activities, the writings, the promotion of Negroes in the 1920s, Harlem had become a racial focal point for knowledgeable black men the world over. To them, Harlem had come to mean what no other place-name could. And so it remained, for a time, a race capital.[7]

By 1925, "nearly a quarter of a million blacks lived in Harlem. By 1930, at least seven in ten blacks living in Manhattan lived in Central Harlem."[8] The physical grace and elegance of one of the successful co-ops embodies this flowering. The building had been the first luxury apartment building built in Harlem intended for blacks, a fact of pride and prominence in the account of the woman most responsible for organizing the co-op. In another co-op, the legacy of black musicians and performers lingers in the minds of tenants and still attracts performing artists to the building who were related by blood and spirit to the place. For others, those years of cultural expression are mainly fond memories, as they are for the retired dancer living in a building resold to a private landlord. After forty-five years in the building, she felt no one would come to her aid if the ever-expected worst would happen and a mugger would catch her on her way into the building, coming home from a jazz concert late at night.

LIVING THROUGH THE DEPRESSION AND EARLY WAR YEARS

H UGGINS HAS written that the optimism of writers of the Renaissance reflected what they had lived through in the twenties. Yet to be experienced was the Depression and the "special vulnerability" for blacks, a war with its "pathological racism," and the years of a "dream deferred."[9]

> The generation . . . was optimistic and progressive. It would take more defeat than they had yet known for them to believe that what they were building would, in time, imprison them.[10]

With the Depression, the riots of 1935 and 1941—the first a result of a rumor that a teenage boy was beaten by police, following an incident in a five-and-dime store on 125th Street;[11] the second the beating of a soldier by a policeman, following an incident in a hotel[12]—a collective disappointment set in. Jane White, a black actress, poignantly described it. In the thirties you felt "that *if* you kept your nose clean, and if you *went* to school, and you *held* a good job, and you *made* a little money, and you washed and ironed your clothes—that it was all going to turn out all right. This turned out to be a fallacy"[13]

But it was a fallacy perhaps more recognized by intellectuals and later generations than by many of the elderly leaders with whom we spoke. For example, a 77-year-old man who had been instrumental in saving his building from becoming uninhabitable spoke of his similar experiences and beliefs. As a merchant seaman, he had been active in black labor union activities during the Depression. As a very involved father, he raised his family very much in the old mold, carefully watching his children and teaching them to keep their noses clean, go to school, and get jobs. Holding a job as a tailor, he encouraged and financed their ability to go beyond his old formula for success by getting educated. For his reward, one son did rise to prominence as a basketball star. He spoke proudly of the son while explaining the presence of his grown daughter just released from a psychiatric hospital and living in his apartment.

Discrimination was blatant during the Depression and post-Depression years. Blacks were the first to be fired from jobs as chauffeurs and maids. Whites haggled over how little money to pay domestics. Adam Clayton Powell, Jr., looking back at the jobs that "Negroes" had before the Depression wrote they "were never the best—bellhops, waiters, porters, red caps, elevator boys, kitchen mechanics and pot wrestlers, with here and there a shipping clerk or a typist,"[14] but they were still jobs. Blacks were not even hired for federal relief jobs. A small elite—"civil service employees, professional men and their families, social workers, the big names of Harlem's theatrical life, numbers overlords and that mysterious group of the well-groomed and well-fed who never work"[15]—lived on Sugar Hill. The others lived in conditions that to this day have not been completely ameliorated, in:

> hovels along 133d Street where one hall toilet serves a floor of four apartments for as many as twenty-five people, no private bathtubs or public bathtubs. Some owners have installed bathtubs in the kitchens. Along Fifth Avenue, from 135th Street to 138th Street, is one of the worst spots. Here are flats with the old-fashioned toilets, which are usually so broken that the refuse flushes down on the floor below. Gaping holes in the skylights allow cold air to sweep down the staircase freezing the toilets so that for weeks during the winter they cannot be used[16]

POST-WAR CONDITIONS IN HARLEM

HOUSING CONDITIONS did not improve in the forties. Ann Petry's social protest novel, *The Street,* evoked an image of what was available in post-war Harlem on 116th Street between Seventh and Eighth avenues.[17] Petry's protagonist, Lutie, looking for an apartment for herself and her son contemplates the layout of a building: "One A must be the darkest apartment, the smallest, most unrentable apartment, and the landlord would feel mighty proud that he'd given the 'Super' a first-floor apartment."[18] Reminiscent of Karl Marx's reporting of children and grown men who would sleep in shifts at their work-place, or the science fiction movie, "Soylent Green," where stairways and halls were used as bedrooms, Lutie stands in reverie, thinking:

it was really a pity they couldn't somehow manage to rent the halls, too. Single beds. No. Old army cots would do. It would bring in so much more money. If she were a landlord, she'd rent out the hallways. It would make it so much more entertaining for the tenants. Mr. Jones and wife could have cots number one and two; Jackson and girlfriend could occupy number three. And Rinaldi, who drove a cab nights, could sublet the one occupied by Jackson and girlfriend.[19]

One of the older women leaders of a struggling co-op lived in such a building which was destined to be rehabilitated much beyond its original level of habitability due to her efforts. She and others of the tenants were among those who never really recovered their jobs or health after the Depression. Nonetheless, her ambivalent attachment to Harlem and her home held her there and prodded her to change her conditions when they reached their worst.

In the fifties, in the wake of the Supreme Court decision in *Brown v. Board of Education,* education seemed to be the way out of Harlem, as it was for the basketball-playing son of the tailor. In the sixties, on the eve of the War on Poverty programs, and two years away from the riots and rebellions that erupted in Harlems across the country, Harlem in New York was a place to get away from. Indeed many of the elderly leaders of co-ops stated with a mixture of pride and sadness that their children had gotten out, that they would not return to take over the homes their parents were fighting to save. As it turned out, this was sometimes a wrong perception. Children of old tenants are now returning to one of the successful co-ops in which the older leaders felt this would never happen. The ambivalence of their exit and the surprise of their return reflects the ethos of the sixties as expressed in Rosa Guy's novel *Bird At My Window.*[20] The conflict between choosing to stay as Bubba did, and leaving as did his girlfriend Gay, plays out an internal drama common to the period. Bubba's girlfriend

> wanted to get him out of Harlem. Worked overtime to get him out of Harlem. From the very beginning she showed him she had no intention of living there, she thought that Harlem was a ghetto not fit to live in. It was alright to fall in love and screw around in, though.[21]

About twenty years later, another Bubba is found in Sonia Sanchez' prose poem and education is again introduced as a way out of Harlem for its women.[22] This Bubba is a young man who she, Sanchez' alter ego, used to play handball with. She goes off to Hunter College. Each time she returns, Bubba and she are at another stage.

She: Words. Books. Waltzed me to the tune of Hunter College days. I severed all relationships on my block. Each night I drenched myself with words so I could burst through the curtain of Harlem days and nights. My banner was my tongue as I climbed toward the gourds of knowledge and recited a poem of life.

He: . . . Of greasy overalls. Of two children screaming for food. Of a wife pregnant with another. Of the same old neighborhood.

The tragedy and the irony was that she was able to return while he could not get out ever.

She: One day, after graduation, I returned to the old neighborhood. I recognized a few faces and sat and talked. I was glad to sit down. I had taught all day long. I answered the questions of my former neighbors. And the tension of the years dissolved in our laughter . . .

He: . . . There he sat. Nodding out the day. The years.
. . . He finally pulled himself up off the bench. He stood up with the last breath of a dying man.
"How 'bout a few bucks girl? Gotta see a man 'bout something."

Tenants of landlord-abandoned buildings in Harlem lived through all this history and it shaped their lives, their responses to abandonment, and their expectations of the future. Most clearly, it affected their desire to stay and to take control of their buildings.

Today there are at least two perceptions of reality in Harlem. The Harlem Chamber of Commerce is promoting tourism, singling out the residential stock that writer and activist James Weldon Johnson hailed as one attraction in the early 1920s. A grand new building complex has opened on the north side of Central Park. Well-built, long-abandoned six-story apartment buildings are being rehabilitated. A lottery for city-owned brownstone properties was swamped with people competing for them. There are city requests for proposals for the vacant buildings. Newspapers carry accounts of black young professionals returning to a Harlem their parents left as they sought out safer places to raise their children.

The second reality is that even as very minimal gentrification by blacks, but also by some whites, is occurring at the edges of Harlem, completely abandoned blocks, or ones where a lone building may stand are near-by.[23]

The reality and emotions of people are caught in a tornado-like swirl where the fixing up is happening at the same time as abandonment and the tearing down.

SITUATING HARLEM AND ITS SCOPE
OF ABANDONMENT

THE EXPANSION and contraction of what is Harlem has varied from the 1920s. If there is one part of Harlem popularly viewed as the quintessential core today, it is probably 125th Street. This Street goes from river to river. This is where the visitor will find the Apollo Theater—under new management and being refurbished—where talented entertainers have been discovered; the State Office Building—consciously planned for this location as an employment generator; the old Theresa Hotel where Fidel Castro chose to stay when delivering his maiden speech to the United Nations—now an office building; the station stop for trains to Westchester County and Connecticut, to and from Grand Central Railroad Station. The plaza in front of the State Office Building, while lacking any architectural distinction, has become a rallying place for politicians and entertainers. It is where Jesse Jackson spoke during his 1984 and 1988 presidential campaigns, and where Harlem Week is celebrated. It is the new "Harlem Square," replacing Seventh Avenue and 125th Street where orators once held forth.

Since 1976–77, New York City has had an elaborate land use planning process which mandates that all developers seek approval from members of an appointed community board. The entire city is divided into fifty-nine community boards. Harlem extends into three community boards, numbers 9, 10, and 11, roughly approximating West, Central, and East Harlem (see map 2). It did not take excessive research to realize that there were many city-owned buildings in these boards. Abandonment is not a hidden process and signs of it were quite apparent even before official figures were released. By 1984, the two boards in which we interviewed, 9 and 10, particularly 10, had large inventories of properties the city had acquired from tax delinquent landlords. More than 22,000 units in about 1,500 buildings, about two-thirds in Central Harlem, had become city-owned.[24] In the early 1980s, most of the buildings sold to tenants, nonprofits, or new landlords were also in these two community boards: the sold inventory in 9 and 10 totaled 88 buildings with almost 2,200 units. At the time of our study, only one community group and two landlords had bought buildings in Community

Board 9, and two community groups and one landlord in Community Board 10. We interviewed in all those buildings, as well as in successful and failed tenant cooperatives. Table 2.1 shows the profile of buildings by type of program in which we interviewed.

THE LANDSCAPE OF ABANDONMENT

W E BEGAN our research with the understanding that maps and figures don't reveal a whole story, neither the despair of living in neglected buildings, nor the hopes and joy and pride in fighting abandonment. We interviewed people in their own homes, and the walk or ride into Harlem let us observe it at closer hand. Block after block, the landscape of abandonment continues, and empty brick, brownstone, or wood shells create almost a separate world. Being there, we were better able to grasp the enormity of what tenants were facing. The conditions of the blocks and neighborhoods also revealed what remained to be done. On virtually every block, there was other city-owned property, either vacant lots or vacant buildings or both. One blockfront, for example, out of ten

TABLE 2.1
Profile of Tenant Interview Sites in Community Boards 9 and 10

	CB 9		CB 10	
	Sold	Not Sold	Sold	Not Sold
Cooperatives	2		5	
Tenant interim lease/ leasing				1
Former tenant interim lease now central management				2
Community management rentals	1	1	3	4
Private landlord rentals	2		3	
Subtotal	5	1	11	7
TOTAL				24

buildings, included a tenant cooperative and three vacant buildings, two were city owned. On another blockfront, a building managed by a community group was surrounded on one side by a tenant cooperative and on the other by two vacant buildings. The patterns varied. Sometimes a building backed up to a vacant lot or building. In other cases, one end of a block was completely occupied, and the other was a stretch of vacant lots and boarded-up buildings.

When the buildings are boarded up, windows are filled in with blank gray cinderblock or tin or decorated with colored vinyl decals of shutters, flower pots and curtains in different combinations.[25] The latter is called the Occupied Look program, one many passers-by see as a bureaucrat's folly to beautify abandonment. On blocks where some buildings remain standing, and others demolished, nothing remains of formerly inhabited apartments except the colored walls that were once rooms. On roofs and in abandoned lots where ailanthus grows rampant, the accoutrements of daily life are also abandoned, an old-fashioned bathtub with clawed legs, a rotting mattress or a rusting coffeepot, stray curtain, or a flower pot or hot plate on a window sill.

EXPERIENCING ABANDONMENT

FOR RESIDENTS, daily life goes on among these ghosts of homes, whether they resist the tide of abandonment alone, as a last inhabitant in an almost empty building or resist collectively, in the few still functioning buildings on the block. What they face in their neighborhoods on a spring or early summer day is an atmosphere that can be benign, empty lots turned into community gardens and bushes blossoming in Frederick Law Olmsted designed parks. Much of life in urban communities where there is housing abandonment is familiar. People are on the streets, catch trains and buses to and from work. Kids dawdle on the way to school or bound out of the doors at the end of their day. In the heat of summer, fire hydrants provide watering holes for children, who dash in and out on the street, exhilarated by the relief of the cool sprinkling. Women wheel carts filled with groceries, old people lean out the windows to observe the street scene, mothers and fathers pick up kids, young men and women eye each other's dress. On the major shopping streets, wooden and metal structures are dragged out each day and the goods displayed to catch the attention of passing shoppers. These activities co-exist with more dismal scenes: clumps of people, mostly men, huddling around fires they've started in garbage cans; drug addicts hanging out, their heads flopping down over their chests. The presence of many men on the street during working hours speaks of high unemployment and difficulty in finding even day labor.

Some semblance of a normal life is maintained by those who live in an abandoned building whose deterioration invariably means the loss of creature comforts. Plumbing leaks, toilets fall through rotting floors to apartments beneath, plaster peels, carrying with it the threat of lead paint poisoning, and faulty electric wiring routinely short circuits. Some buildings have a particular smell of neglect. Fires bring lingering odors of charred wood. Where roofs have been burned and rainwater has leaked behind the walls, there is a damp smell; where outer doors to the street are not secure, urine smells permeate the halls. Poorly painted walls with rotting moldings and decaying wooden stairs in hallways with no circulating air give off their own peculiar dank disagreeable odors. Rooms in the oldest buildings, some with no outside window, only dimly lit from narrow airshafts, and kitchens with ages-old linoleum, hold in the smells and dirt.

At first abandonment is experienced as a piecemeal process rather than a cataclysmic blow, like a fire that sweeps away whole blocks and neighborhoods. In many buildings, the onset is initiated either with the firing of doormen, elevator operators, and superintendents, or the lack of heat. Then other services begin to deteriorate. There may be no electricity. With entrance doors no longer secure, strangers may lie in wait in the dark halls or stairwells. In buildings where elevators are still running, a cat-and-mouse game is sometimes played. A stranger will follow a tenant into the elevator in order to see what button is pressed. Then getting out a floor earlier, the stranger runs up the stairs in order to waylay the tenant as he or she leaves the elevator.

How do people manage to live with all the stresses of abandonment, the discomfort and insecurity of their living arrangements, and the fearfulness engendered by the widespread and visible use of drugs in their neighborhoods? How do they go beyond surviving to attempting to take control of their lives and communities? The answers we found connect the daily acts of survival of individuals to the survival of whole buildings. Many of those who lived through landlord abandonment had behind them long lives of struggling to survive. When landlords walked away, the problems they confronted may have increased in quantity, but they presented extreme cases of familiar problems.

As stressful as it is to live under conditions of abandonment, staying in the buildings presented some opportunities. Many of the people we interviewed mobilized themselves and others to improve conditions in their buildings. The process of organizing and becoming cooperative owners drew on the resources of the tenants and brought out the taken-for-granted strengths that had sustained them during abandonment. The social relationships and informal support that made daily life possible served as the basis for learning to work together. Older people, most frequently older women, emerged as leaders by extending the domestic and social skills they had needed to make homes in poor communities all their lives, to the task of saving their buildings. Their positive attachment to the places where they lived and to the people they knew combined with their perceptions of few viable housing options to keep them focused on their goal of achieving control of their housing.

At the outset of our study we also knew that people's lives, affected as they were by landlord abandonment, were also shaped by and reflected a complex web of personal and institutional relationships that centered around race, ethnicity, income, age, marital status, health, presence of children, etc. The population profile in Harlem was of people who experienced all sorts of abandonment by a public sector.

WHO THE PEOPLE ARE IN HARLEM

IN 1980, the overall population of Harlem was nearly 500,000 people. Blacks and Hispanics were a majority, 49 percent black and 34 percent Hispanic, the remainder white (14 percent) and other (3 percent). There are dramatic differences associated with race when Harlem is compared to New York City. In 1980—and it is not much different today—Central Harlem was almost completely black; its median family income of $10,400 was far below the citywide average of $22,000. The figures were reversed for those on public assistance: in 1979, 43 percent of families in Central Harlem received public assistance compared to 14 percent citywide. Between 1970 and 1980, New York City lost 10 percent of its population; Central Harlem more than one-third. One person households predominated in Central Harlem, about one-third compared to 29 percent overall. Fifty-eight percent of the households were families with children, higher by 10 percent than citywide. Only about 7 percent of all families were large with six or more persons. In 1980, Central Harlem's age distribution with about 16 percent 65 and over ranked among the highest of all community boards in Manhattan; citywide this elderly population was only 13.5 percent but overall was increasing at a fast rate. At the same time, Central Harlem's approximately 40 percent of people between 15 and 44 years was the lowest of all Manhattan boards, and its 25 percent between 45 and 64, the older working age population, was one of the two highest in Manhattan among an age group that has been increasing steadily.

In 1980, Community Board 9 which includes West Harlem also suffered a decline in population but, at about 9 percent, was lower than the citywide average. West Harlem's age distribution revealed a younger population than Central Harlem: there were about 18 percent 14 years and less, 50 percent between 15 and 44, 20 percent between 45 and 64, and 12 percent 65 and over. Community Board 11, however, which includes East Harlem had a 26 percent decrease in overall population, and also a young population. The age distribution in East Harlem was 24 percent 14 years and less, 46 percent between 15 and 44, 20 percent between 45 and 64, and 11 percent 65 and over.

Later figures from April 1985 by community board are available for programs such as income maintenance, medical assistance, day care, special services for children, and home care services.[26] These figures reinforce the trends among the community boards evident in 1980. Community Boards 10 and 11 have higher percentages of persons served as a percentage of the entire borough of Manhattan and of the city, either ranking first or second, in every category except persons in nursing homes where Board 9 follows Board 11. Of the three boards, Board 10, Central Harlem, has a higher percentage of persons served by foster care and findings of child abuse and maltreatment. Board 11 has higher percentages than the two other boards for persons receiving public assistance, food stamps, medicaid, Supplemental Security Income, child care, and nursing home care.

Aware of all these factors, but with very little prior information about the profile of tenants in landlord-abandoned buildings in Harlem (the first systematic survey of tenants by Alternative Management Program was analyzed by us but that data was unavailable until after we began this study), we proceeded to pick buildings in which we would interview tenants.

PICKING THE BUILDINGS:
INTERVIEWING THE TENANTS

W E WANTED to start with those who had bought their buildings from the city.[27] The process of making contact with building residents, knocking on doors and being welcomed or turned away gave us firsthand experience with the social norms, the fears and expectations residents had for interactions with neighbors and strangers. The first person contacted was always a tenant leader.[28] The leader would give us a picture of the kinds of tenants living in the building—age, sex, working or not, with children or without, and sometimes information about the level of participation in the co-op. Then she or he would contact a few other tenants specifically to ask if we could interview them or tell them we would be calling. More generally leaders put out the word that it was okay to talk with us. After that, we would follow-up on contacts the leaders suggested. We would also knock on doors and talk with whoever answered. We would solicit new contacts from all those interviewed. Non-leaders were almost as willing as leaders to speak with us. Sometimes we could not arrange a suitable time, or in the case of residents selected at random, an interview was sometimes impossible because we happened to arrive at an inconvenient time. However, we never spent more than a few minutes finding someone who was willing to participate in the study. As we found out later, this openness to answering unexpected knocks on the door and talking to strangers was an indication of the social connectedness of tenants and their general sense of security in the building.

None of those we contacted in co-ops or prospective co-ops refused us. The high regard tenants had for the technical assistance received from the nonprofit Urban Homesteading Assistance Board (UHAB) and for the individuals we worked with had much to do with our reception. In addition, the cooperation of city staff and their interest in ameliorating problems we identified gave us credibility with tenants. We identified ourselves by our academic affiliations and said that we were interested in finding out about the tenants' experiences of forming limited equity co-ops in landlord-abandoned buildings. We explained that we thought existing evaluations of the city program through which they had bought the building did not contain enough information about the tenants' contributions and problems; therefore, we would like to talk to them. Tenants were justly proud of what they had done. They wanted their stories told. We spoke with 88 people, mainly in face-to-face interviews, primarily in their homes. We asked about their personal history, the history of the building's physical conditions, landlord's and manager's responsiveness to requests, neighborhood conditions, intentions to move, their friendship within the building and in the community. (See appendix C for the interview schedule.)

The early interviews raised concern for us because most of the stories we were hearing were success stories. Although tenants struggled against enormous difficulties, those we had talked to were beginning to reach a condition of greater stability. Tenants had gone through the fights and reversals in their relationships with the city and had accomplished substantial rehabilitation of their buildings. The city views these first buildings as unusual in that the tenants who first entered the program were more organized and sophisticated than those who came later. In order to be sure that a full range of experience of tenant cooperators was included, we asked city officials to identify some buildings in the tenant-oriented program that they thought were in trouble.

At about this time, it became obvious that many of the interviews were with older people. With the support of a National Institute of Aging (NIA) grant, interviews were added with elderly people living in buildings sold through the two other city programs with the largest volumes. These were buildings where the transfer of ownership was to a nonprofit community-based organization or a landlord whose management practices were screened. This direction allowed further investigation of two findings that came out of the first set of interviews. First, older people, especially older black women, played a critical role in the development of the cooperatives studied. It seemed important to determine how their experiences compared with those of similar older people who lived through abandonment. Second, it appeared that the cooperative structure strengthened supportive social networks that had already existed in landlord-abandoned buildings, thus providing a framework for the emergence of leadership as well as sustaining the well-being of tenants. Elderly tenants especially seemed to benefit from these aspects of the cooperative.[29]

The response was different in rental buildings. When a building was owned by a community group, we first interviewed staff members in charge of the buildings, then were introduced to some tenants by the staff. Usually the tenants to whom we were personally introduced agreed to be interviewed but the circle of cooperation was usually narrower, reflecting the smaller social networks in these rental buildings. When entering landlord-owned buildings, we first obtained names of tenants from city records and personnel who would also tell us if they knew any of the tenants. Sometimes we would have to knock on most of the doors in a building before finding someone receptive. Often those who we did interview knew few or no other tenants who they would be willing to suggest we interview next.

Our initial sample of 54 in 17 buildings included 36 leaders, 25 of them female, 21 of them black, and 18 non-leaders, 14 women and 12 black.[30] Table 2.2 details the number of respondents by sex, ethnicity, leadership status, and program. Leaders were defined as people who currently or in the past held office in a tenants' association or block association.[31]

Funding also allowed us to expand the perspectives that we elicited be-

TABLE 2.2

Interview Sample: Program, Ethnicity, Gender, and Leadership Status

	Male		Female		Subtotal
	Leader	Non-Leader	Leader	Non-Leader	
TENANT INTERIM LEASE PROGRAM (TIL)					
Hispanic	3	0	1	5	(9) (4 bldgs)
White	4	0	3	1	(8) (3 bldgs)
Black[a]	4	4	21	8	(37) (10 bldgs)
(Subtotals)	(11)	(4)	(25)	(14)	(54) (17 bldgs)
COMMUNITY MANAGEMENT PROGRAM (CMP)					
Black	2	3	2	8	(15) (9 bldgs)
PRIVATE OWNERSHIP AND MANAGEMENT PROGRAM (POMP)					
Black	1	7	2	9	(19) (5 bldgs)
(Subtotals)	(14)	(14)	(29)	(30)	(88) (31 bldgs)

[a]The 21 black female leaders includes one woman interviewed in a preliminary stage of the study; the 10 buildings include 2 that went from an Alternative Management program to Central Management.

cause we were able to hire a black male interviewer who had grown up in Harlem.[32] An additional 15 residents in nine buildings bought by nonprofit groups and 18 people living in five landlord-owned buildings were interviewed. Reflecting the racial and gender composition of the buildings, all were black; 12 were male and 21 female.[33] Among this group, four women and three men were or had been leaders of tenants' organizations or neighborhood associations.

THOSE WHO REMAINED: THE POOR, THE WOMEN, AND THE OLD

T HERE WERE a few surprises about who remained in landlord-abandoned and co-oped and non-co-oped buildings, but not many. We knew it was a poor population. Housing activists and community leaders, technical assistance staffs and bureaucrats, as well as two reports on neighborhoods in Harlem and the Lower East Side,[34] left no doubt that, as common sense would suggest, it was a poor population. We were not surprised that so many people contacted were women even though it was not until 1982 that statistical data was available to substantiate this.[35] Given the feminization of poverty, it would have been surprising if they were not sheltered in landlord-abandoned housing. City reports in 1984 on the status of its rental stock confirmed that almost 60 percent of the households in all city-owned buildings were female-headed.[36]

At first we found it somewhat puzzling that so many leaders were older people. The city's data revealed a median age of about 42 years in all city-owned buildings, middle-aged but not older. Moreover earlier studies of co-ops in landlord-abandoned buildings had viewed the elderly as a group less likely to be interested in co-op ownership.[37] Looking more closely at the profile of Harlem's population, it made sense that its older residents had aged in place, had come to New York City when it was a better place to get jobs, found work, and stayed. We came to understand that their longevity of tenure played a role in their staying through the abandonment process.

There was also some additional information about who remained in our analysis of the 131 interviews conducted by city staff.[38] Table 2.3 reveals that certain characteristics of tenants were more prominent in one program compared to the others. For example, in tenant cooperatives (TIL), the resident was likely to be female, black, and employed. Not surprisingly, the employed status carried with it higher incomes. One half of the sample

TABLE 2.3
Profile of DAMP Tenants in Three Programs

	DAMP		Nonprofit Community Groups (CMP)		Private Landlords (POMP)		Tenant Interim (TIL)	
	N	%	N	%	N	%	N	%
Sex								
Male	35	26.72	6	15.38	4	18.18	22	44.00
Female	96	73.28	33	84.62	18	81.92	28	56.00
Race								
Black	64	48.85	17	43.59	16	72.73	25	50.00
Hispanic	44	33.59	19	48.72	3	13.64	11	22.00
White	23	17.56	3	7.69	3	13.64	14	28.00
Employment[a]								
Unemployed	44	33.85	16	42.11	10	45.45	10	20.00
Employed	51	39.23	3	34.21	6	27.27	26	52.00
Retired	35	26.92	9	23.68	6	27.27	14	28.00

	N	%	N	%	N	%	N	%
Income[b]								
5000	33	31.13	10	30.30	5	25.00	12	33.33
5-7.5	24	22.64	11	33.33	5	25.00	3	8.33
7.6-10	16	15.09	4	12.12	5	25.00	4	11.11
10.1-12.5	13	12.26	6	18.18	3	15.00	3	8.33
12.6-15	8	7.55	1	3.03	2	10.00	5	13.89
15,000 +	12	11.32	1	3.03	0	0.00	9	25.00
Age								
Under 25	9	6.87	6	15.38	1	4.55	1	2.00
26-40	46	35.11	15	38.46	9	40.91	17	34.00
41-61	41	31.30	7	17.95	6	27.27	19	38.00
62+	35	26.72	11	28.21	6	27.27	13	26.00

DAMP Division of Alternative Management Programs. It includes 2 smaller programs not analyzed in this study. One, Management in Partnership (MIPP) is no longer existing.

CMP Community Program

POMP Private Ownership and Management Program

TIL Tenant Interim Lease

[a]N = 130

[b]N = 106

earned $10,000 or less. One-third of the tenants earned $5,000 or less.[39] Thus the cooperatives sampled housed the largest number of the lowest income tenants in the sample. More than half the tenants interviewed were 41 years and over, and about 60 percent had no children present in their households.

The residents living in buildings sold to new landlords (POMP) were also likely to be female and black, but more likely to be unemployed or retired, although of those who worked some were in higher economic brackets. Half the sample was earning $7,500 or less and the other half was earning between $7,500 and $15,000. Fifteen of the 20 respondents, however, were earning $10,000 or under. The age breakdown was less concentrated in the lower ranges: one half was either 40 years or less, the other, 41 and over. Half the sample had no children and of those with children, almost half the households had children six years and under.

The residents living in buildings bought by a nonprofit community group (CMP) were likely to be female, Hispanic, unemployed or retired, earning under $7,500 a year, 40 years old or less, with two children under six years of age.

Certain demographic factors tended to go together in the population when the 131 interviews were looked at as a whole. Women were less likely to be employed, and to report having lower incomes, less education, and more children. Blacks in the sample were older, and had fewer rooms in their apartments. Hispanics, on the other hand, were younger, less educated, with more children, and lived in apartments with more rooms. They also had lived in their buildings a shorter period of time.

As with figures about abandonment, these associations of traditional socioeconomic data—age, race and ethnicity, marital status, presence of children, employment record—cannot do justice to the people who manage to survive in landlord-abandoned buildings. Statistics do not convey what it was like to sit in the one-room apartment of an 84-year-old woman and note a pair of shoes neatly lined up at the edge of the wall, the backs worn down and frayed, and listen to the strength of her voice as she bantered with the former superintendent who still lived in the building and just dropped by to see how she was. Nor do the statistics adequately capture the infectious rapport and rich relationship among four women leaders seated around a table in an apartment converted to a meeting room, its walls not yet repainted and plastered, all of them answering the questions at the same time. How can numbers, powerful as they may be, paint a picture of the apartment of 74-year-old Mr. Bridely, anticipating his third marriage to the woman he first married and divorced down South, with his suits on hangers decorating the french doors of his apartment while he got ready to leave? Or the apartment of a woman who had been a maid to Zsa Zsa Gabor and had colorful flower paintings hung on her walls. There was the apartment whose tinyness was exploded by floor to ceiling wallpaper of a lake and trees; the dark apartment where high school trophies with polished brass plates, awarded to the now well-known professional basketball-playing son, were prominently displayed. It wasn't only that people talked about abandonment, but that in letting us into their apartments they showed us how they lived and what it meant to save their homes.

II

TENANT RESPONSES

THREE

Tenant Cooperatives

THE TENANTS we initially spoke with had been the first to complete the recovery from landlord abandonment. All the co-ops discussed in this chapter purchased their buildings prior to our interviews. We soon discovered that the cooperation that went on in the buildings had begun long before landlord abandonment. The people we spoke with had come to these buildings for the most part prior to the 1960s, most of them before World War II. Their friendships extended back decades. Their histories were the history of Harlem.

The six co-ops described in this chapter reflect the variety of experiences the history of Harlem has accommodated (see map 1, buildings 1–6). A turn-of-the-century building (1) on the edge of Morningside Heights, and an easy walk from Columbia University, once housed white professionals. Another still attractive building (2) built in the 1920s had ushered in the concentration of blacks in Harlem as its first all-black building. Tenants in a third co-op (3) located on tree-lined Convent Avenue near the City College of New York described their building as a link, through the black entertainers who had lived there, to the Harlem Renaissance. Two other buildings (4, 5), one on West 113th, the other on West 146th, shared more of the unglamorous side of Harlem, housing the domestics, the practical nurses, and others who do the work of physical caring for little pay. But there were also newer, younger tenants who came into better jobs that opened up through successful legal battles to improve opportunities for blacks, civil service jobs for the most part. The sixth building on West 115th presented an undistinguished facade and public spaces but beyond the apartment doors, relatively spacious, well-kept and cosy apartments revealed the unusual continuity of good services the landlord provided until he lost the building through tax foreclosure. These buildings lacked the physical and cultural distinctiveness of the other three, but they revealed just as clearly the underlying history of cooperation and hard work.[1]

Not only tenant's relationships, but also in most cases their struggles for decent housing extended back many years. Tenants in all but one building had come together to make demands for repairs as building neglect had mounted. Their efforts led them through housing court, rent strikes, and then into conflicts with their new landlord, the city. City officials tended to see the leaders as the main force moving the buildings from landlord abandonment through city ownership into cooperative ownership. We discovered that indeed the leaders were outstanding, often inspiring individuals. What conversations with city officials had not prepared us for was the finding that in each building, older people, sometimes in their eighties, played a critical part in saving the building. Most often these older people were women.[2] Yet our interviews made it clear that the leaders drew on a matrix of support embedded in the social life of the building and the broader community.

Patterns of social relationship differed. In the building on West 113th Street, the social networks that gave rise to the tenants' organization focused on Mrs. Wilkins, a retired hospital worker well over 70. She had brought some of the tenants into the building, including another long-term resident who became one of the leaders. Her cousin who lived in the building also became a leader. Mrs. Wilkins recruited Connie Byron to help form a tenants' association one day as they were passing time doing the laundry together. While Mrs. Wilkins knew all the leaders except Connie well, the others formed their relationships during the fourteen years in which the tenants gradually came to manage, then own, the building. In contrast, all the tenants in the building on West 115th knew each other well, many being related by blood or marriage. Indeed, these close relationships may have had to substitute for the years of struggle against the landlord that promoted friendships and tenant organization in the other co-ops. The other buildings revealed mixed patterns of relationships with a core of old tenants who knew each other well and the majority who had exchanged gossip and small favors as well as help in times of crisis for many years. When we speak of the importance of pre-existing social ties, we do not necessarily mean best friend relationships, although leaders usually had some of these among tenants. The sense of ease, of knowing and trusting people, combined with overlapping networks of kinship and friendship; material as well as social support provided the matrix for the more intensely cooperative relationships of tenant ownership. The process of organizing tenants' associations usually extended the informal support to a wider group. However in some cases, differences in goals and other conflicts strained preexisting relationships. In one building, those who would not buy into the co-op were asked to move. However even there, those who remained had been linked by prior ties that grew stronger in the process of co-oping.

A system of communication, trust and support in a building might have begun very casually as Connie Byron described:

> Maybe passing by and coming down, they introduced themselves to me and that's probably how I got to know everybody. They would come down and say I'm so an so. . . . Because then things weren't like they are now—I mean with people. There were really nice people living here . . . I didn't do too much visiting. As a matter of fact I still don't. . . . But I see everybody downstairs and we sit and talk, and we have meetings.

Connie came from Georgia to New York in the 1950s. Then five of her sisters and young cousins followed her to New York as they graduated from high school. One sister moved into the building and became the fundraising committee chairperson in the tenants' association Connie helped found. Connie herself gradually went from a friendly young woman active in the Eastern Star club to an organizer who helped save her building from landlord neglect. The people we talked with in these successful co-ops were similar to those we spoke with throughout the study. Most had come from the South, Louisiana, Alabama, Georgia, North and South Carolina, Mississippi. Their ties to the South remained strong despite the years that had intervened. Two of the middle-aged women leaders sent their teenaged girls back to their home towns for high school, hoping they would do better away from the problems of the city. Yet these ties to the South were ambivalent. The racial discrimination from which many fled was also vividly recalled.

A typical story was that of 89-year-old Mrs. Hill who had moved to New York from New Orleans in 1919. Working as a personal maid for an actress, she seized the opportunity to get away from the South. After a series of "living in" jobs including travel to Europe with one of the families, she met and married a chauffeur. They had an apartment in the Bronx, but she continued to "live-in," going home on days off.[3] When they divorced, Mrs. Hill moved to the building on 126th Street, the first apartment building for black people in Harlem. She remembered the neighborhood when it was mainly Finnish. The blacks who moved in included singers and entertainers like Billy Eckstine and Juanita Hall. Mrs. Hill worked as a personal maid for wealthy and well-known people until the last woman she stayed with died, leaving her some money and personal artifacts. After that she worked sporadically, helping at parties, sewing, being, as she said, a personal maid to all those she helped out every once in a while. Mrs. Hill's apartment, full of cast-off expensive rugs and furniture and photographs of nieces and nephews, provided a comfortable setting as we talked. But more than that, she used it as almost another person in the interview, to remind her of her life, to tell us about her accomplishments and relationships and to convey the preparation she had made for old age. She had space for her nieces when they came to stay. She still visits an old friend who moved away from the building to Jamaica. A newer tenant, a young woman with children looks in on her every day. Mrs. Hill stated in her interview the security that it was obvious her home gave to her:

> I didn't think I'd ever own nothing. I was lucky to live myself. I mean way back in 1919, who thought about it. The little money I made, I sent most of it back to my mother. . . . I felt when I bought this that I would have a place to live the rest of my life. I don't know how long that's going to be.

Mrs. Hill was not a leader; she was grateful to Mrs. Knotts, the woman leader who had first knocked on tenants' doors to organize them. Mrs. Hill had known Mrs. Knotts' mother-in-law; it was her apartment that Mrs. Knotts and her husband now lived in.

The ties of kin and friendship that bound tenants in these buildings prior to landlord abandonment were the first line of defense against threats to their homes and security. When we remarked in the interviews that it seemed like people really helped each other to survive, the people we spoke with were uneasy. They usually rephrased the sentence for us to indicate that it wasn't really a case of helping, they all just were the kind of people who cared about each other. This fabric of care made possible all the achievements that we are to describe.

We should not, however, give the impression that this care was always sufficient. To some extent, these histories of mutual aid arose out of insufficient resources, as an alternative to the money economy.[4] The co-op ownership form in many ways reinforced this informal exchange, but it also linked the tenants to the money economy, for better or worse. Thus some of the strengths of cooperation were undermined in the process. For example, in two of the buildings, the city's requirement that rents be restructured so that the income could sustain the building led to conflict. The way in which leaders handled these crises turned out to have important effects on the network of relationships that existed. At the same time, the kind of relationships that existed prior to co-oping also determined the leaders' responses and effectiveness. The preexisting social life of the building was intertwined with the more easily identified work needed to organize and sustain a cooperative.[5]

TENANTS FIGHTING FOR THEIR HOMES

THE TENANTS' association with the longest history began, behind the stained glass windows of the turn-of-the-century building (1) on Manhattan Avenue, during World War II when rent control started. The 60-unit building is on an irregular-shaped block, next door to another tenant cooperative. Across the street a row of brownstones, six of them vacant at the time we were there, reflects the way abandonment spreads in Central Harlem. In the building, decreased services and the elimination of a twenty-four-hour-a-day elevator man sparked the first actions. The founding president of that association, Mr. Williams, was again the president of the cooperative during the time of the research. He had occasionally been out of office, though never inactive. Mr. Williams and his wife moved into the building in 1937. He first came to the then predominantly white neighborhood in 1921 as a Columbia University student of architecture. Although he later transferred to another university to finish as an engineer, he stayed in the neighborhood and participated in politically significant community organizations.

The same family owned the building from the time he moved in until the tenants took over.[6] Unlike his descendents, the first landlord took a real interest in the building. However, not until the third generation did services seriously decline. The tenants' association began a rent strike in the 1960s and hired a lawyer who suggested that they try to get control of the building. A core group of thirteen tenants worked to save the building. They collected rents, managed the building, made repairs, paid the super, and bought oil. Mr. Williams' wife read about the Urban Homesteading Assistance Board (UHAB) in 1974. For the next six years they worked with the organization to gain control. In 1977, the building went into city ownership. Within seven months, the first interim lease was signed with the city. Tenants purchased the building in 1980. Since 1974, Mr. Williams established an office in the lobby next to the entrance and spent what he described as all of his time on the building. At the age of 87, he reluctantly decided he could no longer continue leading and acknowledged the need to hire a management firm.

The physical condition of the building equaled that of many middle-class buildings on the upper West Side of New York. The stained glass windows were intact as were the mosaic tile floors and other architectural details. Mr. Williams had begun researching the best way to clean marble and methods for retaining the stained glass windows while installing thermal sealed replacements. He had also invested the building's reserve fund in money market accounts. The city had made no major repairs, since the tenants' association had already replaced systems in need of work prior to city ownership.

Just as the building had changed little during landlord abandonment, the tenantry had also remained about the same. Most of those who considered moving out found that they could not find comparable apartments at comparable prices. The length of residency averaged about twenty years, with many of the tenants living there much longer. Although several tenants were on welfare, the bulk of them either worked in or had retired from working-class occupations or professional jobs, mostly in public agencies. A few were in business or worked for the telephone company, a railroad, or other large corporations. The actual jobs they held ranged from domestic, bartender, and so on through secretary, social workers, and teachers. Mr. Williams' job as an engineer was among the highest status occupations of those in the study.

For the majority of successful co-ops, tenant struggles with neglectful landlords dating back to the 1960s led to rent strikes in the late 1960s and early 1970s. In the wake of landlord abandonment, the city replaced the landlord as the target of tenant organizing, again because of poor services. However, as the years went on, tenants experienced their ability to run the building themselves and began to seek not just improvements, but also control.[7]

For example, the 39-unit building (3) on Convent Avenue historically occupied by musicians and performing artists had first been organized in the early 1960s by a professional housing organizer we will refer to as Mr. Bridely. He had worked for the NAACP (National Association for the Advancement of Colored People), organizing tenants since the early 1950s. When he moved into the building in question in 1956, services were not good. He repeatedly took the landlord to court to try to force him to improve services. After seven times, the judge encouraged the tenants to organize a rent strike. They did so that month in 1971. At first only seven tenants joined the strike. They collected $3,000 to make repairs and used their own money for oil. Eventually, others joined them. Tenants began to meet regularly. They cleared out part of the basement for a club room for meetings. It had a kitchen, so they also held parties. Mr. Bridely became the 7A manager (7A refers to a municipal ordinance permitting a court appointed manager, or as it is known, a receiver). He and the tenants operated the building for ten years before they bought the building in 1981.

Mr. Bridely served on the Board of Directors of a fairly powerful community organization that was well-known for its housing organizing. In 1976, when the building passed into city ownership, a politically connected lawyer served as pro bono legal counsel for the building. Nonetheless, or perhaps because of the politicized nature of the situation, acquiring the building proved difficult. Mr. Bridely tells the story as follows:

> [A City Commissioner] said you all go and operate the building. Just tell them that I told you to operate the building. So the gentlemen that was with HDA [Housing Development Administration] at that time, he came up and he would bring the bills, the gas and electric bills and everything at one time, so we operated the building and we kept negotiating, and then they organized HPD. Then after HPD got in, we got in with HPD and we complied with practically everything that they had.

The tenants suspected that racial discrimination underlay the otherwise inexplicable obstacles they encountered:

> See, if we had been white, we would have gotten the house much earlier. Well, every time we sent it [the request for ownership] up, the least little thing they found wrong, they would then put us off.

When asked about HPD's response to accusations of racial prejudice, he replied:

> Well, they would say no, no, no, don't feel that way. Don't feel that way about it. We'd say, well what else could it be? We've complied with everything you asked us to do, and everything has been done, and as I

said, I went down twice to the Metropolitan Council. Miss Benedict had
me on her program on Sunday morning, and who else was it? I forget
the other program. . . . I went on a radio program, the housing TV
program, and I gave the history of the building and how we had suffered.
How many times they sent out papers upstairs to receive the building,
some kind of fraud.

Whether or not his allegations were accurate cannot be determined in hind-
sight in such a large, complex, and frequently inefficient bureaucracy. Such
incidents of racial discrimination are not unknown within the city administration. It is easy to see how widespread racial discrimination in the society generally and in the experience of these tenants shaped the tenants'
perceptions of their struggle to take control of their housing.

The city invested little in the building while it was in city ownership,
despite the fact that even after two years of ownership, the tenants were
still trying to bring the building up to a more habitable standard. Mr. Bridely
viewed the city's excuses that they didn't have the money to help the
building with skepticism:

> They made us all kinds of promises. The only thing they did, they started
> a roof, but everything else, they couldn't get money, and I still have the
> clipping that HPD turned back $9 million dollars to the federal govern-
> ment, unused money. And we went right down to them, right down to
> HPD's office. We had a very stiff board, seven of us. One was a retired
> school teacher, and different people were on this board, and if they couldn't
> do this for us or couldn't do that, why did you turn this money back?

During the ten-year struggle only two or three tenants moved out, all
of them having more money than the average tenant. The board met once
a month alone and once with the tenants during this time, as it still does.
All but one tenant out of 38 units bought into the co-op. Mr. Bridely never
thought of moving out:

> I like the neighborhood, and I knew I couldn't do any better. We were
> working with other tenants and seeing other places. See, when I first
> started in the post office, I was a mail carrier and going into different
> houses. We had a beautiful house here besides the others that we saw.
> I always would quote that to the tenants.
>
> I was delivering mail in so many saloons and houses on Lenox Avenue
> and many different places until I knew that we had something that was
> much better than others had, although it wasn't good then, but after we
> started operating it ourselves. Our rents were so low [$35 for three

rooms in 1971] that I wondered how we could operate, but when the city took over this building, we had spent $95,000 on renovations, and didn't owe a penny.

Mr. Bridely professed that no "segregation" had been used over the years in selecting tenants. In contrast to most tenants in the study, he reported that the teenagers in the building were well behaved and that they never had a graffiti problem. However, one teenager was singled out as a drug addict. Steps were being taken to get rid of his family and also one shareholder who would not pay rent for months at a time.

In contrast to the tenants in the most deteriorated buildings whose activities will be discussed in the next chapter, these tenants were all healthy and active, although some were up in their eighties. Over one-third worked, many in professional or government jobs; one-third were senior citizens. Of the remainder, either the officers were unsure where they worked or they were on welfare. One of the older women, Mrs. Michael, then president of the tenants' association, had retired from a job in a city agency. Her knowledge of the bureaucracy enabled her to find ways to cut through the red tape to get thirteen of the senior citizens Section 8 rental assistance subsidies which they needed. Mr. Bridely and others with experience also helped those in need apply for food stamps and other services. These activities exemplify the ways in which housing co-ops went beyond the provision of shelter to a more general attempt to support the welfare of residents in their different areas of need.

Tenants placed great emphasis on filling vacancies with people who would be active and have skills. The one vacancy that occurred after co-oping was filled with John Paynes and his wife, Martha. Paynes, who had some experience with housing organizations and city agencies, became the bookkeeper for the tenants' association. The women on the board were trying to help the wife set up a day-care center to bring in income for the building. A beautification club to do painting and cleaning was formed and involved many of the young people. Here, we see the extension of domestic activities from the individual household to the building.

The new officers, three older women and one woman in her forties, had joined the strike in the mid-1970s. They prided themselves in continuing the work. The court ruling to turn the building over to the tenants had been a landmark decision. They described how banks arranged a $45,000 loan for a boiler, new windows and repainting through a city loan program. Mrs. Michael described her other efforts to improve the building's financial resources:

I was trying to get a day-care center organized but the person that I thought might do it was not qualified because we have to have a licensed teacher for preschoolers. . . . And we're trying to form one so we can make some kind of small start at an income from outside sources rather than from the rent.

She had thought through the physical requirements of a center in detail:

The day-care center would be in the club room downstairs on the main floor. But, well I don't know if it's going to materialize or not. But we have a vacant lot right here and there's a vacant building, a brownstone. So I have some people looking into that for me to find out whether the house has been sold, because it was on the city auction, and, since I haven't seen anybody bothering with it, I don't think it was sold. So, what I wanted to do, was start the day-care center here and eventually move it there with the parking lot next to it. And this way we could use part of the building for offices and so on, because we really want to do something to keep the rents down.

The day-care center was actually established after our interview and operated successfully. However, Mrs. Michael did not put all her eggs in one basket:

And we are looking into a municipal bond. I don't know anything about it either, but I figured if you send for information maybe somebody else will know something. So, all these things are in the works, but I don't know how they're ever going to materialize, but we have these plans for them.

The new officers recollect a bit more city help than Mr. Bridely, in that they said the city installed 220 wiring in the kitchen, some fire escape repair, and was promising to install new doors. Yet they felt pressure to do more renovation than they could afford. Having fought to own the building, they were now obligated to bring it up to standards the private landlord had long since given up on.

Once you buy the building from the city, they tell you that it has to be upgraded to regular housing standards. That's putting too much pressure on tenants that have just bought, and are supposed to be low- to moderate-income people. Because if we had to do it out of the rent roll, our rents would triple, or it would never get done, and once they sell you the building, they say it must come up to the housing standard and that's it. Just like now, we got the fire insurance paid, and I got a letter saying we've got to put fire extinguishers on every floor, the party room, and the basement room.

Rents at this time were a little over $60 per room. A fire in the one vacant apartment at the time of purchase further strained their resources but was fixed out of rent rolls and sold for $5,000. The $5,000 was put into the building's reserve fund.

Besides money, the current officers worried about participation. They had a sickness committee to send cards when people were ill and to collect a little money to help if the person needed it. They estimated that about 70 percent of the tenants were supportive and sometimes active, as they put it "50 percent showing and an 80-percent agreement level."

Of all the buildings with a majority of black tenants, residents here had the highest expectations for the future. Indeed their area presented an almost prosperous aspect with quiet, winding, tree-lined residential streets of old brownstones and modest-sized attractive apartment buildings, adjacent to a designated historic district. Signs of rehab and construction were on every block. Mrs. Michael thought some day soon the area would be "like the old Harlem." Mrs. Brent, the younger woman officer, said her daughter had asked her to leave her "her jewels and her apartment" when she dies. This was the only building in the study where several people spoke of leaving their apartments to their children or grandchildren, although in several, children and other relatives lived in the building.

We found that when the tenantry taken advantage of by a venal landlord was even poorer and the building lacking in special cultural or architectural distinction, the conditions became even worse. This was the case in the 35-unit building (5) on West 146th Street between Broadway and Amsterdam avenues. Carolyn and LouAnn, two older women leaders, recounted their experience:

> The city took over the building from the landlord. Mr. X was a bandit. The landlord did not take care of the building. We have apartments where the ceiling was coming down, bathroom was sinking . . . the toilet was drawn away from the wall. I had to use the bathroom on another floor. We decided that we weren't going to pay him any money until he took care of the violations. Well, at the same time, he wasn't paying taxes. . . . In 1976, the city came in and gave us notice that the building no longer belongs to the landlord, it belongs to the city. They should be paid the rent. But at the same time, the city did not take care of any violations. So we who were running the building, ten of us, we refused to pay the city until something had been done. So we kept the money.

From 1972 to 1975, the ten tenants had run the building out of their own rent money, often paying advance rent to buy fuel. The other tenants had continued paying the landlord, who did nothing. In 1975, a court-appointed administrator, one of the ten rent strikers, was assigned to the building and began to collect rent from the remainder of the units that were not vacant by then. (At one point only sixteen apartments were still occupied.) The 7A administrator had since been forced to leave because of failure to pay rent and attempts to deceive the city. The two women leaders had been the other tenants' association officers. They had been paying rent and were shocked to discover that the administrator did not. They carried on and attempted to buy the building through the city's direct sales program, which only allocated a minimum amount of money per apartment. Meanwhile they began repairing the vacant apartments, doing as much of the work themselves as they could manage in an attempt to get the rent rolls to a level that would really support the building. Since 1972, they relied heavily on the advice of Metropolitan Council on Housing (Met Council), a housing advocacy group that had been active in rent strike organizing. Their building received among the most city rehabilitation money prior to sales of any in the study; a new boiler, new plumbing, new wiring, and a new roof were paid for by the city.

This co-op demonstrated that the road to cooperation was not always smooth, especially when money was involved. The rent increases required prior to the purchase of the building led to a rent strike by twelve tenants of the then fully occupied 35 units. The leaders took the tenants to court when they refused payment and refused to buy their apartments. The leaders asked those who did not buy their apartments to move out and most did. Senior citizens could stay by law, but the leaders gave the impression that they had asked all non-cooperators to move. Rents ranged from $179 for three rooms to $332 for six. The two women involved in the original rent strike made most decisions, kept books, and handled repairs.[8] The Board of Directors met only once every three months. The whole association gathered only twice a year. However, groups of tenants made key rings and things to sell to raise money for the building and went on picnics and outings together. Most of the tenants worked, including the two leaders, although they were in their early sixties.

The 47-unit building (4) on 113th Street, led by Mrs. Wilkins, Connie Byron, and two other women, presented a particularly unusual case. It was here that we conducted some of our first interviews. Our initial visit on a bleak winter night showed the building projecting the only interior lights onto the street. Otherwise abandoned and apparently vacant build-

ings lined the street that was geographically so close—about ten blocks—
to the booming real estate market of the upper West Side. We entered
the lobby that was still under construction to meet with a board of four
women who had been running their building for over a decade. The landlord
had actually turned the building management over to the tenants long prior
to city ownership. Connie Byron described how this transition occurred
around 1968 when tenants began to feel that they were not getting the
services they wanted in exchange for the frequent increases in rent. Then
the rhythm of abandonment quickened:

> He started to let the elevator stay out over weekends, and on cold days
> he would let the oil run out and we just got together and organized a
> tenants' association.

However, here the experiences of these tenants contrasted with those
living in buildings owned by more resistant landlords:

> And we started to work with him, so he explained to us that he didn't
> have enough money to buy oil or to pay the superintendent and things
> like that. So we really started to hold the rent, and we did the things.
> And if there was anything left over we gave it to him. So he went along
> with that because he said if we think we could do it, go ahead.

The real success of the tenants lay in their ability to work with each other,
a skill that spilled over into their relationship with the landlord.

> We had a board meeting and it taught us a lot about people and other
> things, and then we just started to work there together and about three
> or four years later the landlord just let us collect the rent and we would
> call him when repairs were needed, what was needed, and who needed
> it the worst. We would put priorities on things, and he worked with us
> for about three or four years like that. And he was very pleased with
> us, so then when the building went *in rem* from taxes, he turned the
> building over to us. The landlord himself turned the building over to us.[9]

After Mrs. Wilkins approached Mrs. Byron to start organizing the tenants' association, they invited a tenant organizer to speak; a full house
turned out. From this meeting the Board of Directors emerged, all friends
of Mrs. Wilkins, but otherwise not well acquainted with each other. They
met together on all decisions and often just to work out their approach.
Tenants were involved in active participation through a system of committees and responsibility sharing. Eventually even the landlord participated in the system of tenant control until he discontinued paying his taxes.

Despite high levels of cooperation and good relations with the previous landlord, the group faced many obstacles when the building became city-owned, as Mrs. Wilkins explained:

> I find it has been a very trying experience because we met with so much opposition. The first thing, when we were taking over the building, we couldn't get credit. So what we had to do in order for us to get oil, and get the boiler fixed, the three of us . . . we cosigned for the building in order to get these things installed and so we can develop some type of credit.

The lack of credit reflects a lack of standing in the wider community. The public sector often acts in equally oppressive ways. Mrs. Wilkins explained with pride how they fought against these attitudes of officials they dealt with in the city bureaucracy:

> Also the city didn't know anything about us for a while and then when they discovered that we had the building, they said give them the money. We were required to come downtown. They were very surprised to find out that we were taught to keep records. And we went down with our books to the office. I felt very bad because the head, he would not come out and talk with us. He let his side henchman talk to us. And one of the side henchmen, when he looked at the records, he said you keep better records than we do.

Even when the leaders in this building proved themselves competent, city bureaucrats, predominantly men in this case, were helplessly caught in a morass of procedures and forms:

> So then he said that, well, just give us the money, so then he said he's giving us a dispossess. So we said give us the dispossess. He sent us a form and we answered it. We went downtown and answered 'em, so by the time we went to court and everything, they decided that we would not have to move. But this is the way, the attitude that they give us. The men did not respect us.

Mrs. Wilkins brought in a lawyer from a now disbanded community organization that helped the tenants. He advised them, made court appearances, and responded to whatever problems came up. Finally, the tenants went on rent strike against the city, a move suggested by one city commissioner:

> What he told us was to go on rent strike from the city. Just don't pay any rent, act like we don't even know that they exist, but to make sure

that we collect all the rents, put them in the bank, pay all the bills that come up, just go along as if it was management, and that we manage ourself and that we learn from whatever we do, learn together, but just continue to operate the building on that order.

Mrs. Wilkins said:

And we stayed on rent strike for almost a year. When they found out, the city came back into the building. She [one of the leaders] said we had kept a record and we had did so much until they couldn't say anything about it. So when one of the commissioner's inspectors came down, they told us just to continue on doing what we were doing and he would take the papers and put it underneath a pile, and if they find it, they'll find it, and if not, they won't bother us, and in the meanwhile for us to apply for one of the management programs, and at that time they had a direct sales program which we applied for. Then from the direct sales program came the interim lease program. We were I think the second building in the interim lease program.

The building went into the direct sales program, and, even without the later tenant interim lease cooperative program, these women felt they could have found a way to keep the building. Mrs. Wilkins explained their belief as follows: "I think that there were interesting people that were interested in us down at HPD that would probably of helped us to find a way."[10] Unlike Mr. Bridely, they focused on the eventual support they received, dismissing the earlier city resistance as bureaucratic inefficiency, and unfortunate but not unusual male chauvinism.

The tenants' determination was strengthened by their assessment of the building and their lack of housing choice:

We were gonna get it one way or the other because number one, it was a necessity that we did stick, and it was a necessity for us to really work because at that time we had a full building, and I mean the building was in excellent shape. It wasn't a bad building, and you know it was just hard to go out trying to find apartments and everybody was used to the big rooms. I don't think anybody would just jump up and leave unless they had to. Unless the building just went kaput down the drain. But we were doing pretty good managing the building. So I think everybody would of stuck right here.

Connie Byron summed up the attitude of the tenants as follows:

I think it's that we have a certain amount of pride as a black person, or people here, that we were able to succeed in getting something, as they say, a piece of the rock. And that piece of the rock, we can be able to make it work for us if we go on a little further.

"WE ARE A FAMILY"

THE YEARS of struggle that culminated in cooperative ownership led not only to a sense of achievement among tenants, but also, often, to a kind of group bonding. Over and over again tenants told us that those who lived in their building were like a family.[11] The last building we described was a particularly good example of how leadership first emerged out of strong interpersonal ties among leaders. The four leaders agreed to be interviewed only as a group. The way the leaders structured the tenants' association reinforced and extended these relationships. They developed a sickness committee to aid those who were ill, a fund-raising committee, and a housing committee that dealt with the rent arrears, tenant screening, and the like. Mrs. Byron explained the board's philosophy:

> If you feel if you are involved, it ties your building into the project. Then they don't have time to say "well, well, you are getting everything."

The committee structure reflected this philosophy:

> We formed another group. We have a chairman, a secretary, and members, and you give them a certain amount of responsibility. Then we formed another group, and we got them their chairman and their secretary. And they have to answer to the board. They report back to the board.

Committee members handled much of the day-to-day contact with tenants:

> If the problem occurs in somebody's apartment, then the building committee goes in there and looks at it, and says okay, we've got to get a man to fix so and so. Then they can't say well, those four did it or those four didn't do it. . . . This way we felt that if we had a tenant that didn't want to pay their rent on a regualr basis, instead of one of the board members going in to talk to them, we would let another person go in and talk to them. Then that way they would know that we are not the only four that know they are not paying their rent, somebody else in the building knows it now.

Mrs. Byron's account of their use of the management fee shows how the leaders' commitment to participation affected their approach to the always sticky issue of money:

> You take the four of us; if we did everything, then we felt that there would be animosity among the other tenants. They would say that we were doing everything. We did it without pay. We don't get paid for this. We worked all these years without money. We pooled the management fee because we always needed it. We were never able to take the management fee. Because it had to go back into the building for oil or for something to pick up the slack for somebody who wasn't keeping up with rent.

But tenants did not always perceive these sacrifices:

> When the people saw the prospectus and thought that some of their dollars were paid for the management fee, then some of them went crazy. 'You all got that money, you all made that money.' So we sit down and show them that now, we didn't get it. It went here and that money went there. I would loved to have it sometime but we never got it.

This approach seems to have worked well since the building has been remarkably free of conflicts during the fourteen years it has been organized. In comparison, the structure the leaders established best exemplifies the close ties between successful participatory organization and pre-existing social relations. In comparison, Mr. Bridely and Mrs. Michael's building, with a somewhat similar organization, also built on friendships and solidified them into participation in the building through a formal set of duties. Mr. Williams' leadership in the oldest tenants' association described in this chapter approximated this kind of shared responsibility through a floor captain system. However, tenants had fewer activities which they worked on, and Mr. Williams was definitely the final authority.

Of the eighty people in the 47 units, Mrs. Byron reported only one did not cooperate. They let him go his way and they went theirs. He paid rent and they delivered services. Otherwise people were involved with each other according to the time they had and their personal preferences. A single mother with a full-time job who also went to school helped out in the summer with activities, bought dinners from the fund-raising committee, and found friends and security in the building. An older man claimed his wife should be the one to participate in the monthly tenants' association meetings, but he dropped into the community room many times a week to socialize. The board members were named by several tenants as people they would turn to in an emergency. One of the retired women filled out forms to help those needing social services get them and to get Section 8 or a Senior Citizen Rent Increase Exemption (SCRIE).[12] The building committee bought flowers for all the senior citizens on Mother's Day and had a New Year's Eve party for them. The oldest tenant in the building earned the nickname the "warden."[13] She watched the door, checked on school-age children, let in repairmen and made sure everyone behaved properly— no graffiti or loud talk.

Only twice had it been necessary to take a tenant to court:

> What happened is that the only time we go to court with a tenant is when . . . we can't think of no other way of handling it, when the tenant doesn't make no kind of agreement and doesn't meet with us and doesn't make no kind of effort.

They do not see their relationships to tenants as similar to those of a landlord:

> We usually try to meet with them, talk with them, make some kind of agreement so that they'll be able to catch up cause a lot of times we do find that some people have a hard time, and you may have a hard time, and I may have a hard time at one point, and that it wouldn't be a co-operative if we just did as landlords did.[14]

The leaders acknowledge that most tenants can pay the rent and do so. The problems in rent payment that exist are treated as moral rather than fiscal issues:

> We don't really have much problems because most of our tenants are paying the $286. The only people we have that's not doing that is two . . . and the reason why they are not doing it is because they're sickly and Mr. Smith, he's about 85 and he don't have nowhere to go period. And he's a stubborn man. . . . We hope we can get a tax abatement cause it's the only thing we can do. We could start some kind of proceedings against them, but as a board we figured that they been here a long time and they may not have a long time. We're just carrying them, more or less. It's a hardship, but it's something that we really are ready to deal with, with the mental state of trying to throw an 85-year-old man out or a sickly lady with cancer out on the street.

No doubt the fact that the tenants are all employed except for the elderly people and two households that have occasionally been on welfare prevents the non-payment or rent from arising as a constant serious problem. A number of the tenants seem to be using the financial and emotional security and support of the co-op to seek training for better jobs in the future.

The leaders distinguished between a landlord's approach to owning a building and their own. For them, the money that goes to profit in a private rental building was going instead to realize the vision they had of better homes for themselves and their neighbors:

> We are not trying to be landlords, the only thing we are trying to do is just make sure the money comes into the building and that we are able to be self-sufficient so that we are able to have a home. . . . [If] we don't put nothing into it, then it won't be anything, but if we all work and put something into it, then we can have a mansion, a palace. We have hopes for mansions.

Their goals went beyond merely achieving security:[15]

> We want to try to go around into our store and invest in our stores and eventually take over all our stores and make some kind of work for people that's not able to go to work, for when I get tired of doing my job, I'll have somewhere to come. When Ruth gets tired of doing double shifts in the hospital, she can just sit down after a while and say the hell with it. You know, it's some kind of investment that we're trying to look for. One parent at home, teenagers, college students, it's hard. But eventually we figure that after we get over the hump, we'll be able to do it. It's hard getting over that hump.

Two of the leaders extended their efforts to save their building into the community by founding the Harlem chapter of the citywide coalition of tenant cooperators in the interim lease program. The goal of this voluntary group was to support buildings getting started and to act as a watchdog on city policies affecting tenant-initiated cooperatives. One also worked with a state-funded organization to help tenants take over their buildings. Connie herself demonstrated the expertise acquired from managing the building. When asked if she would like to be a full-time building organizer, she responded affirmatively. Somehow she already squeezes time in between two paid jobs to do volunteer organizing with other buildings.

Just as some families fight, so do members of some co-ops. The four women leaders just described demonstrated real skill in orchestrating cooperative relationships, as attested to by their approach to and success with the landlord. The structure they put in place was the most elaborate system of cooperation we encountered, and the most successful. Yet even less cooperative buildings were characterized by the feeling of being a fam-

ily. In one case, the leaders saw themselves as the central figures, overlooking the problems this might engender when hard decisions had to be
made. Even in this situation, informal support in daily life co-existed with
bitter rivalries.

In the Art Deco 48-unit building (2) on 126th Street at the eastern edge
of Central Harlem, the long history of tenant organization included periods
of apathy and conflict. In 1971, Mrs. Knotts, an outspoken, energetic older
woman had rallied tenants to protest the landlord's neglect. The tenants'
group had managed to win a few victories, a new intercom, and some
minor repairs, but services continued to decline. Around 1975, Mrs. Knotts
described the association as having "petered out."

> That was because the tenants did not show interest, I mean not enough
> interest. Maybe we'd get eight. This is a 48-unit building. . . . But the
> few of us that did come got a few things done, and so they started not
> coming to the meeting, and I became disinterested and I just let it ride
> until the landlord lost the building in 1978.

She conveyed a sense of personal insult about the city's takeover and the
ignomy of how she found out about it:

> When the city took it over, once I knew that the city had it, my husband
> and I were away, and when we came home and found the note stuck
> downstairs and the elevator was out. We had to walk up the four flights
> of stairs with our bags and got a booklet that said "apartments for rent."

Her despair in the situation reflects the poor reputation the city had as a
landlord:

> I thought this was it; if the city has it, this is the last word and the
> elevator is out too. Mr. Graham, who is now the chairman of the board,
> because of his management, had been working off and on in the house
> with the tenants and taking pictures of the tenants washing the wood-
> work, marble, and whatever. And so he got us all together and told us
> to go over to the [state] senator's office.

The tenants told the senator they wanted to take over the building. At
that time only the direct sales program existed. The interim lease program
was however being planned. The tenants indicated they wanted to be part
of it, if it became official, and that they would do whatever was necessary.
Mrs. Knotts had become chairperson of the tenants' association. She and
the secretary signed the lease but not yet with full tenant support:

We took it [the building] over and we weren't ready to buy it. There were so many things that had to be done in here, until the tenants, you know, were not able to buy anything until they could see some improvement.

As in the case of the Convent Avenue and 113th Street buildings, legal assistance provided a critical support in the early stages of co-op formation:

So, therefore, I negotiated with the city's very good lawyer from Legal Aid. First, we went to the Community Law Office. They gave us all the help they could until our problems became a little bit more complicated. Then they assigned us to a Legal Aid lawyer, and I think we got one of the best in the bunch. He's been devoted, and he really helped us any-time we've had any problems. He's come to our aid and it hasn't cost us anything. . . . We could not have done it [without him] because there was no one in here that was knowledgeable enough, you know, to help me [even though she had helped her mother run three or four rental brownstones].

At first, the city did not fix the elevator and the tenants couldn't, be-cause the company refused to deal with a non-owner. Mrs. Knotts ex-pressed the lack of control she felt about sending rent to the city as she told of the rent strike the tenants called:

By the first of August, we had stopped paying the city any rent. . . . We had opened an account in the bank, and we put the money in the bank, and we were not sending it to the city because I asked them why it is we couldn't get our building fixed.

We were paying the rents and they told us the city didn't do that that way, that money was sent to the Commissioner of Finance and they fixed what they felt like they wanted to fix here and what they wanted to fix there, and our things were still going unfixed and we were paying the rent.

Mrs. Knotts had to reduce the anxiety of some of the tenants:

Some of the people, a few of the older people, they were hard put to understand and they kept on paying because they were afraid. We said, well, if they put us out, they are going to have to put out the whole building, and we didn't think they were going to put out the whole building.

During the rent strike, tenants paid to get the elevator and some plumbing leaks fixed. The rest remained in a fund that was used for repairs after the lease was signed. Rent-striking tenants managed to save $15,000 by the time they signed the tenant interim lease. The city never reclaimed the rent money despite having provided other services during this time. The city also repaired the roof and replaced the windows and the boiler. With the help of UHAB, Mrs. Knotts figured out the expenses associated with running the building and beginning to make needed repairs.

Mrs. Knotts' handling of rent increases particularly demonstrates her less participatory approach to sensitive decision making. Whereas in some cases tenants' associations had fought rent increases, she went to the city and asked them to do the rent restructuring. As in other buildings, when the city took it over, rents were often very low, below $100 for even good-sized apartments. In order for tenants or anyone else to manage and maintain the building, the rents needed to be raised. Ultimately the city developed a more careful process, forced by a lawsuit over due process issues for tenants.[16] In Mrs. Knotts' building, rents went up 100 percent; they ranged from $150 to $300 after the increases. Some tenants threatened a rent strike *against the co-op* but did not follow through. As a result of the rent increase controversy, a new slate of officers was elected. As oil prices increased, and the salary of the "super" and doormen, the rent roll once more became inadequate, requiring that the service people be let go. Thirty-two of the forty-eight tenants bought into the co-op, the remaining renters paid slightly higher monthly charges. To make apartments more affordable for the poorer elderly, the equity tenants were required to pay to become a cooperator was less than $250; non-elderly people in larger apartments paid a higher equity, so that the cost averaged out to $250. Apartments sold to those who had not been original tenants went for between $6,000 and $9,500. Profits were returned to a reserve fund to be used for additional repairs.

Mrs. Knotts also claimed that private landlords were interested in acquiring the building and had worked to create dissension among tenants so they could step in. One outside group even claimed they were the managers. The building might indeed warrant such interest. When it had opened in 1938, it was an Art Deco showplace. These features would no doubt also have value in today's real estate market. Tenants we interviewed appreciated the quality of the building as well as its history as the first building "for colored people" in Harlem.

Eventually, the new Board of Directors accepted the higher rents when the city provided Section 8 for those needing subsidies. When we interviewed Mrs. Knotts, she and some supporters were planning to try to gain a majority in the next annual election and try to change over to an outside management firm. In this building, the board paid itself as well as the super from the 7 percent management fee allowable. Some tenants' associations waived this fee. Those that did not seemed to have more frequent internal conflicts and disputes about mismanagement. In this case, the dispute seemed far from settled. Mrs. Knotts viewed the future of the building with concern, believing that the internal conflicts could play into the hands of private real estate interests:

> I want you to know some of the things that go on in these buildings after you buy them. It's not all milk and honey. It's terrible the way they fight each other and battle forth and they complain and carry on, and you would think that they would be grateful that they would be able to get something like this, and then work at it to keep it, you know.

In many ways, this building was run somewhat like a landlord-owned building. Court actions had been taken against several tenants for nonpayment of rent as well as to try to get possession of apartments no longer occupied by original tenants. Less active tenants frequently spoke of Mrs. Knotts as the one responsible for the building becoming a cooperative, regarding her somewhat as they might a benign landlord. Indeed, her handling of the rent increase issue had circumvented tenant participation.

A number of tenants who had participated in meetings told us they quit going because they disliked listening to the bickering. They regarded the conflicts as personality issues and preferred not to be involved. One elderly woman, Mrs. Crawford, who did not attend meetings or have much to do with the tenants' association, reported that she did however clean up public areas and try to help keep the building up. She also watched from her first floor apartment to see who came in and out and let in repair people. Since the building became a co-op, she has had the keys to different areas. A former hospital orderly, she also helped tenants who were sick: "I'll go to the store, I'll cook and take them their food. I'll go to the basement and wash their clothes, fold them up and take them."

Another elderly woman, Mrs. Hill, whom we described earlier, and Mrs. Sweeny, a young mother of three who were interviewed, talked of visiting each other and helping out. The younger woman made sure the older one was well every day and did her shopping. The older one watched the youngest child and checked that the teenagers came home on time when the parents were out. During the course of the study, Mrs. Knotts' supporters were elected to the Board of Directors and as officers. She herself seemed to be in charge again although this time working with the elected officers. Generally tenants expressed satisfaction with the way the building ran. Those who earlier refused to purchase and organized dissident groups had begun trying to buy into the co-op.

The tightly knit social relationships of tenants in the co-op on West 115th Street (6) provides a clear example of how social ties and generous amounts of technical assistance can hold a co-op together in the absence of strong individual leaders. At the time of our interviews, people in the co-op still maintained intense and usually supportive relationships with each other. But as Louise Carroll, one of the ex-presidents of the tenants' association, explained, tenants' close involvement with each other now included a strong dose of conflict. Before, she explained, life in the building was "beautiful":

> Everybody here was friends, neighbors, and everything. But we went into interim lease, we started falling apart.

She blamed the 7A manager for the trouble.

> She came in here and it seemed like the devil walked in. Everybody started fighting between each other. She came in one day, and she came in really nasty. You know, because at first she told us she wasn't taking money. She wasn't taking nothing out of the rent roll. She was just doing it to keep the building going, and then when we looked up she was raking 6 percent out, and that's really, you know, when people started talking and fussing between each other.

Mrs. Lyons, the last president to serve during our research period, echoed previous leaders in her lament:

> Our place has changed a lot since we got into an organization. It used to be beautiful here. We were just one big happy family. Everybody knew everybody, and everybody was friendly. But since we got into organization, I don't know what happened. It's not like it used to be. . . . It just started. . . . They started to fool around with each other. One wasn't doing this right, and the other one wasn't doing that right, and actually none of them wasn't doing anything right.

Many of the residents lived in the building fifty or so years before abandonment. Louise Carroll's husband had lived in the building since he was 13. He was the only person to do rehab work himself and to pay for oil out of his pocket. New tenants came to the building over the years mainly through in-laws, relatives, or friends. Despite the conflicts associated with cooperative ownership and management, tenants still shared meals, did errands for the sick and elderly, and looked in on each other.

The building presents an odd situation; people were attached to each other and the place so they tried to do the will of the majority. But they had little faith in their own and each other's abilities. Mrs. Winston, a somewhat nervous and timid older woman who had been elected treasurer, explained her dilemma:

> There's no sense in saying you are going to move out, and you can't find a place as nice as this for the rent you are paying. Believe me, nobody is trying to fool themselves or fool me and say they are trying to get out. It doesn't make sense. Now, where would I go, a lone woman looking for another apartment? . . . I was thinking sometimes that I might move before my sister decided to come here. But why move into a place when I have been here for so long, and I don't know the neighbors. And the people are watching for that lone lady, you know?

She did not want to follow the example of her predecessor and move to senior citizen housing. She thought it was "not as nice." In this, Mrs. Janes, the ex-president, who did move, agreed.

Perhaps this building can best be understood as similar to an extended family in crisis. Too many of the members' interests, needs, and attachments depended on mutual cooperation for people to be willing to cut their ties. Yet the sources of conflict resisted resolution. As time went on, simply the history of conflict led to ill-will. Even after five years of conflict, Mrs. Lyons, the last person we interviewed, stated: "Everybody in here is very enthusiastic about going to see about the others—like if something happened to them—like if they were sick or something like that."

During the interview, an elderly man stopped by to "look in" on the older woman we were talking with. They had been friends since 1940. At first she was going to say that the house had changed in this respect, but then she changed her mind: "Oh this whole house was like that once. If anything happened . . . well, that may not be gone, you know what I mean!"

Like many family conflicts, the very strength of attachments compounds the stress of disagreement. Louise Carroll had had to start taking tranquilizers during her term as president, a practice she stopped as soon as she was out of office. Mrs. Janes took up residence in a new public housing project for seniors and the disabled, about two blocks away. She regarded it as an inferior place to live, but preferred it to facing the daily strain of the co-op. The treasurer reported increased frequency of illness associated with the stress of her job in the tenants' association.

Despite the disappointments and conflicts that tenant cooperation introduced into the social life of this building, tenants still derived satisfaction and a sense of security from their mutual ties. As we will see in later chapters, quite the opposite was the case in buildings that had initially faced landlord abandonment without a strong sense of solidarity among tenants.

TECHNICAL ASSISTANCE, ORGANIZATIONAL DEVELOPMENT, AND LEADERSHIP

A LL THE co-ops received extensive technical assistance. However, in all cases except the building on 115th Street (6), tenants initiated the contacts and began organizing against the landlord prior to abandonment. In this building, tenants did not experience escalating neglect of the building prior to abandonment. When abandonment occurred, the impetus for organizing came from the church next door rather than from the tenants. First the pastor and then a paid manager provided early leadership. This history appears to have been insufficient to develop a confident leadership core and a smooth functioning organization. In his earlier study, Kolodny noted similar problems in co-ops initially sponsored by outside groups. Kolodny also identified the issue of "freeloaders" as one that plagued some co-ops. Yet in this case, the tenants were able to buy their building and manage it despite problems.

Here, younger working tenants like Louise Carroll felt that older tenants were "getting a free ride" because they would not pay the increased monthly costs it took to run the building. The tenants' association had had three presidents (Louise Carroll, Mrs. Janes, and Mrs. Lyons) in less than two years. In every case, some tenants thought the leader had been unable to handle the financial records. Nonetheless, repairs had been made, rents collected, and the necessary negotiations gone through to purchase the building. The younger people did not want to get rid of the older residents, no matter how frustrating they found them. If the Section 8 subsidies that had been applied for came through, many of the conflicts might subside.

The first president of the tenants' association, an older woman, now dead, had to work hard to get people to participate. Throughout the years, tenants have felt a sense of inadequacy about managing the building. This feeling has led to anxiety among the officers of the association and to frequent changes in leadership.

Louise Carroll, the young former president of the tenants' association who was replaced because tenants were not happy with her leadership, looked back cheerfully on the experience:

I enjoyed every bit of it. It was really an experience for me to meet other people and to go . . . to the classes and fight with HPD, and walk out and we are happy. We had our troubles with our management, and we had a lot of ups and downs but we walked out from behind the door laughing, so it was beautiful, really.[17]

Indeed, according to one UHAB organizer, Louise improved her reading and writing skills in her determination to make the co-op succeed. She took classes the city requires with the Urban Homesteading Assistance Board. There she and the other officers learned to keep books, tend boilers, and follow the rules of the interim lease program. Personnel from UHAB also attended tenant meetings and helped them weather their conflicts.

In contrast, Mrs. Winston, the treasurer, described her anxiety about the job:

It's an awful load because, if you don't have the know how, it's a load. This is a responsibility that you need some kind of experience, some kind of know how. It definitely needs people with an attitude for people to do certain kinds of work. . . . Nobody is perfect. But you have to have something. I know I didn't have it, that's why I wouldn't take the presidency. They wanted me to take the presidency and . . . I didn't know how to carry the job out. I mean at least know something about it, and I wouldn't take it.

Despite her position, she felt the building would be better off not being a cooperative:

If it had continued under the leadership of the pastor, it would have been better. But after it had got out from his control the "know hows" tried to carry it on; it would have been better to stay in the hands of the city.

Mrs. Lyons, the 70-year-old president was the last one to hold the office during the study. She shared many misgivings with the others:

I didn't want to [become president]. I told them, don't put me in there. I don't want it. Nobody wanted to be the president, and nobody wanted to do anything. You know what I mean. I told them, I don't know. Nobody knows nothing. I had no commitments with nothing. And everybody wants to just sit back and live on flowery beds of weeds.[18]

When asked how the tenants responded, she replied:

Oh, you know what you are talking about. You're doing a good job. Well you see, the trouble with a place like this is that you don't know, but

I'm willing to learn. I have some people that I can go to and ask questions to. They give me a little advice on it, and then if you got some ideas in your own head, you know, you can't just stop at one thing. Now I tried to tell them, we're here, and this is our home. We are supposed to care. You are supposed to think about it as much as I think about it, and I'm supposed to think it as much as you think about it.

Mrs. Lyons believed the building would be better off under a good private landlord although she doubted that a landlord could retain the rent levels tenants were paying. Her evaluation of the benefits of cooperative ownership is important because she identified may issues that did indeed trouble tenants in buildings owned by private landlords. As she saw it, owning the building had some clear financial advantages:[19]

We think we got high rent but we are paying low rent, and we can control this rent as long as the inflation don't boost or raise the rent. . . . As long as we give the city and whoever gets these taxes, that's all they want from us, right? . . . As long as we do that, this is our home. That's what the lease says, ninety-nine years. As long as everybody pays the bills and pay these people and take care of the building, you got a place to stay until you die, right?

Screening tenants was also important to all those in the building. Many of the residents interviewed in landlord-owned buildings, for example, complained about their inability to contribute to tenant selection and dissatisfaction with the landlord on this score. Since the building had been tenant run, the one vacancy that occurred was filled with a working couple carefully selected to bring necessary skills to the building. The man in the couple they chose worked as a certified public accountant. He immediately became treasurer and straightened out the books, a long-standing anxiety for tenants' association officers. From the interviews it seems likely that participating in building affairs was a requirement for a new tenant. The accountant somewhat begrudged the amount of time the task took, but was in office still at the end of the study. Consensus appeared to be building that contracting with an outside management company would be a prudent thing to do.

CONCLUSIONS

ALMOST ALL of the tenants believed that they were better off living in a co-op than in a rental building. Most especially valued control over living conditions. The rewards of co-op living included both a strong sense of belonging and social support, as well as choice about financial expenditures. The importance of both early struggles against landlords and technical assistance confirmed Kolodny's findings and to some extent those of Lawson.[20]

The important role of elderly leaders and the influence of women in cooperative organizing challenge some of the earlier assumptions about successful cooperative development. Previous studies describe in much less detail who tenants are and how they go about leadership and participation. In these, our first-co-op interviews, the intertwining of race, age, and gender in the specific actions and communications involved in co-op development began to be apparent. Additionally, we began to understand the empowerment and social support many co-op residents experienced as an important aspect of co-op living. These themes continue to appear in the next chapter in which we describe the efforts of tenants to take control of buildings they have not yet bought from the city.

FOUR

Struggling Co-Ops

A SECOND group of buildings was organized more recently, under more desperate circumstances of physical deterioration and landlord neglect. Whereas tenant organizations that began during the first signs of landlord disinvestment had succeeded in staving off the worst building conditions, those in the second group had not. These buildings posed more problems. There were that many more crises to face, and empty apartments to fill, as a precaution both against further vandalism and occupation of the building by non-residents in search of shelter. Here leaders fought for other tenants to move in. These tenant leaders frequently had to overcome health problems, but they found the strength and inner resources to do so. In these desperate fights to resist abandonment, people regarded by the society as practically without resources showed clearly how wrong that assessment is.

In many of the worst buildings, even the oldest tenants could not recall a time when the building had been more than shelter of last resort. All four buildings in this group stand out because of the physical desolation of the blocks on which they stood (see map 1, buildings 7, 8). For example, we remember clearly jumping over the patches of accumulated snow and ice while trying to avoid rusty cans, broken glass, and piled up debris on our way to a small tumbling down 15-unit tenement on West 123d Street (7) in Central Harlem. Mangy-looking dogs on the street added to the desolate atmosphere. None of the narrow brownstone buildings on either side of the street looked fully occupied, even the one we were to enter. Most were boarded up or partially falling down, remnants of a block that had not been very good for a long time. The tenant leader who met us, 75-year-old Mrs. Miller, looked back on her first days in the building thirty-nine years ago, and recollected that she had never liked it: "It just didn't look . . . you know how things look when it's burned out. And I looked at that dirt all day, and I looked at the windows and I called it the dark hole of Calcutta. I thought that I would take it until I got something better."

Unlike most of the other black tenants, she had moved to the area fifty years ago from Vermont. She described her life as a hard one. Before her first marriage she worked, doing as she said "the usual thing, housework." After her marriage she became ill and never held a job outside the building again for more than a short period of time. Her husband died, she remarried, and then divorced. This led to her moving with her 4-year-old son into the building she never liked and still occupied. To earn a living, she had worked inside the building as a super despite serious back problems.

Many of the leaders and non-leaders in this building shared similar histories of physical and psychological disabilities. Out of fifteen households, only four or five included someone who worked. Most tenants were described as having specific illnesses or vague complaints that made it impossible for them to find jobs. In the same building as Mrs. Miller, we interviewed Yvonne, a middle-aged Hispanic woman whose attempts at suicide dated back to her twenty-first year. After having been evicted from a previous apartment because of her son's criminal behavior, her social worker had helped her find a place in this struggling co-op. She managed to break her ties with the son who caused trouble and she found support and company in the building. Mrs. Miller became a person she turned to with particular frequency. Discussing the relationship, Mrs. Miller stated that she was the only one who turned to her so regularly for help, and added with a laugh "and that's enough." From our interview with the younger woman it was clear that she needed a lot of help. Another tenant who looked after her own grandchild helped Yvonne by accompanying her younger child to and from school. Mrs. Miller viewed Yvonne as putting the child off on the grandmother and said that they were trying to "wean her away from it." Yvonne herself found the co-op much more supportive and friendly than her past residences.

In the other three buildings in this group, many tenants also reported these patterns of disability.[1] We met a young man with a withered leg on crutches in the stairs in another building where most of those we interviewed were older people who had suffered some chronic health problem. In other cases, tenants in their eighties and late seventies had lived active lives working and raising families but were losing much of their strength and vigor. In these buildings, too, the impact of the economic recessions of the 1970s was most clear in human terms. Older people were laid off as businesses closed, hospital aides were forced onto welfare as the health system cut back expenses, single mothers employed through the poverty programs of the 1960s could find no other jobs as the programs folded.

The burdens of poverty and ill health borne by tenants made all the more remarkable the tenacity of their struggles to control and renovate their buildings. These factors combined with the terrible conditions in buildings led to the stories of the most heroic if not always successful fights to co-op.

LANDLORD NEGLECT AND ABANDONMENT

MRS. MILLER'S building on 123d Street was typical in its record of landlord negligence and speculation, although it was by no means the worst case.[2] During her tenure, the building had had four landlords, the first two selling out in quick succession, the third holding on for nearly thirty years and the final one lasting only a year before the city took over. She saw the first three landlords as nice people who tried to keep things up but had trouble making it (although later in the interview she said she never trusted landlords). Mrs. Miller found it difficult to understand why the last landlord would have bought the building in the first place, given its condition. She described a classic pattern of speculation, even though she did not label it that way:

He didn't do anything for the building. I don't know whether he knew, he must have known what he was doing. He couldn't possibly just be coming in and not know what he was doing because he'd come in here and tell us that he was going to make this building a show house, you know, on the block. Well, that takes a lot of work plus money.

In fact, services had become almost nonexistent and the landlord showed no signs of remedying the situation. The building had always had heat and hot water except in the final disinvestment period. The building had never been properly wired. Rather wiring for lights had first been put in, then as people got more appliances, refrigerators and so on, jerry-rigged solutions were added. In the 1980s, Mrs. Miller still had to stoke the coal-burning furnace. At the time the landlord walked away, the wiring, roof, windows, and boiler all needed replacing. The grimy, dark quality of the public spaces in the building and its fifteen apartments had only increased in the almost thirty-nine years since Mrs. Miller moved in. Nonetheless the building had always been fully tenanted.

Other buildings identified by the city as managed by tenants' associations still struggling to buy their buildings turned out to have much in common with the building just described. The conditions in these buildings had deteriorated to an almost unlivable point over a long period of time. The tenants were very poor and many of them elderly, disabled, or chronically ill. As in all of the predominantly black buildings we studied, the leaders were mainly older people.

The 61-year-old president of a second tenants' association, Mrs. Oilers, almost through sheer will, ran two connected buildings (8) on a vandalized and partially abandoned stretch of Lenox Avenue with nine apartments each and two commercial uses.[3] Paralyzed in one arm and suffering from cancer, she managed to bring in two other women tenants who later became the vice-president and secretary-treasurer. Sadie Barton, the vice-president, had been living in a welfare hotel with six of her twelve children after having been burned out of her apartment. If she had not been able to find an apartment, her younger children were to be placed in foster homes. Elba Jones, the other woman, lost her job as a nurse's aide when the hospital she worked for ran into financial trouble. After going on welfare, she was assigned to work in the New York City Department of Parks as part of a "workfare" program. Eventually she managed to become part of the paid staff and to advance several civil service grades.

Involved with the Harlem rent strikes of the 1960s, Mrs. Oilers had been the last person to leave another city-owned building (around the corner from her present home) in which she had tried to organize the tenants and community so as to save the building. It had been the place she raised

her five children and lived for thirty years. When she moved into the building she now occupied, she chose it because she needed lots of room and
wanted to stay in the community. Shortly afterwards, the landlady died.
For about ten years a number of "supers," "ministers," and other vaguely
identified people collected rent, and provided spotty service.

During the interviews, tenants repeatedly mentioned the terrible condition the building had fallen into during this time. Elba, the parks worker,
gave an especially vivid picture, similar to Adam Clayton Powell's evocation
of earlier times:

> Like I said, if you could have seen my bathroom . . . I could stand in
> my bathroom and look into the apartment over me, the kitchen. The
> ceiling was gone. From leaks and water pouring down. The wall here
> and around it would have made you throw up from water pouring down
> here. It looked like somebody had tobacco juice and something else up
> with it running down these walls.

The toll on tenants under conditions like this is chronic stress:

> I couldn't take it no more. I had to try and get something to do to it. I
> just couldn't take it no more. That's a horrible thing, looking at something
> like that every day. . . . I could be in my bathroom and look at the
> tenants in their kitchen and somebody up there was looking at me. And
> when I sit on the toilet with an umbrella over me to keep from getting
> wet?

The public areas of the building and the exterior showed the same signs
of complete neglect.

COMMUNITY ORGANIZERS: LIFELINES TO SURVIVAL

THE TENANT leaders in all the buildings in this chapter worked
closely with community organizers, community groups, and politicians in their struggles toward ownership. In most cases, their
involvement differs markedly from that of the more successful co-ops in
that the leaders had few previous political or organizational contacts. In
three of the five cases, an organizer of some kind first introduced the leaders to city programs that could help the building survive. However, unlike
the tenants described in the last co-op on 115th Street (6), in these buildings leaders worked actively with the outside groups from the beginning
and maintained primary responsibility throughout the process.

Mrs. Miller was typical among these tenants in that she only vaguely recollected and understood how the initial contacts were made. When asked about the early tenant opposition to the landlord's neglect, she denied any tenant organization but clearly remembered an activist politician. She asked us about her: "Do you know anything about Marie Runyon? Have you heard of her?" Mrs. Miller was uncertain of a second woman activist's first name: "Another woman, [Luana] Robinson. The two of them are the ones that got us started with the courts and all of that." She recounted the first meeting as if it were almost accidental:

> She was on the block here, for some reason that I don't remember what it was. They have a center down the street here. And she was down there at the center, and I don't remember how we got in touch with her, but however it was that we got involved with her . . . she came here and talked with us and got us headed to go into court to make him do something.

In another case, Jack Fuller, an ex-leader we interviewed, was a young man who had moved into a city-owned building (9) with the explicit purpose of organizing it.[4] He belonged to a community organization dedicated to increasing community control and fighting racism and poverty. Jack's living in the building was a part of the group's plan, although tenants were unaware of this motivation.

In other buildings, the leaders took active roles in seeking out organizations to help them. However, they did so in an almost haphazard way, based more on personal history than on knowledge of the political alternatives that existed in Harlem. They never seemed completely clear about the organizational affiliations of the individuals they worked with.

In all the struggling co-ops, contacts with political individuals and groups were absolutely essential in keeping the building out of city ownership. In contrast to the extensive networks of many of the successful co-ops' leaders, these leaders depended much more on chance discoveries and meetings. As we learned later, the nature, adequacy, and continuity of the help they received was the biggest factor determining their success or failure.

ORGANIZING FOR SURVIVAL

AFTER THE first contacts with outside organizers, the tenant leaders exerted themselves mightily. It is impossible to overestimate the strain and demands placed on leaders in the most deteriorated buildings. Participation was rarely very high. Financial resources practically did not exist. The buildings needed everything. The city was usually unresponsive at least for several years. Despite the outside help obtained, most of the burden fell on one or two people who were willing to assume the leadership role. Mrs. Miller's story of how tenants came to control the building presents one version of the repeated themes of landlord unresponsiveness and city opposition: "Because they started putting pressure on him to do something, he just left. When it came to going to court, he never showed up in court for anything. So I guess you would say that we got it by default or whatever."

The tenants had organized to keep their shelter, mainly at Mrs. Miller's prodding. Finally, she was appointed as 7A administrator to run the building. Marie Runyon, then the local state assemblywoman, steered her through the court appearances into the 7A program. After two years, the city reclaimed the building. Again under Mrs. Miller's leadership, the tenants organized to take back control through entering the city program to sell buildings to tenants. At one time, the city notified the tenants they had returned to city ownership. However, Mrs. Runyon helped them contest the city claim. Although the building was regarded by city officials as one that might fail to become a co-op, the elderly woman who had given so much of herself to the building viewed the future optimistically. The city had repaired the roof, new windows were promised, and the tenants' organization had hired a management firm to handle its financial matters, thus relieving Mrs. Miller of the part of the job she felt least confident about. Some apartments had been rehabilitated. The extent to which the organization seemed to depend on her leadership did suggest the likelihood of future problems, although at least two other tenants were somewhat active as vice-president and secretary-treasurer. Most tenants participated in meetings, supported cooperative ownership, and attended screening sessions for prospective tenants. In 1986, tenants succeeded in buying the building.

In contrast, Mrs. Oilers (building 8) initiated contacts with people who could help her through the local community board. With the aid of a woman who worked for the board at that time, Mrs. Oilers organized the building, tried to find out the identity of the owner, and eventually took over the management of the building. Working with the local community board and other connections she had developed during her earlier organizing efforts, she got the building into the tenant interim lease program.

Mrs. Oilers, like Mrs. Miller, was responsible for most of the initiatives taken to get the building into the program. But for her, this kind of struggle was not new. During the interview she repeatedly described herself as a fighter and told stories to prove it. For example, she described her first experience in organizing tenants in her previous building:

> I was the president, the head of it [the tenants' association]. I hadn't any experience but they used to have me fight with the landlord, you know. I was a fighter.

Asked if she saw herself as a fighter, she responded:

> Well yes I do. I will fight. I'll fight to the bitter end whether I get defeated or not. I've always been a fighter. I've always felt like that whatever I was entitled to, that I was going to get it one way or the other.

Like the successful co-op tenants, her first fight was with the city over heat. That fight she lost. But she continued:

> The rent wasn't much, like I was paying $30 a month, very cheap. And some of the people stopped paying the rent, and when the city stepped in, they said one dollar a month. . . . I assumed okay, one dollar a month. So then the next thing we knew they stuck a sign up there, vacate. . . . And I was still fighting with them, and I was the last one to leave.

Her efforts to get her good friend and next-door neighbor into her present building was also a fight as well as a sacrifice of personal needs:

> I went to the landlord and I asked him about an apartment. He said they all were rented. Mind you, I don't have no place to go. I said they are all rented! He said yes. I said well, I have a lady who lives in the community and she needs a place. I said you know what? . . . If you don't rent her an apartment, I'm going to organize the tenants and I'm going to throw a picket line up here, I said, because she lives in the community and I feel like you should give community people the first choice . . . if you don't give her an apartment I will get every black person in Harlem and we will picket this site here. . . . In a couple of days, he said he had an apartment for her.

Mrs. Oilers recounted the confusion about owners during the period of city ownership. She speaks of her battles with one of the managers:

> I forgot the woman's name who was manager. She come to tell the people to pay the rent. But only one person would pay her the rent. The rest of the people would pay their rent to [representatives of the community board working with Mrs. Oilers].

There were meetings with the city at which Mrs. Oilers battled the manager:

> So then we would have meetings with the city, and I told her, I said, we are going to get the building. . . . So she is fighting me and I am fighting her. I told her in the meeting, I'm going to get that building. She said, evidently, we weren't going to get the building.

Since it was not clear who the manager worked for, it is impossible to know why the manager wanted to fight except, according to Mrs. Oilers, "she just didn't want us to have it."

As in the previous case, the tenants had to fight the city to gain control of the building. In the four years of tenant control, the city had provided a new roof, a boiler, and materials, as well as pointing the bricks on an exterior wall. They did not pay for labor for apartment renovation. At the time of the interviews, there was a waiting list for seven of the sixteen apartments that still needed work before they could be occupied. Vandalism of the halls and one apartment caused a serious drain on operating expenses and on the morale of the active tenants. The recently painted halls had been vandalized by local youths, who got into the building because the new front doors had been broken down. One apartment had been destroyed by a tenant. That experience seemed to have contributed to a prejudice against welfare recipients. Mrs. Oilers described the problem as follows:

> She got angry because welfare was paying her rent and she was not paying us. When she found out that we were going to dispossess her, she did a job on us. . . . and we had spent $3,000 to get that apartment fixed up. She knocked holes all in the wall. She even took the tiles and tore some of them up.

She went on to say that it was costing about the same as the previous renovation to fix the apartment so that it could be rented again. Both times the cost had to come out of the rent rolls.

But the apartments we saw had been transformed from dilapidated rooms with holes in the ceiling, falling plaster, and nonfunctional plumbing to comfortable, attractive places. The three leaders had used their own money to install customized and highly individual bathroom tiles and fixtures in their own apartments. The bathrooms looked like photographs in *House Beautiful*.[5] The Parks Department worker, Elba Jones, proudly displayed a photo mural of the wilderness that dominated her small living room. She explained her attachment to her apartment, as follows:

I'll tell you one thing, I'd be kind of sick if something happened and I would have to go, and I don't get my money back. I had to do an awful lot of sacrificing just to get the two rooms done.

After detailing the state of deterioration her apartment had reached, Elba described her decision to save her own money to make repairs:

The association wasn't able to pay for it to be fixed. . . . We get so many complaints about leaks and about this, about that. And the only money we have to work with is the rent roll, and it don't go but so far before it's gone, and in the winter most goes for oil, and then we pay the people we owe.

Throughout the four-year process, the leaders had chipped in their own money to buy oil for the burner when the rent rolls were insufficient and missed days at work when they had to appear in court or at a city agency. Because of Mrs. Oilers' ill health the tenants now paid an 8 percent management fee to a professional manager who had been helping them all along in her past job with the community board.

When those interviewed spoke of the future, they looked forward to securing the front doors, steam cleaning the building facade, fixing the sidewalks, painting the hallways, as well as fully renovating all apartments. All agreed that the neighborhood would improve as well. Mrs. Oilers saw signs of improvement in contrast to the decline of previous decades.

I think they are going to build it [the neighborhood] up. It started going down in the 1960s. Burned out by absentee landlords. Cheap rent. And the city stepped in for tax. They grabbed the buildings in a minute for tax.

She had only to look around the neighborhood to see improvements:

Now I see a lot of building going up. A lot of them that are renovating. And I see that they are really building up Harlem. I know . . . by the post office they are putting up a building there. I noticed that at 137th Street, the people done moved in there . . . and a lot of churches are building too. . . . (Where I lived before) it's like a ghost town, but I heard that they are surveying the block and they are talking about fixing it up.

Sadie Barton, the vice-president, was a bit more apprehensive about the building's future: "I just hope and trust it's going to get better. That's all I could say." Yet she also saw signs that the neighborhood was getting better because other groups and churches were also renovating "like we have here."

These struggling co-ops managed through a combination of determined leadership and competent technical assistance to operate as tenant-controlled buildings. The level of tenant participation and leadership skill was high enough to keep the buildings heading toward co-operative ownership. They differed from the co-ops that had already bought in that their tenant organizations were formed later and the buildings were in much worse shape. Both leaders and tenants suffered from disabilities but persevered nonetheless.

As tenant managment progressed, levels of social support in the building increased but the background of interconnected social networks was not extensive. Leaders, however, did have more of these social ties and worked hard to gain trust and participation. Three years after we collected the data, tenants in Mrs. Miller's building on 123d Street (7) had bought their building as a co-op. The building on Lenox Avenue (8) had survived well enough to still qualify for the TIL program but tenants had not yet purchased.

CO-OPS THAT FAIL

W E INCLUDED one building (9) in this chapter that had gone back into the city's Central Management inventory prior to our interviews. Another (10) went back into city ownership between the time interviews were completed and final follow-up information on the building was obtained.

The Central Management building (9) had all the problems of the buildings described above. In addition, Jack Fuller, the ex-tenant leader we interviewed, reported that many tenants were involved in drug dealing and other illegal activities. He rented an apartment in the building because it was part of the city's interim lease program. As part of his work with a community organization committed to the empowerment of the black community, he actively participated in the tenants' association and became the president. He took on most of the responsibility for maintenance and renovation, mainly doing it himself or working with other activist contractors. To take over leadership, he and two other tenants had challenged the management organization that previously signed the tenant interim lease when it was discovered the group let the lease lapse. They accused the previous leaders of misusing their positions to obtain better apartments and evade rents, and of hiring incompetent contractors. The young ex-leader described the experience of physical exhaustion caused by the hard labor and long hours he put in. He felt that the mental strain of dealing with untrustworthy people, both those for and against him, was more than he could bear. A fire that gutted the apartments of two of the more solid households in the building coupled with the death of his father drove him to a nervous collapse and near suicide. After dropping out of Columbia University to recover, he has since returned to the Harlem community to work and engage in less intense political organizing. He still kept in touch with the building and reported that some of the older women continued to try to organize the tenants to save it. They had been the most responsible members of the tenants' organization although keeping a low profile in the fights for control among tenants. He also recalled the personal support and occasional hot meals they had given him to keep him going. However, the building had returned to the city's Central Management portfolio.

Tenants in the other building (10) went through some of the hardest struggles only to come to a sad end. This would-be co-op located on Adam Clayton Powell Boulevard toward the northern edge of Central Harlem stands out as having reached the lowest level of habitability of the building in our study. Of the fifty-two apartments, only eighteen remained occupied, the others being subject to vandalism, fire, and use by drug addicts as shooting galleries. Across the street, a wall of largely abandoned and rapidly deteriorating facades extended down almost as far as we could see. All of the tenants left in the building, a gray brick structure in the middle of a block, were older people, ranging in age up to the nineties. The building had no heat, hot water, or electricity. The roof leaked, the plumbing broke, and the elevator did not work. For years the ownership of the building had been unclear and the services variable. The last to lay claim to the building were two men who collected rent and occasionally supplied heat and hot water. As in Mrs. Oilers' building, who actually owned the building was a mystery to the tenants in the years prior to city ownership. A 75-year-old man, Mr. Grayson, retired from the postal services, and a 57-year-old ex-merchandise buyer, Mrs. Baylor, who had been laid off when the store she worked for went bankrupt, began to organize other tenants. The few households left barricaded themselves in their apartments. At first, they worked with a community organization to learn about the city program and get themselves started.

Mrs. Baylor explained how the tenants had tried to maintain any level of habitability by running extension cords from their apartments to the halls. Tenants had to fall back on their own resources:

There was no super here. And if one wanted to give somebody twenty dollars to sweep the building down and mop the building down and that was it. Everybody just keeping this building whatever way they could. Everybody was just heating the building with whatever they could, gas, electric, whatever. There was no heat in the building, no heat at all.

The amount of work required on the building to bring it up to even low standards was staggering:

When we took the building over, we took it over with thirty-four empty apartments. Now if they had just been empty and needed painting, it would have been fine. But they were all vandalized, and when I say vandalized, I mean to the bone. There was no water, and no apartment, no light switch, no nothing, absolutely nothing there. So we had . . . to rehab all the way.

For the most part, tenants did the first rehabilitation without outside help beyond friends and kin:

We did a lot of our own work. There is a gentleman who has been in construction all of his life and now he's a man about 56 or 57, so he was the number one man because we certainly didn't know anything about it, and we got a few people together and what he could do and we would go into an apartment and work there until we got it together. But those were apartments, at least they had a bathroom floor. See, some of the apartments were without bathroom floors and that was where we couldn't work because we weren't ready for that.

Mrs. Baylor spoke here, as she did throughout the interview, of the lack of training and knowledge she felt in facing the overwhelming job of bringing the building back:

I was absolutely lost. Had I had any experience, . . . I just feel that it would never had been into the condition that it was because we would have known to close up the apartments when people moved out, and see to it that they were nailed up so that no one could get in there. But we didn't know. We were locked in this apartment and that was it, you know. Mr. Grayson [the president] was downstairs and we really didn't know to do anything until after we had really been hit very hard.

Her courage comes through as much in her denial of fear as in the descriptions of the conditions she and the other tenants faced:

As the people moved out, the vandals came in and took everything even down to the face basins off the walls. . . . I really wasn't frightened too, too much. But of course at one time when the landlord first walked away, it was terrible. The drugs, and the building was a haven for it because of the empty apartments and as I said there was nobody to close up the doors and try to put a little protection on us. . . . But they didn't bother us, but they were here, and that was fearful right there, you know.

Mrs. Baylor had lived in the building forty years. She remembered the early days as a complete contrast:

The place was always nice and warm. It was kept nice and I'm talking about a long, long time ago when I was just a very young girl. Well, this was a nice building, you know. The main floor was carpeted and we had a switchboard operator, and we had elevator operators and whatever. We had a night shift and a day shift. And it was nice, but then as the years went by, it started to crumble, crumble, crumble.

The building had been in the interim lease program for five years. When asked about the city's attitude to the building's extension of the lease, Mrs. Baylor said:

The building was so bad, I guess they probably felt that they would have been better off to pay us to get out . . . the building was so bad and we was doing the very best we could.

She recounted the importance of the tenants' solidarity in those early days:

Had it not been for those few people in the building who helped [six men worked every evening and week-ends], and we had ladies too in there with a paint brush in their hand, or a roller or something. Nobody really stood by and they did what they could you know. . . . At that point I think most everybody was older. There wasn't too many young people here. . . . They ranged up to, I would say 93, the last lady who passed away.

When asked what the city could do or could have done in the past, their simultaneous response was swift:

Mrs. Baylor: They could give us some money.

Mr. Grayson: No, if they could just supply the material . . . give us oil, and give us material. We wouldn't want them to actually give us a handout or any money, but those are the things that we have needed so much. . . . We need the doors very badly.

They spoke of the endless effort required the last winter to get just a small amount of oil. Mrs. Baylor concluded that she would rather be cold than go through that again. Mr. Grayson explained as follows:

> Of course it's routine, and it's something that has to be done. But it is just so taxing on you. It makes you feel like a beggar.

Yet signs of hope were still abundant. Mrs. Baylor's apartment was busy with younger women making signs about meetings, others stopping by to report on jobs underway. A copy of *Architectural Digest* lay on her coffee table in front of the beautiful old small-paned glass doors connecting the living room and dining room that she had carefully maintained. Mr. Scott, the construction worker who played so critical a role in the building renovation felt strongly about the building's future:

> That's my fantasy. To see the halls [clean] and stop the outsiders from coming in and destroying the building. . . . See we had locks on the door and they all broke the locks off. But this is my fantasy and I feel like that one day I'm going to see it. You know with the windows and with the building being steam cleaned, and when you walk there's nice clean halls. The walls are fixed. They have tile on the floors all upstairs. This is my fantasy. And I believe that my fantasy is going to come true.

By the middle of 1986, this building was once again managed by the city. As we were checking some data on the buildings against city records, we made the discovery of the change in programs and decided we would investigate further. City officials indicated that fiscal mismanagement played a major part in the city's decision to terminate the tenant interim lease. Conversations with UHAB staff confirmed that the impression was widespread that Mr. Grayson had diverted city materials and perhaps other resources to a building or buildings he owned elsewhere. We returned to the building to reinterview those we spoke with and to talk to tenants who might represent a point of view missing from earlier interviews. We had learned from other sources that the tenants' association had history of factional conflict much more serious than we had understood from earlier interviews.

The new information we obtained did confirm that the tenants' association had weathered factional dissension since our earlier investigation. Apparently a group emerged to oppose involvement in the interim lease program when it became clear that timely payment of rent and rent increases would be required. However, by the time of the later interviews the conflict had been transformed into a struggle for leadership of the tenants' association with both groups agreeing on the goal of cooperative ownership. The Baylor-Grayson faction had more support and continued in office until the building was returned to city management. The less powerful group continued to express its opposition through nonpayment of rent which they explained as an appropriate response to the slow progress those in office were making toward complete renovation.

As we arrived at the building, we were told that Mr. Grayson had died a week before. The new people we spoke with mentioned that some financial irresponsibility had occurred but they did not commit themselves on how it had occurred. One older woman attributed many of the problems to the group that would not pay rent, saying this action had made impossible the meeting of financial commitments. However, she described herself as unknowledgeable about the tenants' association. In reinterviewing Mrs. Baylor, a different picture emerged. She told of how first Mr. Grayson fell ill and then she herself was hospitalized for several months because of a stroke. As Mr. Grayson had been losing strength, he had resigned from the office and his close associate, Mr. Scott, was elected in his place. With the decline in his health, Mr. Grayson had sought help with management. A reputable technical assistance organization recommended a certain manager who was hired. He took over financial management even though the president who followed Mr. Grayson co-signed checks. As Mrs. Baylor told it, the building repairs seemed to be going more slowly. While she was hospitalized, it came to light that the manager's records did not account for the expenditure of a sizeable amount of funds. The extent to which the manager actually swindled the organization was cloudy because of lax bookkeeping practices during an early period when the organization hired and then quickly fired a first manager. She acted as if Mr. Grayson had not contributed to the swindling of resources. The illness of Mrs. Baylor, who was treasurer, further obscured problems with the records. However, the manager had not even appeared in the building for many months prior to his ultimate disappearance, claiming that he was afraid to come on the premises.

In our final interviews, the opposition faction was trying to begin a new tenants' association to attempt to reenter the leasing program on the way to becoming a co-op. Those we spoke with were uncertain about the building's future. They did not know whether the city would continue to run it or try to sell it to a private landlord. The city had made some repairs and the building condition was slightly better than it had been three years before. There was a steady supply of heat. Nonetheless, much remained to be done. None of the tenants we spoke with were trying to move despite the change in management. Mrs. Baylor, despite her possible association with financial mismanagement, accurately summarized the situation in many of the most struggling co-ops: tenants in buildings like hers can do a lot, but they need support, money, supplies, labor, and, above all, training and management help.

CONCLUSIONS

I T IS these struggling co-ops that pose the greatest challenges to the development of workable low-income co-ops in landlord-abandoned buildings. On the one hand, the conditions of the building and the lack of tenant resources place incredible burdens on the tenants. Reasonable levels of public investment could compensate for these strains as noted by the eventual success of Mrs. Miller's building (7). Here the city in the long run invested around $73,000 in Community Development Block Grant funds to bring the building up to standards adequate for sale to the tenants.[6] In addition, Section 8 rental subsidies continued to be a necessity for the building to operate.[7] In contrast to other low-income housing development schemes, the cost is not great. Yet in today's climate of fiscal austerity, Section 8 subsidies are ending with no clear replacement in sight. The city reported making similar investments in the Grayson and Baylor building only to be "defrauded." The importance of management assistance then is on a par with the need for financial and physical aid.

These buildings came later to the struggle for tenant control. The tenants of successful co-ops had developed their skills in tenant management and had in the process augmented their social support networks for an average of fifteen years. It is not clear that the final chapter on tenant control has been written in any of the buildings in which tenants have not yet bought, or even in those that went back to city management. At this point, the one building that became a co-op found the skilled assistance needed and was endowed with sufficient leadership skill and tenant participation to move forward. The stamina of existing leaders, the emergence of new ones, and the future of the social networks that bound tenant organizations, as well as access to adequate technical assistance—these are the factors which will determine the future of the buildings. To the extent that the self-management experience affected tenant perspectives, improved building conditions, and began connections to other groups and institutions, some hope for future tenant control exists.

In the next chapter we will see that even some rental buildings that had gone through landlord abandonment, city ownership, and resale were the site of tenant activism. However, in all these cases, social networks, leadership skill, and the connection to technical assistance had been even less adequate to the demands of co-oping than they were in the case of the struggling co-ops considered in this chapter.

FIVE

Renters and Abandonment

BUILDINGS THAT return to the market from city ownership as rental property housed tenants whose experience of landlord abandonment had quite a bit in common with those sold as co-ops or still in tenant or city management. The stories of deteriorating services match those in the co-ops. The histories of the tenants and the buildings told also the story of the conversion of Harlem to a black community, its ambivalent ascendence to cultural vitality, and the road it followed into the present state of abandonment and crime, combined with rebuilding and hope. In all these ways, *except* the prevalence of hope, renters and co-op residents shared the life of their community.

In some rental buildings, tenants went on to organize to fight for their homes. As in struggling co-ops, they often floundered from insufficient resources and deteriorated building conditions. In addition, the factors that weakened tenants' associations in co-ops and prospective co-ops also could be found, often to a much greater extent. The absence of organizational sophistication among tenants was frequently a major stumbling block, one that seems harder to overcome through sheer determination. In such conditions, the ties among tenants sometimes sustained a certain level of organization but the translation of such informal cooperation into building management was much harder. In other cases, lack of trust among tenants eroded the efforts of emerging leaders, who often exacerbated the mistrust through factionalism, a sort of perceived elitism, or incompetence. The clearest difference between tenant organizations in rental buildings and those in co-ops and prospective co-ops had to do with technical assistance. None of the tenants' associations in buildings that returned to the market as rentals had access to adequate technical assistance comparable to that found in successful co-ops or even in struggling co-ops. In the latter cases, some outside group usually informed the buildings of the existence of the city tenant interim lease program. Even this initial step had not occurred for most of the rental buildings. Further assistance was always necessary for a building to enter the tenant leasing program, and even more for a building to be sold to tenants. Again, most of the renters never received this second and third level of assistance.[1]

The tenants we interviewed in five buildings where tenants' associations arose viewed their situations very differently, depending on the city program the building got into (see map 1, buildings 11–15). In contrast to the tenants in the previous chapters, these seemed to feel that the building ended up in a particular program more through the actions of others than through tenant initiative.

PROGRAM ACCESS

THE HISTORY of one building (11) and its tenant organization came closest to the histories told in the preceding chapters. This 55-unit building on the corner of St. Nicholas Avenue was eventually acquired by a long-established community management group with numerous buildings in West Harlem in its portfolio. Mrs. George, an older woman who herself reached out to the group, had lived in this building on St. Nicholas Avenue in Central Harlem since 1919. Her years in Harlem paralleled those of Mr. Williams in the first co-op we described in chapter 3, and apparently the building had once been of similar quality to the one he helped save. Mrs. George gave her view of what had happened during the decline of the building:

> It was beautiful, beautiful. We had carpeting from the door on to the
> window, where the mailboxes are. And we had men that used to run the

elevator in uniform, and we had one in the morning that worked from
six through until one. . . . Oh, it was beautiful. We had a lovely table
over there with two lamps. If you came in and were tired, you could sit
down there until the man came down in the elevator. It was very nice
then, after, everything just changed.

She remembered a sharp shift in services as the landlord began to rent to
more black people and welfare residents. Physically, the building remained
in reasonably good shape until the 1950s.

Then the familiar changes occurred. The landlord died, a son took over.
He let things go somewhat. The building changed hands. Finally the landlord quit repairing the plumbing, pipes froze and broke.[2] A child was killed
in the elevator shaft. The landlord stopped providing heat. Vandals moved
in and many tenants fled. Some of the older tenants contacted a woman
who managed 7A buildings. She came in to help the tenants organize and
began to clean the building and make repairs.

The few remaining tenants that we interviewed gave much credit to the
woman manager they had contacted, as can be seen from the following
account:

> The building just started to deteriorate, and that was that. Until my friend
> came in here and she resurrected it, we both worked in here; we mopped.
> I did a lot of work in here and so did she, day and night. . . . Quite a
> few of them that was living here came to meetings.

The repairs did not go fast enough for some:

> Some of them moved out. Now they regret their move, after they see
> how the place is being rejuvenated.

Mrs. George described their process:

> We would go to different tenants, and she would have her meetings; and
> we would go downtown to different courts and charities to see what was
> doing, you know. Some of us work very hard in here. . . . We paid
> rent to the house. And we put the money in escrow in the bank. And
> whatever money that we had there went into this elevator here, $28,000
> we put into that. . . . We fixed the boiler every week. . . . And we
> mopped, went up on the roof where, what you call it, the thing up there,
> the tiles got frozen. In the winter we didn't have no heat in here. And
> the winter wasn't like this winter here, just like . . . so bitter.

The landlord continued to harass them during their efforts to improve
conditions:

And those people who worked for the landlord came in here and they would sabotage the building, sabotaged everything. You think you have heat and they would sabotage it. Anyway, we would go back and report this to the courts and he fought with us and so forth.

During the time tenants began the court procedures to have a 7A manager appointed, the woman manager went to work for the 20-year-old local development corporation that had a community management contract. The building became part of the contract. As soon as the community management group took over, their crews began to work on the building and the tenants' association faded away. Progress on rehabilitation was slow but the tenants regarded the community group as a benign landlord. The chief difference between this building history and that of some of the successful and struggling co-ops seems to be the orientation of the technical assistance received. Tenants apparently did not know anything or much about the city's tenant interim lease program. The woman manager whom they contacted did not direct them toward the goal of self-management but rather gave her energy to solving the building's many fiscal and financial problems. The length of the rehab process, which was not longer than in tenant-managed buildings, eroded the commitment of many tenants who moved away. We cannot say whether those who moved were less tied to their neighbors and the place they lived or whether the absence of participation in tenant control lessened their commitment.

Tenants in three of the four buildings sold to screened private landlords had organized during the period of landlord abandonment and the transition to city ownership. All these tenants experienced a brief period in which heat and hot water were cut off. At least some tenants rallied to maintain basic services on their own. Conditions were similar to those in most of the struggling co-ops. But in all cases the level of tenant involvement and cooperation required for co-op ownership seemed wanting. In addition, none of the tenant groups managed to find or be found by technical assistance groups that were so critical to struggling co-ops.[3]

In trying to understand the problems these tenants' associations faced, an examination of the social life of the buildings provides a good starting point. One tenants' association in a building eventually sold to a private landlord seemed to have the foundation of mutual support associated with successful cooperation. Many tenants regarded each other with underlying affection and trust. People also engaged in the little favors and daily exchanges characteristic of the more successful co-ops. In contrast, the tenants' associations in buildings marked by hostile and indifferent relations among tenants never went beyond an immediate response to crisis.

SOCIAL LIFE AND TENANT ORGANIZATIONS

W HEN TENANTS viewed each other almost like family members at the time of landlord abandonment, they reacted somewhat like a family under threat. This aspect was similar to the successful co-ops. Whatever their normal ways of organizing and supporting each other were, these relationships extended into the formation of the tenants' association. In one building (12) on West 139th Street that was bought from the city by a private landlord, Mr. Keen, an elderly man, aided by his wife, built on his informal caretaking of the building to become a tenant leader. The Keens had been pivotal in a network of older tenants also sentimentally attached to the building and the social world it housed. These friends approved of the couple's efforts to organize the 134-unit building, and told us with pride of Mr. Keen's efforts to fix the place up. But they did not participate in the struggle. For them, the friendships that existed were enough. One elderly woman, Mrs. Pratt, gave the following account:

> Everybody in here has been here fifty years, more. . . . The least they've been here . . . fifteen years. . . . They don't leave here. . . . This is one house, one family. We live like a family here. Everybody will help you, and rescue you. If somebody is dead, we go in their houses and get them envelopes and go and get money, and who lives here has got a flower as big as this, or whatever they want. We go in the house and fill it up with food, and tell everybody to come.

For her, the physical condition of the building was secondary:

> The house is falling down, and it needs fixing; the landlord don't want to fix it, but we don't want to go 'cause you know why? Why do you need a beautiful place, and every other thing if you don't have no companion. Old people get sick, and they ain't got nobody to say nothing to during the night, and nobody's bell to ring.

While she still felt protected by her friends, she recognized a change in the new people who were replacing the elderly as they died. "These people don't want to hear from you, because they don't want to make friends."

Mrs. Keen, the ex-leader's wife was more bitter. During the interview with the couple, Mr. Keen expressed a feeling that maybe a tenants' association could still work with the new landlord to improve conditions, although he himself felt too old. Mrs. Keen believed that the mutual concern people had for each other in the old days no longer existed for most of the people:

> It could make a difference but you got so many people in here, the new people in here, they're not interested in anything. They don't give a John Brown. They are not interested in anything. And the older people, they're dying out. We're all dying out.

The disappointment that most dominated their conversation was the fate of the building. Mr. Keen clearly felt that the steady decline he saw ahead was inevitable:

> I believe the condition of the house in five years, that would be the landlord's problem . . . I don't know if he intends to sell the building or walk away or not do anything. . . . I can't remember when I saw him doing anything as far as the building is concerned . . . the house will get worse all the time.

Mr. Keen contrasted the landlord's inattention to the care and affection he had lavished on the building. The refrain "I did all that work" speaks of his involvement of time, effort, and emotion:

> I used to do all the painting of the railings, the flower boxes, we had a flower garden down there. I did all that work. You can ask all the people in here. . . . I used to paint those signs out there, wash the court and all that kind of stuff. . . . I did all that work. I'm the one that did it. . . . I just wanted to have something to do, you know what I mean? That was the idea.

The friendships that existed in this building had given Mr. Keen a base from which to organize, but they were insufficient support for the struggle he confronted. He described the early phases of organizing very similarly to more successful co-op leaders:

> I had quite a few meetings and reported to the Commissions downtown. Had a lawyer with me and I did have quite a bit of the work done in the house here. But at the time it wasn't the same landlord as it is now. . . . Then he gave it up, you know, he walked away and the city took it over. They sold it to this owner now. But at the time the city had it, when I went down to the Commission, I was with [the lawyer] and he suggested that the tenants take the house over at that time, and it wouldn't cost us a cent. . . . He said it wouldn't cost us a dime, and all the rent that we collected, they wouldn't want a dime. It would go

back into the house. And there wouldn't be no taxes. . . . I thought that was a good deal. But what it turned out to be, with tenants in this house, they weren't, you know, that aggressive.

But, perhaps due in part to the size of the building, the small core of supporters could not sustain him in his efforts. He saw meetings as being poorly attended:

There are 134 units in this house. Out of 134 tenants, we may have had twelve or fifteen people. And there was no backing at all there, none whatsoever. So we wouldn't go through that, really because we know that it wouldn't work. It wouldn't have worked.

He did get aid from the community board, but somehow the landlord bought the building without the tenants' being able to make an opposing bid. Mr. Keen told of how the landlord made promises to fix up the building to the tenants but never followed through. He described trying to bring about a confrontation:

And we used to go to their meeting down there at the community board so the board wanted to know what happened to the money. So every week they'd have a lawyer with them . . . every week they'd say well, we'll have the books here next week and we went two or three weeks after that, and every week they'd have excuses, no books. So the last thing I heard was that Board 10 said they was going to Washington. I stopped going to the meeting and just what happened after that I don't know.

The community board was somehow unable to help and the landlord took over. Lack of tenant enthusiasm was key in Mr. Keen's mind.

In two privately owned buildings, tenants expressed active distrust of each other. In one of these, tenants talked to us through closed doors, most refusing to be interviewed. Located on Edgecombe Avenue (13) on "Sugar Hill," the 84-unit building close to West 145th Street had once been one of the best in Harlem. It was named after Florence Mills, a noted black stage star of the Harlem Renaissance. Physically, it retained none of its past splendor but appeared in good condition. But the barking dogs, frightened voices, and suspicious looks we encountered spoke of social deterioration. One interview with an elderly man was abruptly terminated when he suddenly decided he was being involved in some kind of illegal solicitation. During one visit to the building, we were told that a woman had been found raped and killed. Her body had been in the apartment four or five days. Ethel, the one woman who would agree to an interview stood at her door for the two hours we interviewed her, apologizing for the condition of her apartment. She said:

> I've lived in this apartment for forty-five years but if I had to holler, I'm sure no one on this floor would open their doors. People are frightened, they just wouldn't want to get involved or anything like that.

Apparently a tenants' association had been formed some years before to co-op the building. A number of tenants had gone on rent strike before the landlord abandoned the building, but had lost their case in court. When the city took over the building, a few meetings were held, one with a lawyer, but tenants did not agree to buy. The new landlord provided heat and hot water but apartments seemed to need repair and painting. Ethel described the building as having had carpets down the stairs, a canopy to the street, and an awning that was changed every year. There had been no "nicer house" in Harlem. She seemed to blame the decline of the building as much on the change of people as on the landlord. Now, she stated, the landlord let anybody in, everybody had been robbed, and no one could be trusted. Still, she loved Harlem. A former chorus dancer, she continued to go to jazz clubs at 74 years of age, even though she feared being attacked coming into and going out from her apartment to the elevator to the street.

LEADERSHIP INADEQUACIES

I N SOME buildings, distrustful relationships among tenants were clearly made worse by an absence of effective leadership. When leaders lack experience, skills, and sometimes the personality characteristics that would make them successful, isolation from technical assistance and political connections can be fatal to the tenants' organization.

In one of the privately owned buildings (14) on 152d Street, with 30 units, factions had formed along racial lines. Most of the black tenants interviewed commented on the large number of Puerto Ricans in the building, some saying only that they would not speak English to them if other Puerto Ricans were around. Others were most overtly critical of their habits and child care customs. Spanish-speaking tenants did not really tell their side of the story, being more reluctant to be interviewed and keeping the interviews brief when they did consent. At this point the absence of a Spanish-speaking interviewer undoubtedly created barriers to getting the whole story. The leadership was primarily black although a Hispanic woman was named as having been active. She gave a very brief interview that essentially added little information. What was clear was that tenants felt distrust for many of their neighbors, sometimes including the tenant leader.

One tenant in the building, Mrs. Johnson, gave the following description of the tenants' association. "It's all right to have an association when you got people who really know what they're doing. As far as I'm concerned, these people actually don't know what they're doing." She had been involved in some court transactions that eventuated in the tenants "signing something," apparently without any one understanding what it meant.

Distrust of Mrs. Saunders, the black president of the tenants' association, made cooperation even within the primarily black tenants' association difficult. To some extent, the new landlord remained a main target of hostility for many. The building was being renovated during our interviews. Tenants complained about the disruption in heat, the poor quality of building materials, and the lack of responsiveness to requests for repairs. One tenant, Mr. Loomis, took the interviewer on a tour of his apartment, pointing out cracked ceilings, a torn down wall that had yet to be replaced, and other places where repairs had been made and were already broken again. When asked what the building would be like in five years, he replied, "If it lasts that long. I don't think it will last that long." Mrs. Johnson, another tenant, gave an even longer list of examples of failed or inadequate repairs. At the same time, she worried about the increasingly high rent.

Mrs. Saunders, the tenants' association president, felt that the new landlord had snatched the building away from the tenants while they were running it. Her description supported a concern tenants expressed that the tenants' association leaders did not really know what was going on. The president was unfamiliar with the city's Alternative Management programs. She stated that she had been working with someone to collect rents, but she did not know (or would not reveal) who they represented. She continued to try to block the rehabilitation by writing letters to the person at the Housing Preservation and Development Agency who had signed the notice of sale through the Private Ownership and Management Program and by putting out a newsletter for tenants.

A 24-unit building (15) on 129th Street now managed by a relatively new community organization (which was also managing two other buildings on the same block, and a third one a block away) had much in common with the landlord-owned buildings with histories of tenants' association organizing. Many of the tenants had moved into the building thirty to forty years before. The landlord who owned the building for most of this period died, his son took over but seemed to care little about the tenants. The next landlord never kept the building up, and some tenants began to withhold rent. One tenant spoke of being afraid to go into her bathroom because of the rats that lived there. By 1975, some tenants organized to collect rent themselves and pay for oil and electricity. The tenants' association never really got off the ground because many refused to cooperate. Then conflicts broke out among the leaders, eventually resulting in the dissolution of the cooperative organization.

One of the leaders of the now inactive tenants' association, Melvin Fontaine, recounted his view of the abandonment period. A small group had saved the building for the new landlord. The other tenants would not cooperate with them:

> The landlord was gone so we stayed and the people wouldn't work with you. We had to buy the oil and all that. We had to buy it because we took over. We had to pay the bill for the hall lights. . . . No one would come up except for a few of us. There were four of us up here. The rest wouldn't pay for nothing. That oil was $400 and something. We used to get, I don't know how much a gallon is now, but it cost us good money . . . it may last us only two weeks. . . . And the other tenants wouldn't give us a dime. They would go and hook on people's lights downstairs and everything. Man it was terrible, but you don't know. That's why the landlord walked out. They all hook up down there. They don't pay no rent.

The four elderly leaders, two men and two women, carried on until the community organization bought the building. Only two of them remained through the renovation. Mr. Fontaine, the remaining elderly man, now 80, had mixed reactions to the community organization's effort to encourage a tenants' association. He felt he would leave it to the younger folks, although he would go to the meetings. He still distrusted some of the old tenants who remained and doubted whether the younger ones would have the commitment. At a critical point when the community organization stepped in, it seemed that three other families had tried to make the building into a co-op but failed. Mr. Fontaine refused to go along with the move because he didn't like the man who would become the leader. In addition, he remembered some of the supporters of the co-op had refused to help pay for oil and electricity during the period when the tenants ran the building. Therefore he felt they might not be responsible co-op owners. He summed up his attitude now as follows:

> Just pay my rent and do what I'm supposed to be doing, and that's all.
> Nothing to worry about. That's the way I like it. I don't want no re-
> sponsibilities now. I'm an old man.

Mrs. Howard also had a negative view of the tenant's ability to run a
co-op:

> They had tenants' meeting with the people in the house. I've never both-
> ered with it. . . . The door was wide open, they had these teenagers
> running in and out and everything. So why complain to the man about
> this and about that when their own children were doing the dirt. Yes,
> messing up everything. Between them and the grown-ups too. The grown-
> ups would do it and blame it on the kids. You know what I mean? They
> were throwing trash all over the house, in the hallways and everything,
> mailboxes broken in and everything else.

Yet she thought there were improvements brought about by "cracking down
on that and they had all these tenants' meetings." But "The leader was
back in her rent and quite a few of them was back in their rent." The
future looked somewhat better: "Now it's working out all right, it's working
out good. Before, you'd be scared to come in here. The little old woman
you just saw out there, she used to be scared to come in here."

Dorothy Monroe, a young single mother who moved in only after the
community group renovated, knew nothing of the history of conflict. In
fact, she had no social involvement in the building at all. She described her
relations as follows:

> I know the man across the hall. I'm very rarely here. My schedule is
> totally different from everyone else's. So they don't see me coming and
> going. . . . I'm home in the daytime when everyone else is working.
> There's a lot of people I don't know.

She lived in the apartment next to the entrance door. Therefore she felt
that she probably recognized tenants, but she clearly did not play the kind
of gatekeeper role frequent in successful co-ops:

> Well, I would recognize them going in and out of the building and I would
> assume that they live here because I see them regularly. But I don't
> know them, their names or what apartments they live in because I never
> go up the steps. I just come in the door and go in the house.

She completely rejected the idea of buying her apartment and being a member of a co-op. Where elderly women and men used a first floor window

or lobby as their vantage point to ensure security, she regarded her location in the building as an invasion of her privacy. She described what she wanted:

> I would buy a house, not an apartment. Because I like single units. See, like down South you don't come into a building. Everybody comes through the same door here, but in the South you have your own door, your own private entrance. And I'm used to privacy, and this is not private to me . . . not to me. . . . I can see every time everybody goes out the door. . . . and I can't see paying all of that money, talk about seventy, eighty thousand for a condominium or a co-op and it's not really yours. Not directly, you just own a piece of the building. I want to own the whole thing, you know? I'd rather have a house so that I could have a yard and everything.[4]

She also stated that there were no places in New York City that she thought were good for raising a child.

Clearly the internal conflicts combined with inexperienced leadership created serious impediments to cooperative ownership. However, looking back to the co-op on 115th Street (6), we can see that sufficient outside help plus strong underlying social bonds could at least in that instance sustain tenant control and give leaders additional time and aid in developing the necessary skills.

NEW LANDLORDS BUT NO SIGNS OF CHANGE

FOR SOME tenants, landlord abandonment appeared to be part of a continuous process in which serious neglect and lack of services ebbed and flowed according to forces beyond tenants' knowledge or control. Many older residents in buildings owned by nonprofit community management groups and private landlords denied or scarcely noticed that former landlords had abandoned their properties. They perceived the new owners as just the most recent in a string of landlords, some better and some worse than the new management. Other tenants were younger working people or were older but new to the building. For them the crisis period in the building's history was a memory of the past. The younger working people were busy with their lives and usually declined to be interviewed. Much of what we learned about them was from interviews with middle-aged and elderly people. But we knew from the analysis of the 131 interviews that working people were more satisfied than non-working people with landlord and community-group ownership. Tenants in two privately owned buildings (16 and 17),[5] fit this pattern, and in six community management buildings (18–24) owned by two different groups (see map 1).

The older respondents shared some experiences and differed from the interviews of other people we have reported. Theirs were also stories of an odyssey from the South to Harlem, although they had more of a negative view about the future of the building and neighborhood, and were less inclined to be friendly with their neighbors. While some people were either unable or unwilling to move, or both, they did not organize to fight their landlords or form a cooperative. Some felt they were too old to get involved in any new organization. In contrast to their earlier lives when they were mobile and able to undertake the adventure and risk of coming North, they may have become too physically and psychologically tired once more to sally forth. Age alone cannot explain their collective lack of energy. It was the older people who were often prominent as leaders in successful cooperatives. More likely, personal factors, including their health, what had happened to them during the course of their lives, and a debilitating reaction to changes in the neighborhood combined to prevent action.

The stories of two tenants in a landlord-owned building reveal a classic stereotype on the one hand, and a potential resource for sustaining a social network on the other. An elderly black woman, Mrs. Harry, lives in a six-story 50-unit building (16), its yellow bricks dulled by grit and soot. It is on a block fronting Jackie Robinson Park (formerly Colonial Park), where it is one of two similar buildings on Bradhurst Avenue. The surrounding frontage facing the park, on other blocks to the north and south, is marked with vacant lots or abandoned buildings interspersed with occupied structures. Across the side street a cannibalized automobile sat on an empty lot. Mrs. Harry's building showed signs of repairs to the outside, but the carelessness with which its pediment had been secured indicated that aesthetics were not a motivating factor. The interior was intact, and the lobby with a large birthday card with space for changing names, showed signs of some neighboring. There was a working elevator and the building plan was organized around two inner airshafts with apartments opening onto a hallway. In one of the airshafts a well-tended flower box was adjacent to a broken window covered with a wooden board in a makeshift arrangement. Except for a couple of apartments with two rooms, the majority are one and one-half rooms.

Mrs. Harry had a stroke ten years ago. When she recovered and was walking outside, a youth knocked her down on 150th Street. The youth and his friend were going to take her to the park, but a friend of hers came along and prevented this. The incident has had a marked effect on her. She admitted she can go out but she is frightened. "I'm really afraid to walk in the street too much." She will cross Frederick Douglass Boulevard, a block away, for milk but will not travel any distance. She referred to a tenant group that may be in the lobby every night but hasn't worked up her nerve to ask them what they do. This attitude extended to her conjecturing about her response to other activities. When asked if she would join a community organization to fight against drugs, having said that the park used to be nice but dope is sold there now, she replied, "Boy, I would have to make my nerves better first, because like I first said, I'm afraid." Mrs. Harry has lived in the building for twenty-eight years. She stays to herself, and, even before her accident, hardly associated with her neighbors; she spoke of feeling lost, and of not knowing other people. When told about the formation of tenant cooperatives and the $250 equity needed, she responded positively to the idea but didn't know where she would get that kind of money. She also liked the idea of a retirement home, in part because moving there would mean she could afford it. Her association of the retirement home with seeing people every day was in contrast to her current loneliness and isolation. She told the interviewer that she had checked out retirement homes and whites have better places than blacks. "They are all out of good places. If you don't have money, there is no good place."

In contrast, Mrs. Jefferson has lived in the same building for almost half her 93 years of age. She was aware of the tenant patrol. She thought they did a pretty good job and helped out with papers and applications. Although she claimed that she thought a lot was going on but didn't know about it because she didn't bother with it, she was aware that the senior citizen center across the street had closed. The center had helped with papers about rent and utilities. Mrs. Jefferson also had a stroke about four years earlier. She too thought that a senior citizen building "or something like that" would be a better place for her to live. At the same time she appeared to have a more positive manner about herself and the building on Bradhurst. She thought the building had stayed nice or "not too bad." She took a walk every day, knew where all the markets are and their relative quality of goods, called people who couldn't get out to cheer them up. She expressed a genteel contempt for a 62-year-old male friend who had a back problem although he was "not an old man." Her behavior was guided by her feeling that you have to help yourself because "if you just sit and get in a rut, if you sit and complain you'll be by yourself." When asked about the building's future in the next five years, Mrs. Jefferson expanded on an earlier point she had made about parents supervising their children more. She felt that people had to do more for themselves.

> Some of the people . . . they . . . live in a place and they . . . work and . . . don't bother about it. They don't bother to paint. . . . Even the apartment where they live; they just don't take pride in it. . . . You can be poor and your job's dirty, but you can be clean and take pride in what you do have.

She offered advice about a way of life she had clearly followed.

> If you don't have but one dress or one pair of shoes, you can put some polish. If you don't have polish, you get some bacon grease or get any-thing and rub that shoe up, and wash that dress and press it, and make a good appearance. And it don't have to be something so fine and so this or that or other. If you just got one dress, you got a bed, you got a dresser, clean it up.

Of the two women, most of the tenants interviewed in buildings man-aged by a nonprofit community group or a private landlord were more like Mrs. Harry. Already beleagured by problems confronting them because of their race and class, other events in their lives had left them with little resources to mobilize themselves or others. They were not in Harlem by accident, but in their later life they were accidentally living in buildings that experienced lack of services if not abandonment. They had moved into the buildings because they were the best that they could afford at the time. Most of them made that move when it was easier to find apartments, and had stayed for upwards of twenty years. Mr. Wallis, one respondent, saw progress because he had found a building owned by a private landlord rather than the city. He took the opportunity to move into Mrs. Harry's building when a vacancy arose because his friend passed on. If these respondents moved, it was most often within a few buildings or blocks from where they had been.

Some of the buildings they were in were as good or as bad as others where there had been efforts to form tenants' groups. Indeed, even in some of the buildings discussed in this section, there were scattered ref-erences to "off and on again" tenant groups. But there were neither the internal or external resources to form a cooperative, nor the desire to do so, although there may have been a latent possibility. The tenants per-ceived new owners as just the most recent in a string of landlords, some better and some worse than the new management.

LANDLORD CHANGES: TENANT RESPONSES

ONG-TERM residents invariably remembered the turnover of landlords in any one building or the switch from one landlord to the city to another landlord. When tenants moved to a relatively stabilized building, their comparisons with life in other abandoned buildings were vivid. Tenants characterized their previous buildings as "conditions they escaped from." One elderly woman's comments were echoed by others.

> It got so bad. The landlady started taking anybody. Those boys came in, and she rented rooms, you know, and Lord, I was robbed three times. These people came in here, you know, and they were robbing the whole house. It got so bad over there so I kept praying to the Lord to help me find somewhere to go.

For a number of tenants, the community management buildings provided a refuge from prior living conditions. Jesse Harrington, an older woman in a 20-unit community management building (18) on West 114th Street, who had moved in eight years ago when the abandonment process had long since been over, found conditions when she got there "pretty good." The house she was previously living in was condemned, the water pipes were stolen, and she didn't like the newer tenants. She worried about stopping fires without access to water. When she went looking for another apartment in the Bronx, she found the "most dilapidated places," and then she ran across the building in which she lives now.

Another tenant in the same building for only two years had similar experiences. Fiona James had been living in one building on West 115th Street for thirty years and was forced to move when that was torn down. She moved into a building on 126th Street but couldn't remember the address, saying, "I really want to block that out of my mind. I don't even know the number of that house." At first conditions in the unnumbered house of her memories were "alright" but then the landlord gave it up; her son advised her to get out and just take her clothes. She stayed with a girlfriend, storing her newly purchased bed in her friend's building, and waited until she got a call from the community group.

In a building (19) on 129th Street with 24 units, Terry Jones, an elderly black woman, reviewed her residential history. She had been the tenant of a father-son team with the promising name Progressive Operating Corporation. They had an uptown office on 126th Street and Lenox Avenue.

After two months, they moved her from the top floor of one building on Seventh Avenue because she was robbed, to a ground floor apartment on Lenox, where she stayed from 1941 to 1953. She had been moved again because "I was afraid of rats."

> The rats ran all over. . . . my brother . . . bought me a big rat trap. . . . I came home from work. I was working then at Club 65 . . . but nobody was home but me. . . . I rested on my couch for a few minutes . . . And I had one arm hanging down off the couch . . . something woke me up nipping at my hand, and I jumped like that. Then a big rat went to the bathroom.

Terry recalled that plumbers had been working in the bathroom and had left a big hole. She took the trap and "laid back down, pretending like I was sleeping again . . . but after a while I heard something say screams, like a child." When she got up, the trap had "cut him right across his neck," and "he had splashed blood all over the walls." In the next building she moved to, she recounted taking an active part in organizing a rent strike and court appearances in the building she lived in before 1975.

> The landlord just disappeared. . . . the building was condemned. . . . We had a, what do you call it . . . a tenant strike. And we went to court, the tenant court, but nothing was done. I worked with, I forgot the name, the one on Lenox Terrace. Whatever the name, that's where we worked but the strike didn't materialize. . . . Everybody began to move out, we had no steam, no hot water. During cold weather like this, we burned the oven until the oven burned out. It wouldn't even bake bread because it burned the oven out.

The apartment on West 129th Street where she was is now managed by a community group.

In a fourth case, Mrs. Pritchard found the building (20) on West 142d Street in which she now lived when it was still owned by a private landlord. Having moved from a city-owned building, she twice experienced the process of landlord abandonment, but the transition was less extreme the last time. She didn't move, and witnessed improvements under city management and subsequently the community group's:

> When the landlord had it [the building], we didn't have the service that we got now. We didn't have the remodeling, which [the community group] did. They did a very good job here. . . . They put in new bathroom

fixtures, sink, new stove, refrigerator. They painted the walls, put in storm windows. When the landlord had the building, services were terrible. When the city took it over, it was pretty good.

She saw no need for a tenant organization in the community management building since conditions were comparatively good. Her energy went to decorating her apartment and attending crocheting classes at a local church sponsored senior citizen center.

Where a community management group has been doing a satisfactory job, restoring essential services like heat and hot water, responding somewhat quickly to requests for repairs, tenants were likely to restrain their criticism. Mrs. Harrington, the tenant living for eight years in a building managed by a nonprofit community group, rated their services highly! "They're good people. . . . they take care of the heat and hot water. And the repairs. . . . All you have to do is just tell them a problem and they will fix it."

Tenants generally praised the organization for trying, even though repairs were sometimes slow. Heat and hot water were reliable and rents reasonable, even though some were just making it on inadequate Social Security checks and in some cases Section 8 rental assistance.

Mrs. James thought the same community group was doing a "beautiful job."

> I like their promptness. I like the service they give and I like the security they give here. . . . The super's always here on the job, and the door stays locked. If the door gets anything wrong with it, they are here to fix it. And . . . they don't let anybody move in here. They have to go through a good investigation now and everybody in here is very quiet people. They don't have that running in, drinking, and hanging around in the halls.

But there were others whose complaints about previous landlords included the present one. In the same interviews where they may comment how glad they were to get into the building, there may also be complaints about the size of kitchens, the extent of rewiring, insufficient replacement of stoves and "fridges," and general resignation about where poor people can live. Opinions about housing conditions were intermixed with life chances and the relation of race to income. For example, Jesse Harrington, who moved in eight years ago because the last house she was in was condemned, understood the difficulties of trying to find a place in the 1980s, that poor people have nowhere to live, and that things can't get much worse. If you closed your eyes, you might have thought she was Petry, the novelist, describing conditions forty years ago.

Terry Jones, the elderly woman who had been moved four times and is now in a community management building, found that the group did not respond quickly to her complaints. Indeed this community group, the same one as in Jesse's and Fiona's building, faced a daunting task. They would have to make up for fourteen years of neglect during which the apartment had not been painted, the ceiling had fallen in, the refrigerator door had come off, and holes appeared all over. Terry coped by trying not to think about it and, despite her problems, spoke of a network in the building and people she knew. Her socializing, it seemed, was only restrained by her inability to climb stairs. In the past, Terry recalled that her block work with the PAL (Police Athletic League) brought her into contact with kids for whom she found a place to play, even letting them come upstairs to use her bathroom.

Terry knew almost everyone in her 24-unit building. As she went through each apartment in her mind, she recounted the history of tenants and remarked on those who attended meetings. She felt that although she could call a meeting and get tenants involved, she had too many health problems of her own and her husband's to deal with. She could more easily imagine playing a supportive role:

> When I see myself clear, I would continue to talk with some of the younger groups and tenants out here, especially the people living in apartment 6. There are two nice younger girls up there. And Mrs. Jones' daughter and her son and a few others I know. I'd call them together and leave it like this, and ask them, "Are you a chairman or a manager? I will stick with you and I will back you and do anything I can to help you, but please organize yourselves a tenants' association. Get yourselves a secretary, a treasurer, what do you call it—a board. And get yourselves everything you need and have yourselves a little group that you can fight and do anything you want, and we could really take the landlord to court."

Mrs. Jones, who was interested in a tenants' association, opposed purchasing the building because of its rundown condition. It was not clear that her optimism about helping to form a tenants' association was well-founded. From some of her descriptions of youth programs she had organized on the block, it sounded as though she might have been one of the persons another tenant saw as letting undesirable young people into the building.

Interviews in the two privately owned buildings (16 and 17) on Bradhurst, down from Sugar Hill and across from Jackie Robinson Park, had quite a different cast, although there too tenants reported little or no awareness that the previous landlord had abandoned the building. Mr. Wallis summed up what seemed to be the prevailing attitude: "There's no point of speaking about buildings because they belong to someone else." Most tenants had lived in the buildings from twenty to fifty years. Even the newcomers we spoke with had been there a dozen years. However, many of the newest tenants, mostly working people, would not be interviewed, or, after agreeing to an interview, canceled because of work schedules. Mr. Taylor who lived for twenty-five years in the same building as Mr. Wallis, summed up many of the attitudes tenants expressed: "When I moved in here, everybody knew everybody. What I mean by that, there was more communication with one another. Now you don't know who's coming here and who's who. They don't say anything to me, but it's all right."

The building's facades and hallways presented a better-maintained appearance than most. Tenants reported reasonably good service, although other statements in the interviews sometimes contradicted this. One man said he would never buy an apartment in the building if it were to become cooperatively owned because it was in terrible shape. Others in his building were more satisfied, but several hoped to move. Despite the fact that Section 8 was provided for tenants, many believed they might not be able to afford their apartments in the future.

Tenants are not completely satisfied, either in these buildings or the ones described earlier. But in these buildings, there were no signs of either tenants' associations, interest in co-oping, or assistance by community organizations. Without the co-oping process, there is one less opportunity to develop a building-wide social network, although there were signs of some neighboring.

KNOWING YOUR NEIGHBORS

WHEN RESIDENTS in buildings managed by nonprofits felt the organizations saved the buildings from further decline and were improving it for the future, this feeling spilled over to their opinions about their neighbors. Generally tenants liked each other and trusted the organization to fill vacancies responsibly. When younger people moved into the building with senior citizens, the age groups appeared to get along. The older women interviewed all named from one to several close friends in their buildings. The men kept more to themselves but reported general good will among neighbors. The following description of tenant relations was fairly typical for male tenants: "They [the tenants] are friendly. They share the rent and look out for each other and we get along good."

The following quotations exemplify the range of women's responses, from noncommittal assertions that people don't bother each other to more positive feelings. For example, Mrs. Harrington stated the following:

I do very little visiting around here. We are all to ourselves mostly. I always stay in the house. That's the best policy. Why disturb each other and get in each other's business. And this and that, and that only causes problems. . . . I think everybody's friendly.

An elderly woman in another building also stated, "I don't know nobody but the super and Mrs. R. upstairs. I don't know everybody 'cause everybody stays to themselves and I do too."

But Fiona James, a more outgoing older woman in Harrington's building, enjoyed her relationships with younger tenants, saying they treated her like a mother or a sister. She described the socializing in the building as mainly casual, and in a time-honored tradition in New York City of bringing chairs—usually aluminium with plaid plastic patterns on the seats and backs— to sit outside the building on the sidewalk and chat. She advised us to "pass by here some day and you'd see everybody out there. We know each other and we sit down there and talk." James talked of other tenants as being almost like family, but did not apply the sentiment to the whole building as in cooperatives. She observed:

I think this is the tightest floor. We had one tenant right over there who died. Now the four of us on this floor were just like that. And that one . . . me and her is closer than the others. We are like sisters.

The building's future did not command much attention from these tenants, but most felt relatively secure against unreasonable rent increases and other threats to their continued residency. In the absence of a mobilizing crisis, these tenants focused primarily on the insecurity they felt in the face of the crime and devastation they perceived as endemic to Harlem.

In the two landlord-owned buildings (16 and 17) adjacent to each other and fronting Jackie Robinson Park, the social climates seemed to differ. Many people in the smaller building refused to be interviewed, even after repeated return visits. Of the residents in the thirty apartments, only one person would talk with us. She said that she knew no one else in the building even though she had lived there for around thirty years. Those people she had known had moved out and she had not gotten to know those who moved in. In the other building with 50 units, Mrs. Jefferson was mentioned by a number of those we interviewed as someone to talk to who knew about the building. It was here that a young woman had taken it on herself to put up the collective greeting card and seasonal pictures in the halls. However, her work as a live-in caretaker made it impossible for her to schedule an interview. The networks that did exist apparently did not involve many of the tenants.

William Taylor, who also said he didn't bother to get to know the tenants because they moved so frequently, described others' references to a tenants' association in derisive terms.

> They don't really have a tenants' association. They have a bunch of people sitting around, you know, they don't do nothing.

He thought that all they did was "yak" and sometimes open the door for older people coming in. Mr. Wallis, who lived in the building ten years, completely denied that there was an association.

> Lordy no. There used to be one before I lived here, but I don't remember that. . . . other people wanted a tenants' organization, you know so they organized it. It was just among the tenants. Those that were interested, they moved.

He went on to describe problems he had had in filling out forms, the sort of thing Mrs. Jefferson claimed the tenants' patrol helped with, and stated that he could find no one to help him. Even Mrs. Jefferson, during the course of the interview, went on to say that she didn't often see people from the building, especially the younger people. When asked what the building will be like in five years, she answered as follows:

> Well, that's a hard question and I don't know. It's like a lot moving in and out, and I don't even know the people. I don't keep up with them because I just go in and out and I see them, because they move in and they move out and they keep on the move. So I couldn't even say what their feeling would be like five years from now. . . . I hope it would be better but you see, say for instance, some of the apartments in the building now because of the way people move in, they don't treat the apartments like they should. . . . some of the people, they just live in a place and they just work and they don't bother about it. They don't bother to paint certain times. They just live there and they just don't take care of their apartment.

In the six interviews in this building, about 10 percent of the households, tenants repeatedly said they didn't know what was going on, they didn't know the "new people" moving in and out, and they didn't know what would happen to the building in the future. Many mentioned fear of crime as a big factor in their lives. Mrs. Sheffield, a wheelchair-bound woman, talked of how little she left her apartment: "I don't bother to go sit in the park. . . . And I don't want to. I sit here like I'm sitting and enjoy it but to go out there is too much crime." Most expressed a sense of hopelessness and of abandonment, not by the landlord but by the world. Mr. Taylor described the neighborhood this way:

> You've got a lot of people around here who work for it, but it's still a stinking neighborhood. You could see that, with all the neighborhood burned down and everything. The city don't do nothing except for a few places; just enough to say that people live there.

When asked about the power of the community to change conditions, he replied:

> That the city has to do, the city had to do that for themselves. How the hell can we do it? We ask for different things and we get shit around here. We get our faces washed in it.

Yet his was no stereotypical "welfare mentality." He had earned a living since he was 12, working at a butcher's shop and auto shop to help his parents, subsequently sending several children to college. After retiring at 62, he found his pension and social security too small to live on so he continues to work part-time as well as coach a boys' baseball team.

CONCLUSIONS

NOT EVERYONE wants to live in a cooperative. There may not be enough motivation or the appropriate skills for tenants to work through the crisis of landlord abandonment, resolve conflicts, and sustain enough energy and commitment for the continued involvement co-oping brings. In such cases, a breach is filled by transfer of ownership to a nonprofit or for profit landlord or Central Management. The transition from one landlord to another may be smooth and orderly, conflicts or conditions not having reached an extreme, or the changes may be very disruptive.

In this chapter, tenants described how they thought about and lived through abandonment. There was no simple or uniform response, particularly when landlord abandonment is seen as one aspect, although a major one, of the multiple crises poor people often face. These crises seemed to have interfered with tenants' abilities to extend their household resources to the building as a way of coping with abandonment. In some of the buildings studied, social relationships appear to have once been strong but to have atrophied through death or the moving away of residents. In others, the physical and social decline of the building went hand in hand. For some tenants, efforts to cooperate led to bitter dissension. Regardless of the situation in any one building that became a co-op or at least entered the tenant leasing program, organizations and politically active individuals provided assistance to tenants in all the buildings in a way that did not occur in buildings bought by nonprofit or for profit landlords. It can be argued that the assumption of ownership by a nonprofit represents assistance, as the group is mandated to assist the tenants to form a limited equity cooperative. At the time of our research, and in the buildings where we interviewed, community groups did not actively pursue this goal in a way that affected tenants' consciousness. When the idea of a cooperative emerged as an active alternative, the tenants participated in the process much more than in other buildings owned by nonprofits. Transfer from a nonprofit to a tenants' cooperative has occurred in a handful of cases, although not in our study. Some housing experts have recommended that landlords encourage and help establish tenants' associations in the privately owned buildings. This had not occurred in the buildings in this study nor does it seem to be a goal the city will adopt.[6] Unlike the successful co-ops, there were no, or only faintly remembered, expressions of tenants' indignation about the city becoming their landlord. On the contrary, some tenants experienced better conditions under city management. Others who might have shed light on this had either died or moved away. There was no apparent sign of sufficient camaraderie to mobilize others. Usually, physical conditions had not deteriorated enough, or tenants appeared lacking in the requisite skills to be effective leaders.

Even the most sophisticated tenants in better and worse buildings could not do all the work required in reclaiming abandoned buildings. The importance of community organizations became clear as we reviewed the interviews and analyzed why limited equity cooperatives were successful in some buildings and not in others. We began to see that one thing missing in the non-co-ops were references to individuals or organizations for technical assistance. *None* of the tenants in landlord-owned buildings that had tried to become co-ops but failed because of problems with tenant coop-eration reported working extensively with technical assistance groups. In the next chapters we analyze further the complex patterns and interactions between organizations and how they relate to the household and building organization.

III

THE ROOTS OF ACTION
AND INACTION

SIX

Organizations: A Supportive Infrastructure

A LL THE buildings in this study completed a cycle from landlord abandonment through city ownership to some new form of ownership. In some of the buildings we found that tenants made the transition along with the buildings; in other cases, many of the original tenants left. Relations of tenants with outside organizations proved critical and determined much of the building's fate.

Looking at the interviews as a whole, the period of interaction with organizations extended roughly from the pre–World War II era during which the buildings were constructed through 1985, the end of our data collection. The rise and demise of organizations have been covered in other books, most recently in a book focusing on New York City by Ronald Lawson with Mark Naison.[1] The focus here is on the significance of intervention by organizations and the array of services they delivered to tenants in crisis.

BUILDING, COMMUNITY, AND SOCIETAL CHANGE

S TARTING IN the 1960s the decline in physical and social conditions of Harlem which began in the 1930s, and accelerated in the 1940s and 1950s, began to get even worse. At the same time, political and social activism was on the rise. The tenants who participated in this study were either a part of these changes or affected by them. Some were touched more intimately than others, having had jobs in neighborhood based antipoverty programs of the 1960s, which provided them with a reservoir of experiences to draw from when faced with abandonment.

Housing options in Harlem, as in other poor communities, varied as a function of federal and local programs and of housing deterioration and abandonment. During the 1960s, War on Poverty programs helped shield some low-income people from the impact of urban renewal and the restructuring of the job market. The former had decreased the number of available and affordable housing units and the latter had phased out manufacturing jobs as the service sector began to expand.[2] For those who benefited, programs on child care, job training, employment, and housing provided relief and options for some to assume leadership roles. The alleged War on Poverty, really only a skirmish, was followed by Model Cities with its comprehensive mandate to coordinate resources and develop innovative programs. These were specifically tied to the physical environment—housing, infrastructure, and transportation—bringing in social welfare, job creation, health care, and education programs for a population living in designated poverty areas. The two efforts promised but ultimately failed to provide, for a vast number of people, better living conditions or control over their own lives. Both programs were followed by Community Development Corporations (CDCs) which were to fill in the gaps left by these earlier efforts. CDCs would engage directly in economic development and be controlled by minority entrepreneurs.

Virtually all federal, state, and city programs were tried in Harlem, from programs like public housing in the 1940s to code enforcement in the 1960s, a veritable alphabet soup from OEOs (Office of Economic Opportunity) to CAAs (Community Action Agencies) to CDCs. They were never enough. Tenants experienced decline in the quality and services of their buildings and their neighborhoods. Boarded-up buildings, fires, and vandalism became increasingly common until abandonment reached new highs in the mid- and late-1970s. During this period, the supply of new public housing failed to meet the increased demand. Many Harlem residents and poor people throughout the city wait ten, fifteen, and twenty-five years for an apartment; many never get one at all. As in other cities, the public housing agency has a waiting list; in New York the 200,000 people on the waiting list easily outnumber the 175,000 apartments the agency owns.[3]

At the city level, changes in the economic base translated into more demands for services. People were losing jobs because the firms they worked for had relocated elsewhere, or they lacked the entry level skills needed to fill the available jobs. Earlier generations had benefited from the wartime efforts, and then the expansion of the public sector. When the more recent generation found work, it was likely to be clustered at the menial end and to be minimum wage service jobs. At the same time, the city's property tax base eroded. Efforts to force landlords to comply with building codes and pay property taxes failed to prevent decay and the quickening pace of abandonment. The fast foreclosure law passed by the City Council took effect in 1977 and had unanticipated consequences. This law reduced tax foreclosure proceedings from three years to one, but rather than acting as an incentive for negligent landlords speeded up the flood of buildings coming into city ownership. The Harlem landscape became pockmarked with abandoned buildings.

When in the 1980s certain locations became hot real estate markets and targets for gentrification, landlords paid their taxes, emptied their buildings of poor people, and "warehoused" the units until they could convert them to luxury cooperatives and condominiums. In other areas, like Harlem, speculators bought and sold buildings throughout the abandonment period, making a quick profit. By the late 1980s, signs of incipient gentrification can be spotted at the southern and western fringes of parts of Harlem. In 1987, the white developer of the first condominium project is reported to be having no trouble selling apartments to whites in Central Harlem on 113th Street. Public and private financial interests are waiting to see what other inroads of whites might occur.

The community organizations, political officials, and courts that played so important a part in the formation of the limited equity co-ops we studied reflected the currents of the period. Many of the community groups that aided those we spoke with grew out of the wave of political activism following the civil rights movement and accompanying the opposition to the Vietnam war. A few, like Met Council, go back even further. Urban riots and black consciousness spawned a multiplicity of small and large, short-lived and lasting, successful and unsuccessful groups trying to bring about greater equality and better living environments for the urban poor and for blacks. These groups touched the lives of people suffering from declining housing conditions and influenced their options when faced with abandonment. Table 6.1 locates the larger and more active and successful organizations involved in housing advocacy for low-income people on a timeline from pre-1966 to 1983. Many of the lesser-known community groups named or spoken of by study participants have disappeared from the community. Likewise their names but not their actions have been forgotten by those we interviewed. In other cases, tenants remembered individuals but not organizations. Nonetheless, the tenants' recollections of their fights for housing were filled with mention of people and groups especially those active in the early to mid-1970s.

TABLE 6.1
Timeline of Activities Organizations and Physical Conditions

	Pre-1966	67	68	69	70	71	72	73
Federal Programs	Public hsg.; HUD; Legal aid; Model Cities; War on Poverty							
New York City Programs	Receivership						Community mgt.	Direct sales
Local organizations	Met Council; RENA; churches	Other housing organizations			Proliferation of housing groups			
Housing activities	Rent strikes; demonstrations							Housing court
Forms of Tenant Control	Informal co-ops; Tenants' associations							
Housing conditions	Deterioration				Increasing abandonment			

NOTE: New York City Division of Alternative Management Programs: Tenant Interim Lease & 7A; Community Management; Private Ownership & Management; Met Council = Metropolitan Council on Housing; RENA = Riverside Edgecombe Neighborhood Association;

HOUSEHOLD AND BUILDING ORGANIZATION

S OME ORGANIZATIONS may be understood as responsive to events that take place at the level of households and buildings and spread outward into the community. For example, activities that begin "at home" as personal problems, such as discontent with deteriorating conditions and insecurity of tenure, can either lead to tenant resignation and internalization of problems or to individual and collective actions, such as withholding rent and rent strikes. Tenants in the successful and struggling co-ops were characterized by taking collective action, almost invariably beginning with rent strikes. This was less true in buildings where

74	75	76	77	78	79	80	81	82	83	87
Community Development Block Grants; Section 8							$33.7 billion housing assistance programs			$10.2 billion housing assistance programs
Office of Neighborhood Preservation			7A Tenant interim	Private ownership and management						
ANHD	UHAB			Community Boards						
							Limited equity co-ops		Mutual housing	
			Returning losses to housing stock							

ANHD = Association of Neighborhood and Housing Development; UHAB = Urban Homesteading Assistance Board.

abandonment was almost unnoticed, and where the memory of a strike was an event ages past. Rent strikes became legitimated through programs such as 7A, which permitted the courts to appoint a new managing agent, the receiver. The later establishment of a separate housing court enabled tenants to focus their complaints on a particular branch of the judiciary instead of finding their way through the entire civil court system.

Tenants' associations and informal cooperatives began at the household and building level. If there was a leader or more than one and the association was internally strong, they were able to find technical assistance at a community and citywide level. This was the case when Mrs. Wilkins invited a housing organizer to speak to the tenants and when Mrs. Williams contacted UHAB. Some of the nonprofit community groups that came to manage abandoned buildings had started as tenants' groups themselves.[4]

In some cases, assistance was found by a person like a minister or community organizer who didn't live in the building. This outside party may have continued to play an important role, as happened in Louise Carroll's building, which was under the wing of the pastor from one of the churches next door. He identified a friend of his who became their paid manager. Some tenants thought that she was also the tenants' association president; this is unlikely, since she did not live in the building. When the city restructured rents, conflicts among tenants surfaced. Some of the resentment became focused on the manager, who was then fired. As the tenants asserted more authority, the pastor became less involved, although he still stepped in. One of the past presidents described his role in the conflict about rising rents.

> We had meetings, we went around and the lawyer came in and talked
> to the tenants about the increases and everything. The pastor from the
> Baptist Church, I set up a meeting with him and he came here and they
> promised they would pay it. Then they said no, I'm not paying anything.

UHAB also became very involved in helping this co-op settle its disputes and learn to manage the building. No resolution had emerged at least during the course of our study.

In other cases, the actions tenants took to gain control over their buildings brought them into contact with people knowledgeable about a program. For example, Mr. Bridely described being told by a judge to go on rent strike as a first step toward the appointment of a 7A administrator. Mr. Bridely and Mr. Williams were both active in other organizations dedicated to improving housing and community conditions in Harlem, so they provided a two-way bridge between their buildings and the local political scene. In a number of the buildings, how leaders became associated with organizations was not clear. One leader recollected somehow learning about Met Council: "It was in October, 1972, when we learned about Metropolitan Council on Housing and we were keeping with them all this time. . . . They gave us advice on how and when to strike."

In the years since then, the leaders had continued to attend meetings and seek advice. We surmise that the reason contacts with advocacy groups were vague in the recollections of tenants is because the tenants themselves had not initiated these contacts. To further cloud the issue, it appears that some people took advantage of the situation to pass themselves off as community organizers and collect rent from the tenants. Mrs. Baylor and Mr. Grayson first found out about the tenant-initiated cooperative program from two men living in the building and trying to collect rent. The tenants thought of these men as landlords even though it seemed that the building was already owned by the city at that time. From the information we could gather, one likelihood is that these men worked with some community organization that was trying to save landlord-abandoned buildings.

The tenants' associations became formalized through limited equity cooperatives (at the time of the study, cooperatives in other parts of the city were planning to form a mutual housing association, a coalition of individual co-ops). The transformation of a successful tenants' association into a limited equity cooperative has already been described. The intervention of community organizations was a significant reason why fledgling groups were able to be developed into a more formalized cooperative or went no further than an informal group.

THE TECHNICAL ASSISTANCE PACKAGE

THERE WERE several ways in which organizations related to tenant groups. A single organization may provide myriad types of assistance which take the form of advising tenants about strategies, providing them with information, and lobbying on the tenant's behalf.[5] Advising can range from suggestions about how to organize, which elected official to see, which bureaucratic desk papers are stalled at, what requirements are for programs, and how best to alleviate anxieties about any one of the steps. Providing services can include access to a lawyer to interpret laws, a mortgage banker to establish a line of credit, and to a fuel or insurance cooperative for lower rates. Lobbying covers the gamut from local to national issues. An organization may offer one type of assistance to vary-

ing degrees. For example Met Council and a branch, Riverside Edgecombe
Neighborhood Association (RENA), are well versed in all facets of rent
strikes, 7A court appointed administrators, and rent control. Sometimes a
lesser-known neighborhood organization provides a single service such as
legal advice. Some assistance may occur accidentally, by people whom tenants know casually. Sometimes one set of assistance becomes the first step
into a larger supportive technical assistance package. Other assistance can
be formalized by the city. The Urban Homesteading Assistance Board has
been offering assistance to co-ops since 1975, at first through sponsorship
by the Episcopalian Church. Since the late 1970s, a contract between Housing
Preservation and Development and UHAB requires tenant leaders to enroll
in courses, and for its staff to be available to tenants' associations of sold
cooperatives. UHAB's contract with Housing Preservation and Development was primarily oriented to classes on managing a cooperative and
bookkeeping; its after-sales assistance was intermingled with interest in
tenants' lives, depending on the personalities and styles of UHAB staff.[6]

GOVERNMENT AND COMMUNITY ORGANIZATIONS

OTHER ASSISTANCE is formally structured through government
and community based groups. New York City's fifty-nine local
community boards, headed by a district manager and support staff,
and composed of sixty appointed representatives, is a layer of government
designed to reflect the opinions of community leaders and provide a forum
for the grass roots. The boards came into existence at about the same
time as the fast foreclosure law took effect in 1977. All development decisions are brought before the community boards, although its powers are
advisory and can be overruled by the city's appointed Planning Commission
and the Board of Estimate, an elected body.

In 1976 and 1977, when the city wanted to auction its increased inventory of city-owned buildings, a computer printout listing a profile of each
property was sent to the community boards for action. Rather than respond to perforated sheets of information which obfuscated the impact
abandonment was playing, members of Manhattan Community Board 9 (the
board covering much of western Harlem) led a successful fight for a citywide moratorium on sales. The ability of the boards to intervene effectively
is dependent on the skills of its staff, membership, and the sophistication
of people who participate in the hearings.[7] When a tenants' association buys
its building, one of the first steps it takes is to gain approval from the

community board. The interviews we conducted revealed the weaknesses and strengths of a board. In the interview with the Keens in the landlord-owned building with 134 units, although Mr. Keen was able to identify some technical assistance, he became discouraged by the board's activities which had him coming back week after week. This by itself may not have been an obstacle but combined with the lack of tenant support, he lost heart, no longer went back, and was not clear what had happened. He became resigned to living in a building owned by a private landlord rather than a cooperative. In another example, in Mrs. Oilers' building, a shared arrangement of sorts was found. She contacted the community board to help her find out who owned the building because of the lack of services. A man and woman from the board began to work with her, first searching for the ownership status, then helping organize the tenants, shepherding them into 7A management and then into the tenant interim lease program. The woman ceased working for the board and became a professional manager. She continued to work with Mrs. Oilers and to help with management until she moved to another city.

Churches have always played a significant role in the lives of Afro-Americans, providing platforms for leadership in the broader society for its men, and a social and supportive world for its women who struggle to make ends meet for their families.[8] Tenants interviewed recalled church involvement in their low-income housing problems in the late 1960s and throughout the 1980s. The form of church involvement varied. In one building the tenants were introduced to city programs through the pastor. In another case, a minister known citywide for his role in housing issues offered his church as the place for holding initial organizing meetings. At a more basic level, tenants and leaders frequently referred to the church as a source of spiritual assistance. The churches also sponsored some of the senior centers respondents attended.

Legal Aid lawyers, beleaguered survivors of the War on Poverty days, offered their services to tenants fighting negligent landlords from the early until late 1970s. Tenant leaders seemed to be aware of legal aid from those days, through the Community Law Office in Harlem and from political leaders. Access to lawyers appeared again and again as one of the most consistent needs. Even more sophisticated leaders like Mrs. Knotts, who had helped her mother manage buildings, attributed much of their eventual success to the Community Law Office and Legal Aid. The lawyer didn't cost them anything and, according to Mrs. Knotts, he had been on loan from a "very, very large firm." He was in her words "in the background advising counsel in all ways" at a time when she felt the "laws were changing every day."

Throughout the stories of tenant struggle, local politicians were frequently named as helpers. Political aspirants, local city council officers, state assemblymen and women, and senators and federal representatives gave tenants critical information about legal strategies and housing programs. They sometimes went with them to court hearings and to the offices of housing commissioners. Their aides kept track of the sequence of actions tenants needed to go through to gain redress from landlords or to take control of their buildings. Tenants in different buildings in Central Harlem but the same political district often cited one person as a source of help. There was high praise for Henrietta, a woman on the staff of a state senator, whose offices at 125th Street in the State Office Building were very accessible. The favorable references outweighed the charge in one building that a politician had defrauded them. In several buildings, politicians and city personnel required that the building be organized in return for their support.

Assistance sometimes came from judges or commissioners in housing courts and agencies. During the mid-1970s, housing court judges not only ruled on tenant grievances but some advised tenant groups about confronting legally noncompliant landlords. Similarly, housing commissioners sometimes suggested that tenants continue running their building and by the time other city agencies discovered that, a particular program would be available. In all likelihood, the presence of operating informal and extralegal cooperatives encouraged the development of programs within the housing agency.

Together churches, UHAB, and Met Council were the organizations which had most often helped the tenants we spoke with.[9]

CITYWIDE PROGRAMS AND TENANTS' ASSOCIATIONS

HOUSING CONDITIONS in Harlem generally went from widespread deterioration of buildings in the 1960s to widespread abandonment by the mid-1970s. Only in the late 1970s were city programs fully developed to provide alternative ownership options.

The programs we studied had their roots in the receivership program of the 1960s.[10] In that program, state law permitted the city to step in when landlords were not providing essential services to a building. A receivership law had been found unconstitutional by New York State in the 1930s, but by the 1960s, under conditions of a worsening housing crisis, and with safeguards for landlords' rights, the program was legally sanctioned. But the numbers of receivership buildings declined between 1965 and 1970. Although the numbers climbed between 1970 and 1973—from 15 to 51 to 170—only four buildings were ever redeemed by owners.

At this point the city was not assuming or anticipating any long-term responsibility for abandoned buildings.[11] Those city-owned buildings it couldn't sell were poorly managed through the Department of Real Estate. Stories of people dying in city-owned buildings in the winter were common. Management of receivership buildings was not much better. There were no overall repair or rehabilitation plans for buildings. Repairs were made, only to be remade, either because of shoddy work or discovery of problems when walls were "opened up." Horror stories were told of contractors leaving in the middle of jobs and accounting was in a muddle. In 1972, community workers in Williamsburg, Brooklyn, told the city that they could do the job better. An agreement was struck between the city and a community organization, Los Sures, that the organization would manage receivership buildings from an office in the neighborhood, with a budget for staffing (a director, bookkeeper, and handymen to make minor repairs). The organization would manage buildings until they became city-owned and available for purchase by the community group. Contracts with other groups followed. Between 1972 and 1974, prior to the passage of the federal Community Development Block Grant, the number of community management groups fluctuated between four and nine, and from 19 to 25 buildings. Block grant monies permitted an expansion of all programs, and the city's hands-on experiences with the variety of community groups led to modifications and new programs.

Community management was followed by the direct sales program which sold buildings "as is" to tenants' associations. Tenant interim lease supplanted direct sales in 1978. The program to sell buildings to private landlords was begun in January 1979. (Each program had different mandates and funding levels; see exhibit A in Appendix for details of each program.)

By definition, tenants' associations were mandatory in the city's tenant-initiated cooperatives, nonexistent in privately owned buildings, and by historical inclination found in community management buildings. Reality is more complex. As we discussed in preceding chapters, the mandatory tenants' associations differed by degree of success in forming a limited equity cooperative, handling dissension, and sharing responsibility with tenants who were not leaders of the tenants' association. In buildings now owned by private landlords, some little vestiges of tenant involvement were uncovered. As for community management, the flagship program, though begun with a strong tenants' orientation, the funded groups vary and tenants often regard them as benign landlords.

TENANT SCENARIOS: ON THE WAY TO ASSISTANCE

THERE WERE various ways in which tenants looked for, found, and used assistance. Rarely was the course from abandonment to cooperative a straight line, either from politician to staff aide to city administrator to lawyer, or from tenants' group to advocacy organization to lawyer to politician to the city. The oldest tenants' association was begun during World War II. A relatively stable tenant body and strong leadership in Mr. Williams' building saw the organization through a succession of battles culminating in tenants' buying the building as the first limited equity co-op in 1980. The other more successful co-ops all had active tenants' associations beginning in the late 1960s and early 1970s. In 1968, Mrs. Byron, Mrs. Wilkins, and the other two members of their four-woman board began to run their building with the agreement of the landlord. Mrs. Knotts had become president of her building's tenants' association by 1971 and continued until 1975. By then, tenants had become discouraged and disinterested in activism until they received notice that the city was to be their new landlord. Mr. Bridely brought his tenant activism home to his own building. A volunteer housing organizer with the NAACP since 1952, his building went on a prolonged rent strike beginning in 1971, that continued until the landlord abandoned the property. Similarly the two women leaders, Carolyn and LouAnn, of the co-op that worked closely with Metropolitan Council and Riverside Edgecombe, were part of a leadership group that began a rent strike in 1972 and continued until 1975, three years before the city took possession.

These five co-ops not only became functioning limited equity co-ops by the early 1980s; they also had pioneered the program they eventually joined by being among the examples of successful informal tenant management.[12] Several had been in the direct sales program but had not succeeded in buying their buildings due to legal red tape and problems with the city bureaucracy. Leaders in these buildings described their awareness of the political activism of the period. They also described unsolicited and solicited help they received from activist groups and churches as well as from politicians. Their accounts of struggle included a greater number and wider range of such contacts than those of struggling co-ops. Leaders in three of the more successful cooperatives participated, and one continues to participate, in housing advocacy groups beyond the building, again unlike leaders in the more struggling co-ops and in the non-co-ops.

While the tenants in these more successful buildings experienced real landlord neglect, their continued pressure and involvement kept their buildings from really falling apart. In the mid-1970s, when landlords walked away, some tenants left, particularly those with higher incomes. Thus these five buildings began their struggle less from desperation for housing than from a sense of outrage and their own efficacy. The co-ops that were struggling in 1984 and 1985—buildings in which Mrs. Oilers, Mrs. Miller, and Louise Carroll live—came later to the fight for decent tenant-controlled housing.

The political history of the '60s, '70s and '80s influenced the formation of the still struggling co-ops in less direct ways. For example, in the building led by Mrs. Oilers, two tenants' association officers had occupational histories affected by the succession of social activism and social programs of the period. Mrs. Oilers began her tenant activism through involvement with the rent strike movement in Harlem in 1968 and 1969. She fought unsuccessfully to save her previous building from demolition. Having participated in a program for grass-roots people in the helping professions, she had become a licensed social worker.[13] In both capacities, she gained experience and a political orientation toward confrontation that informed her work as a tenant leader in the city program. Elba Jones' life had been changed through her mandatory involvement in a "workfare" program of the 1970s. Having been placed in a Parks' Department project requiring her to do work traditionally done by male employees, she was the only one of her group of welfare recipients to go on to paid employment with the New York City Department of Parks. While she still missed the experience of caring for others she associated with her former occupation as a nurse's aide, the Parks' Department job gave her a new sense of physical and intellectual capability. For these leaders the decision to try to become a limited equity co-op grew out of the experiences and out of a situation in which their housing crisis was blatantly apparent. Throughout their struggle, the local community board provided critical support and information. Mrs. Oilers' personal contacts with politically involved and influential people in the community sustained and contributed to the progress of the building. Unlike the more successful co-ops, the tenants' association made little impact on events in the building until they were able to become part of 7A and the tenant-initiated program. The structure of these programs solidified the leaders' position within a shifting tenant population characterized most often by apathy and sometimes by destructive behavior directed against the building. If the leaders had not been vested with real control over resources, these factors might easily have overwhelmed the organization and led to its decline.

Mrs. Miller began organizing her building about the same time as Mrs.

Oilers, though slightly more toward the end of the 1970s. Access to housing court proceedings against a delinquent landlord also led to a successful effort to become a 7A administrator. Both Mrs. Oilers and Mrs. Miller relied heavily on local political leaders for advice concerning city programs. Mrs. Miller, however, had no previous history of housing activism or political involvement. Her experience was more typical of those coming later to tenant control in that community leaders were already publicizing strategies and programs that could lead in this direction. The other co-ops followed a similar pattern, discovering the program for tenants' associations through community activists who aided them in entering the program with an appointed receiver. In these buildings initial leaders had no political experience themselves. The tenants in their buildings reflected the decreased political and economic commitment of the era to improving the well-being of the poor. Many were unemployed, many living with inadequate incomes. Most could not afford better housing and were pessimistic about gaining access to housing subsidies or public housing. Their lives were affected by the increase in crime and drug use in their community. In Mrs. Oilers' building, two of the three leaders had lost sons in crime incidents. In Jack Fuller's building, which went back into city management, many tenants operated in the shadow world of drug use and drug dealing. By the late 1970s much of Harlem had, as we described in chapter 2, become a patchwork of abandoned buildings, half burned out structures and empty lots filled with the ruble of destroyed homes and businesses. The City of New York had come through bankruptcy with reduced public services and less aid to the poor.[14] What remained of the earlier climate of political activism against poverty and racism resided mainly within the community organizations that survived and the programs and institutions shaped by that activism. For these late 1970s and early 1980s tenants' associations, the advice and intervention of these proved crucial.

The leaders of later-formed associations whose histories were fragilely connected to the memories of surviving elderly tenants, had fewer resources themselves. They did not join a mass movement in their community as pioneers. Rather, they found themselves or were sought out by those groups and institutions fighting against a growing lack of concern for poor people and minorities. Without the existence of city programs oriented to tenants' groups, as well as the help of community boards, churches, and a much smaller but more experienced cadre of community activist groups, the isolation of low-income minority citizens from access to power and resources would very likely have led to their failure. When tenant leaders were asked what they thought would have happened to them without the city's programs, they often could not imagine. Other times they said they would somehow have come to gain control of the buildings anyway.[15] In either case, it was clear that the program transformed their opportunities for taking control in a number of ways. First, it changed the tenants' efforts from reactive to proactive. Even when the tenants' association had a long history of organizing, even when they had been on rent strike, they had not really been able to define the future for themselves. In the early stages they were dependent on negotiations with the landlord and the recourse of landlord-tenant court. When they ran the building during a rent strike, uncertainty about their legal future prevented them from making major improvements. Plus the legal battle usually consumed much of their energy. When the city took over, the tenants had almost no rights. Buildings could be closed and tenants moved to other city-owned property at the decision of the city through its consolidation program. The Tenant Interim Lease Program changed the stakes. Tenants could achieve the status of control from an insurgency action to a legal step toward ownership. Psychologically this seemed to change tenant attitudes in several ways. Very importantly, it pointed their attention to developing a comprehensive view of the buildings' need for repairs and renovation rather than just trying to cover the costs of fuel and emergency repairs. It also crystalized a positive goal that was attractive to many of those less involved in rent strikes. Sometimes, however, it had the opposite effect. Rent strikes often operated with a sizeable proportion of tenants refusing to pay rent at all. Tenants who preferred this situation even if conditions were not good often opposed entering the program.

Those tenants' associations that sprang up and withered in non-co-op buildings differed from the struggling co-ops mainly in having less information about programs and less support from organizations and institutions. No longer were legal aid lawyers easily available. Fewer politicians beyond those at the local level extended help to struggling tenant groups in an effort to build a support base. Funds for social service programs that would have trained and employed these low-income tenants had all but disappeared, leaving these tenants without necessary support and contacts. New housing programs no longer aimed at empowerment of low-income communities, nor even at providing them with adequate amounts of housing. Rather emergency shelters for the homeless took up the political limelight.

Theoretically, tenant ownership of housing was being encouraged as in President Reagan's 1984 speech advocating the selling off of public housing.[16] In reality however, the capital and rent subsidies of earlier periods that made low-income tenants' control of housing feasible were being attacked and eliminated. For example, all of the Alternative Management programs have depended heavily on Section 8, now phased out, and the Community Development Block Grant program is presently under attack and no longer available to Alternative Management programs. When these were available, they made the economics of running the building possible.[17] Such subsidies are absolutely necessary for programs to serve low-income populations. Thus, while our study of these experiences of abandonment and reclamation of buildings has focused on tenants, the larger economic and political trends in the society are not separate from these experiences.

However, even when the bureaucratic impediments to obtaining Section 8 and stabilizing senior citizens' rent were ironed out, barriers remained on the tenant side. Some very low-income tenants we spoke with declined to apply even though their incomes would clearly qualify them for relief. Some felt that filling out forms was too much of an invasion of their privacy, and, from a sense of self-respect, declined to fill them out. Obviously poor tenants told us there were others who were needier. Some simply did not want to depend on public subsidies, especially elderly people who had worked all their lives but in jobs with no pensions or retirement benefits. Others got confused about the forms and the responses to their applications and abandoned the effort to obtain the subsidy. Often the availability of Section 8 in a building depended on leaders having the time and ability to be sure all eligible people applied correctly, received appropriate responses from the bureaucracy, and followed through when necessary.

The city programs provided financial assistance by repairing from one to three systems before the building was sold, subject to city assessment of need, tenants' abililty to pay for repairs themselves, and a negotiation process. In our study, all but one of the earliest tenant-initiated cooperatives sold received almost no city help. As the buildings coming into the program later were in worse shape and had less sophisticated leadership, public investment increased. This later higher level of investment may also reflect a more realistic appraisal by city bureaucrats of the needs of city-owned buildings based on more experience, as well as sustained pressure by advocacy groups like the Association for Neighborhood Housing and Development (ANHD), the Pratt Center (a.k.a. Pratt Institute Center for Community and Environmental Development), UHAB, and local politicians.[18]

CONCLUSIONS

PERHAPS THE most important thing we learned from our research was that the fate of individuals was inseparable from that of the groups they belonged to—households, friendship circles, others on the floor where their apartments were located, buildings, blocks, neighborhoods, communities, cities, and societies. Planners often start from the larger levels, working down in a way that ignores the strengths of the smallest units. Psychologists and social workers err in the opposite direction. We think there is an argument to be made for understanding the smaller units and how they work in order to avoid or at least inform any top-down planning that tries to be progressive.

The argument to be developed in the next chapters has something in common with the current rejection of government intervention. We too believe that the real solutions to people's problems lie in their own actions supported by organizations, programs and subsidies, not in the services of a bureaucracy that sees them as clients rather than agents. The distinction between support and bureaucratically provided services is critical. The first builds on the strengths of small social units and relates them to the larger community. The latter takes away the resources of the lower levels of organization and centralizes them in hard-to-affect, distant, and impersonal agencies. However, we reject the assumption that market forces can provide the medium through which poor people, especially those disadvantaged also because of discrimination, can solve the problems they face. We also reject the assumption that a community dominated by market forces, as they are now constituted, can be an empowering community. Rather, we think that reformulating the issues, understanding the total lives of people, and focusing on the social categories that place people in their societies—in particular, gender, race, and age—can reveal ways to structure future programs. These must begin with, not end with, who the people are. Empowerment as a real goal, not the trappings or the rhetoric, also has to be central. Otherwise improvements in material conditions may occur but there will have been no gains made against the impoverishment of the total person. In the next chapters we will look at this further as we analyze our findings by gender, race, and age.

SEVEN

Gender and Race

W HAT PEOPLE think about the conditions of their lives, the kind of housing they are in, whether they will fight or move, what type of community they would like to live in, is influenced by gender, race, and age. The problems that can be associated with gender, race, and age come together in the profile of who the people are in city-owned buildings.[1] About five years ago, overall, women headed almost 60 percent of the households in these buildings; a little more than 75 percent of the tenants were blacks and Puerto Ricans. Less accurate information was available for age. In 1982 and 1984, the median age of all residents in city-owned properties was 42. Yet older people figured prominently in the co-oping of buildings in Harlem. Curious, we asked ourselves why facts about who tenants are is barely acknowledged in the formulation of policy.

The city, no less than other levels of government, has paid scant attention to who the people are in different Alternative Management programs. The beneficiaries are usually referred to as poor and minorities. The thinking of nonprofits and tenants' associations themselves reflects the need to satisfy the objectives of program requirements. Were there to be funding available for, let us say, cooperatives designed particularly to meet the needs of female-headed households, it stands to reason that groups would orient their proposals accordingly. There are some few studies that praise tenants. Robert Kolodny's evaluation in the early 1970s of informal cooperatives—those formed without any major city sponsorship—provided clues about who lived in cooperatives.[2] He found families at all stages of the life cycle, low- and moderate-income minorities, in some buildings predominantly elderly, and a few with primarily welfare families. A major evaluation of the Alternative Management programs by the Pratt Center in collaboration with the Urban Institute was aborted after the first year (of a projected three-year study) by the change of administrations in Washington. The project called attention to the "people" or "tenants" as key to the success of limited equity cooperatives. Middle level bureaucrats who administer the programs and come into frequent contact with tenants also are quick to point out their remarkable abilities. Equally remarkable, the city's staff is able to recall many if not all of the tenants' leaders and dissenters in a particular building by name, personality, and background, and recite dates and times of events when tenants badgered or cajoled to gain more renovation dollars.

Thus it came as no surprise to some city officials when we pointed out the prevalence of women or the elderly among the people we interviewed. While city officials readily acknowledged this fact, more problematic for them was what it meant. After all, one way to think about administering the programs is by defining away tenant differences. The argument goes somewhat like this: it does not make any difference who is living in the buildings beyond knowing it is a poor population. The limited number of programs that are available to provide housing assistance in existing buildings are drawn from federal Community Development Block Grant money, and federal, state, and local rental assistance. These are targeted to poor people, with some qualifiers for very low-income, large households, and the elderly. Differences, be they of gender, race, or age, are subsumed under income. Being black and poor, and female and poor, are implicitly assumed.

We think there are ways to go further than this. Research can be structured and findings can be interpreted that go beyond the mandates of programs and thereby transform them. Mandates, by necessity, given funding mechanisms and the mentality fostered in either a fiscally conservative or liberal era, are narrowly conceived and executed in well-established ways. Our evaluation of 131 tenants' perceptions of their housing and neighborhood conditions before and after sale confirmed that the programs do benefit a poor population. But more was learned about gender, race, and age from the interviews discussed in the preceding chapters. In this chapter we present our findings about gender and race; in the next chapter, issues of age. This reinterpretation of data points the way towards using such information in the reconstruction of policy, issues addressed further in the final chapters.

THE GENDER COMPONENT

W E BEGAN our research with questions about housing the poorest segment of the population, female-headed households, especially those from minority communities. Our hunch that women have something special to offer society in terms of new directions for the development of housing and community was initially confirmed by the numbers of women in our interviews with tenants in low-income cooperatives.

Of those who participated in our study of predominantly black buildings in Harlem, 71 percent were women (see table 2.2). If we include those from other ethnic groups, 69 percent were women. These figures come close to the gender distribution in the larger survey of 131 respondents (see table 2.3). In that study 73 percent of the respondents were female. Leadership in buildings sold to tenants' associations reflected the gender composition of buildings sold through all Alternative Management programs. Sixty-two percent of the leaders we interviewed were women. In primarily black buildings the proportion rose to 84 percent. Since our sampling was neither random nor based on a previously established proportion of male and female leaders, the possibility that we picked buildings that overrepresented female leadership certainly exists. We have some anecdotal evidence to the contrary from housing agency officials and technical assistance staff who agreed that, from their experience, leaders, particularly in Harlem, tended to be women.

We also asked male and female leaders about their perceptions of who became most involved in tenants' associations. Both agreed that women did more work. Even male leaders noted that women often provided the backbone of the organization by doing necessary but less publicly visible organizing. The women we talked with by no means held separatist positions with regard to men. They felt themselves to be a part of the black community and to be working for their families and neighbors. To the extent that they thought about gender in relationship to their activities, they focused on problems of getting men involved and of "being taken seriously" by male authorities. The men in the study spoke most forcefully about how women approached housing differently, how they were more committed to saving their homes, even if the homes seemed almost not worth saving to men. The men also pointed out how the time-consuming demands of operating cooperatively conflicted with men's needs to hold "responsible" jobs and see themselves as being in charge.

Our findings fit in with themes that repeat themselves over and over in feminist writing: women handle the daily problems of coping with poverty and crisis routinely but often without acknowledgement of their contributions.[3] Parenthetically we would add that women's ability to cope also renders them better able to handle the potential restrictions of old age.[4] Many women understand their lives in terms of commitment to others more frequently than in terms of individual advancement. Social relationships provide the vehicle through which women most often seek to achieve goals. Many evaluate their activities in terms of an ethic of care and commitment. Often women accept work characterized by unending and conflicting demands for attention, work that is never done and often subject to reversals. Men's activities can also be understood along these dimensions, but the vocabulary in which many men describe their experiences highlights other issues: individual achievement, confrontation, completion of tasks, to name but a few.

Several themes about gender are revealed in the interviews: domestic life compared strongly with the saving and maintaining of previously abandoned homes; emerging leadership styles fostered by the cooperative structure are atypical of hierarchical more masculine leadership, and facilitate a more typically female orientation. Each of these is discussed further. First, however, we should note that the fact that these tenants were primarily black may have significantly determined our findings.[5] While domestic life and a less hierarchical mode of organizing often characterizes women's activities, the translation of these factors into co-op organization also depends on the mutual expectations men and women have of each other. It may be that women within the black community play a larger part in determining the nature of co-op organization and therefore the organizations are more continuous with women's other activities.

DOMESTIC LIFE AND COOPERATIVE ORGANIZATION

THE ACTIVITY still equated with women is running domestic life. This involves everything from cleaning and upkeep to budgeting, preparing food, and resolving conflicts. While the specific tasks may be easily enumerated, what is as important are the responsibilities identified with women and the expectation of others in their households that women will devote their personal attention to facilitating everyone else's life.

The interviews confirmed the similarity between the work of running a co-op and housework. Building leaders often spoke of the constant interruptions by tenants and the endless demands of the building. Much like a busy mother, the leaders had to respond to multiple requests for repairs, emergencies like a burst pipe, stories about financial problems, as well as the expectations of tenants that leaders will be friendly and attentive to them in the numerous casual encounters that occur every day. The boundary line between their own housework and their "building work" was blurred. They also tended to discount the time taken for either. The remarks of Mrs. Crawford, one of the older women in the building organized by Mrs. Knotts, highlighted the casual way in which interruptions were typically integrated into her day.

> I'm home and don't take half the day. Whenever somebody come, you never know when somebody's coming. So they ring the bell and tell me where they're going. The elevator man, I'll give him the keys, I'll go with him. Electric man come, I'll go down there with him with the keys and let him read the meter.

When disputes arise in the tenants' association, the leaders must endlessly listen to different sides of the argument. When they themselves were involved, they were subject to public criticism and gossip. Because of the importance of smooth social relationships to the effective functioning of a co-op, none of the repair and maintenance work could be handled strictly as a task. The individual needs and personalities of tenants entered into every transaction.

The aspect of the situation that most overwhelmed Jack Fuller in one struggling co-op that reverted to Central Management was the slow uphill nature of the renovation work, the setbacks, the lack of support, and the endless amount of work. Women leaders also experienced these as draining. However, being used to the same problems in making their own homes, they seemed to find the strength to carry on. Many also had jobs as live-in companions or nurses, or worked as hospital attendants and domestics, all occupations requiring endless attention to messy, mundane, and repetitive human needs. Indeed, saving an abandoned building through co-oping is much like woman's work in the old saying, "Man may work from sun to sun, but woman's work is never done."

Co-op leaders over and over again conveyed the feeling that the building's problems were their problems. Not infrequently, they felt on the edge of exhaustion as the result of their efforts to respond to emergencies while at the same time working to effect major capital improvements. The following exchange with 70-year-old Mrs. Lyons in Louise Carroll's building typified fairly well the pressures on co-op leaders. She had reluctantly accepted the position of an officer in the tenants' organization, the first time she had done so. When asked why she should not have accepted, her reply indicated that she felt overwhelmed. Yet she was following through on the details to get everything repaired and operating. The plumbing required immediate attention, as did doors damaged by water leakage. She described how an informal network wound up getting relief for one woman who suffered a leak in the bathroom, and what ends a tenants' association must go to insure proper repairs.

> The plumber came and fixed it, but he didn't go far enough in. . . . And you know he wasn't gone long because the lady called us and said . . . "Lord, the water is coming out of here like crazy" . . . we had a time trying to find somebody else, especially that night. . . . Everybody we got were roto-rooters. . . . So finally a lady, a friend of one of the tenants . . . was speaking to some gentleman that was in her place about the water. He said you know, I'm a plumber. And he went and did a beautiful job.

Typically also, the troubles she had did not deter her from planning even more work. A few minutes later Mrs. Lyons went on to describe her plans for lowering the basement ceiling, fixing the floors, making a little recreation room. She wanted it to be clean and beautiful, a place people would want to come and a place that would meet their needs, possibly even having laundry equipment so tenants would not have to go out to wash.

Leaders and, to a lesser extent, members of tenants' associations did not simply manage the buildings they were saving from abandonment; they nurtured them. Their approach to housing development is not based on traditional economic criteria of making a profit, or, in the worst scenarios, extracting a profit by pocketing rent monies without delivering services. Rather the approach embraced attention to every detail, much like an individual conscientious homeowner but with a major exception: the benefits are shared collectively. One woman leader, Mrs. Baylor, described the difference very clearly, comparing it to watering a plant and allowing it to grow. Here too the analogy to domestic life was apparent in the continuous vigilance over details.

The landlords when they had it . . . just owned it and . . . collected
rent. They were not here to see if the knob was off the front door or
whatever, if the steps was broken in the basement . . . that would just
go on from time to time, year in and year out. And finally all these things
accumulated and the next thing you know, the building is on the ground.
But when the tenants own the building, I feel that it gets the attention
it needs.

The predominance of female leaders in the co-ops studied and the similarity between their approaches to leadership and women's traditional roles
provided the strongest link between domestic life and the organization of
the co-op buildings.

Male leaders seemed often to handle their jobs by splitting the social
functions off from the tasks and passing them on to their female co-leaders
or wives. This division reduced the similarity to housework. When attention to detail was assigned to these women also, male leadership took on
a more executive style. But regardless of the leader's gender, the personal
and prompt attention to problems contrasted with the behavior of even the
most responsive community management groups and had little in common
with reports of contemporary landlords' reactions.

RESPONSES TO WOMEN LEADERS

A S A pattern of female leadership emerged, we began to ask what
contributed to it.[6] Some of the women leaders linked the predominance of women in co-op leadership to women's roles in the home,
and to men's reluctance to get involved. For example, the four women
officers of Connie's building all joined in:

I think that a lot of times men feel like the home is something that's for
women, and they don't need to participate. . . . the women's job is to
take care of the home and whatever circumstances happen in the home,
they take care of it.

The men, they thought, devalued the work, much like the way housework
is devalued, and felt that "it's nothing that they have time to be bothered
with."

Several men thought both that the work was beneath them and that
women couldn't handle the job. Mr. Leeds, one of the male tenants of the

building, told us that his wife was the one who attended board meetings, as she should. He didn't want to be bothered.

> I'm trying to get my wife active. And she's trying to get me, but there are a bunch of women down there . . . I said, Daisy . . . you go down there with them.

His other remarks also suggested that he held some pretty negative stereotypes concerning women's abilities. In response to a question about why there were no men involved he replied:

> The reason I believe is . . . because the house is falling down, the women aren't too proud, they look after their home. But women don't know how to get nothing done. They are no good at business, period. Women don't know how to do nothing. I got a wife and she doesn't know how to do nothing. Dumb, dumb, dumb, dumb, dumb, dumb; that's right.

Since the same man lived in a nicely renovated apartment he had recently purchased in the building and he reported good services, we asked him how he thought women could be running the building. He explained:

> They are doing the best they can, but they need a man there too. When they go around to take care of the business, looks like some men try to take advantage of them. . . . I believe if a man was there we would get things done better and quicker. And it isn't gonna be me.

Carolyn and LouAnn, the two women leaders in the building on 146th Street, reiterated the point but felt more optimistic about men's participation.

> It seems as if the men don't want to do anything. But they will work if we bring them out. You know, you have to go and pull them out. . . . But if we take them and show them these things to be done, they will cooperate.

They also noted more of the eleven board members were women; they were hoping that two new male tenants might be candidates for future leaders.

In other women-led buildings, new male tenants that they had selected because of their skills were viewed as possible officers in the future. John Paynes, one such man in the building led by Mrs. Michael and three other women, had a long history of housing organizing as well as bookkeeping skills. He had developed a philosophy of cooperation and self-help that fit in with the mores of the building.

I'm involved so it's nothing to me. I know all the trials and tribulations. It's not as romantic as one may think it is. . . . It's a struggle, it's a fight, it's a hassle.

The same young man reflected on why women always seem to get more involved in "quote unquote civic ventures than men":

tying it to the types of jobs men may hold. . . . Unless the men work, unless that's their profession anyway, less they're the guys on the board of the Chamber of Commerce, he's going to be out there. . . . The guy works from nine to five. He comes home. PTA (Parents Teachers Association) meeting at 7:30. . . . Who's going to go to a PTA meeting 7:30 on Monday night in the wintertime?

He followed the pattern he described. Despite his position as bookkeeper, he did not get involved in the tenants' association. In his home, his wife handled the "familiar" and "ordinary happenings," although even then he thought her familiarity was second to his. He believed that the division of labor occurred in all types of programs, relating it to the numbers of men and women in the community. When he was a teenager, and active, he said that "we had more men than women" but men had a career he thought which required them to stay at the office.

For instance, before I took on this job, I was working for the city. Sometimes, I wouldn't get home 'til 7:30, 8 o'clock, 9 o'clock at night. Okay I had to stay at the office. That's not to say that sometime a woman doesn't have to stay in the office but then you find most . . . men have those types of jobs . . . have more responsibility doing their jobs. . . . "It's a man's world" still prevails.

The bitter irony is that his idea of men working in a man's world differs because of the dual labor market. His sentiment reflects more generally an employment pattern of white skilled men than that of black men like himself who may work equally long hours but at low wages.

Mr. Bridely, who was still active in this same building somewhat fit the pattern of merging building work with paid or volunteer work. He had been a professional housing organizer and a member of the board of three civic organizations. He also noted that women were more frequently active in such organizations, citing their presence in his church. He speculated that there were 3,500 active members in that church, and I'd say almost 3,000 of them are women." Mr. Bridley doesn't see himself as being that different from other men but attributed his activeness to the necessity "to do these things and I've always been a civic worker, and I continue this way. It's in me I guess, a part of me."

Two older active male leaders, Mr. Williams in a successful co-op and Mr. Grayson in another building that reverted to the city during our study, treated their roles as jobs.[7] Williams and Grayson both talked about the way the work on the building replaced their paid jobs when they retired. Mr. Grayson told of his experience this way:

> The landlord retired from this particular thing . . . and as I am retired now, it gives me something to do. Sometimes too much but still in all I enjoy the work, you know trying to help other people live.

Mr. Grayson's female partner, Mrs. Baylor, was the secretary of the tenants' association. Her own remarks echoed Mr. Williams' description of his wife's attention to detail. Mrs. Baylor listed some of the little things she did to forestall larger problems: noticing a broken door knob before it no longer worked thus protecting security and the door from abuse, watching out that the glass panes in interior doors did not get broken during other repairs, and so on. She described herself as only making "the big decisions" when Mr. Grayson was hospitalized for several weeks.

Jack Fuller again illustrated the tendency for men to become involved as a result of career aspirations. Working with a community organization at the time, he had expected housing and neighborhood organizing to be his future. He too noted the prevalence of women in co-op activities, and the problems of involving the young, especially young men:

> In all the cases I know about, it's essentially the women that are the backbone of all this . . . the elderly women that have been in the building for a while or either just moved in like Elvira. . . . The women that are really working with her are elderly women. The women who were doing this were essentially women that don't work any more, that were home, older women, with the exception of one who is in her forties, maybe pushing fifty.

Fuller's observations pointed to some very significant aspects of the leadership. First, many if not all of the people we are referring to as leaders were not previously seen in this way at all. They were often invisible, like housewives, in the more menial service work they did to earn a living and individually wielded no political clout. Second, Fuller recognized their knowledge in a way that suggests alternative educational programs that award academic credit based on life experiences, legitimating domestic and community knowledge. This approach to education, popular in the 1960s, is overshadowed by the emphasis on learning that is more abstract and recognized through accredited programs rather than the "school of hard knocks." Fuller commented: "All these women I'm mentioning essentially voice concerns about the building, seemed to know a lot more about what was going on than you might on the surface give them credit for." Their ability to speak out and lead was not universal. Many of them held back, "still . . . not in . . . themselves ready to take on this responsibility." But in his view they were not simply passive victims but at some minimum level participated by coming to the meetings.

> The women who really attended the meetings and were more quiet about things, even when I ran into them in the halls, were the ones that obviously had very little education, were very intimidated by all this stuff. . . . It was important that people were together which they knew, but they struggled with this because it was about their homes.

Not all of his experiences with women in the situation were positive. One of the leaders he had helped depose was a woman who has allegedly been involved in a deal with a woman-led management corporation not to pay rent and to get a larger apartment in exchange for giving the management group her business.

A contradictory aspect that may be particular to the ways in which poor black families compensate for low income is the help several of the black men actually contributed to domestic life. While male leaders and even male tenants were fewer than females in the sample, many of the men interviewed reported taking responsibility in their household for domestic tasks stereotypically performed by women. Mr. Bridely and another older man who lived in a community management building where he had been active in a now inactive tenants' association both talked extensively of their involvement in raising their children. Mr. Bridely had worked at night and his wife, an entertainer, was on the road months at a time. Therefore, he spent most of his time with his son and cared for him with the help of his mother-in-law. John Dawson, another older man, began to supervise his six children after school when his wife went to work at a restaurant, a child-rearing task he took very seriously:

> You always worry about them, but I tried to channel them into supervised play at all times . . . if I'm not supervising . . . then they must be at some place where the play is supervised. I would take them to the center [run by Children's Aid Society] or I would be with them in the park.

Even the men who depicted themselves as too busy with "important things" to be involved with participating in the co-ops they lived in engaged in domestic activities. Mr. Leeds, the man who claimed women were simply "dumb, dumb, dumb," including his wife, was busy making soup during the interview. He stated that he had always done most of the cooking in the household. John Paynes, the young housing professional who tried not to get too involved in co-op affairs and who included himself among the men he described as too busy with responsible jobs to participate in the co-op, was at home baby-sitting the day of the interview. Louise Carroll, the ex-president of one of the co-ops, received help in her work in the building from her husband. He also worked at his job at night so he regularly did some of the household tasks. She stated: "He's the big cook. In the daytime he would cook and then when I come in, all I would have to do was to warm it up." The willingness to pick up pots and pans or take responsibility for children echoed the tone for sharing that is essential in cooperatives. Whether female partners emerge as leaders or not, there is that much more opportunity to do so when gender roles are less rigidly divided in domestic work to begin with.

LEADERSHIP STYLES

BOTH THE number of tenants participating in co-op activities and the number in top leadership positions varied. The two buildings with the strongest interpersonal relations among its leaders were led by groups of women. In both cases, the presidents insisted that the first interview be conducted with the whole group. The organizational philosophy of one building was articulated by Mrs. Wilkins and Mrs. Byron. They stressed the need for close cooperation and frequent consultation of the leadership group as well as the necessity to form committees for specific functions to broaden the decision making and share responsibility with as many tenants as possible. Their strong personal relationships with each other and with many tenants, as well as their belief that they could accomplish the almost impossible if they worked together, gave a foundation of interpersonal care and trust to the formal structure of the tenants' association. They emphasized the need for communication and for everybody to try to see things from perspectives other than his or her own. As Connie Byron, one of the leaders, said in explaining her success in getting cooperation, "You can catch more flies with honey than you can with vinegar." Yet the structure appears to have had an important sustaining function of providing occasions for the exchange of information and support as well as increasing the number of activities the co-op could sponsor.

Mrs. Michael in the other building also talked about the importance of communication:

> I try to stick to once a month with the board. If I can get across to the ten tenants what is actually going on and that ten can get across to ten more then we got something working. But we have our regular [full tenants' association] meetings once every three months. . . . But when you have a meeting with all the tenants and two or four miss and you're having a meeting, you gotta explain to these two or three what has happened before and you never get to what you want to get done. That's why I feel like once a month is good because every day something happens. . . . So if I can keep all this in perspective at one time and then give it to them in one monthly meeting they know as much about the building as I do and somebody else does, they can tell everybody else.

She was continuing a tradition dating back to Mr. Bridely's leadership that has been successful in assuring cooperation, active participation, and the development of new leadership. The beautification committee has also served the purpose of integrating new, younger tenants into active participation.

Mr. Williams, who in many ways seems the embodiment of the strong individual leader, acknowledged both the significance of his wife's constant vigilance about ways to save the building and her intense social involvement with other tenants as key factors in the building's success. He also helped institute a system of floor captains to insure communication and share some responsibilities. In this building, more of the actual decision making and day-to-day work fell on him than it did on the presidents in the other buildings. Nonetheless, the tenants' association had been able to generate a number of presidents interspersed throughout Mr. Williams' leadership.

In most of the co-ops, a core group of from four to fifteen active tenants had worked hard during critical periods. This was true in the three buildings just described as well as in some of those still struggling to become cooperatives. For example, Mrs. Baylor and Mr. Grayson, the two leaders of the 52-unit building that had only 18 occupied units at its low point referred to six men who did most of the early rehab work and to a smaller group of tenants involved in the decision making and in support. The two buildings still in the most deteriorated condition at the time of the study had the smallest leadership cores. In one case it appeared that the 75-year-old Mrs. Oilers, who had initiated the co-op, dragooned two other women into holding the offices of secretary and treasurer. Elba, who attended UHAB classes with her and took over some of the leg work as the original leader became ill, seemed to be developing the knowledge base to assume greater leadership. Louise Carroll's co-op, characterized by both internal conflict and strong interpersonal supportiveness, seemed to give a great deal of responsibility to the person designated as president. Yet since the officers rotated so often, an unanticipated benefit was that over a quarter of the households had held offices. The officers and ex-officers spoke of exchanging information and of people they could rely on.

Participation by the entire tenantry only occurred on a regular basis in Mrs. Byron and Mrs. Wilkin's building. Here, the existence of three standing committees (sickness and courtesy, fund raising, and housing) provided regular responsibilities for another twenty or so tenants in addition to the four leaders. The kinds of things the committees did, give parties, call on the sick, organize dinners and bake sales, as well as screen tenants and deal with rent arrears, required them to call on even more tenants for help. The committees also did things that required large amounts of contact and communication with the other tenants, increasing the involvement of those communicated with. Thus, the leaders estimated that seventy-nine of the eighty tenants actively participated. Mrs. Michael, with only one committee for physically improving the building, relied on more passive forms of participation such as attendance at meetings and agreement in decision making. She expressed concern about the situation:

> We're getting stuck in a position that each tenant should be having input into. That's why I want them to be knowledgeable of what's going on so that they will know what we are going through, and then somebody else can take over the job and we can sit down and rest. I'm tired.

She went on to say that about 50 percent of the tenants came to meetings and about 80 percent reached consensus regarding decisions. The women leaders in this building had followed Mr. Bridely and his board in office. He had described the earlier group as a pretty forceful lot that had directed much of their efforts to dealing with the bureaucratic and political problems of gaining ownership. The women leaders speculated that many of the old tenants were accustomed to the affairs of the building being handled competently without their participation, so they had developed the habit of expecting the leaders to do all the work. There were suggestions in the interviews in Mr. Williams' building that a similar phenomenon may have occurred.

The goals embedded in a cooperative when it goes from being a reaction to crisis to a self-conscious commitment to a way of living, shift from the provision of mutual aid to include empowerment of individuals and the community. The two buildings with all-women boards best illustrate the difference. Here, leaders talked of rebuilding the community, creating shared homes they can really be proud of and extending their efforts outward into local economic development and the renovation of other buildings. Nonleaders spoke of sharing this vision and described ways that their lives have improved as a result of living in the building: space to spend more time with grandchildren,[8] security about children's health and well-being so that the mother can go back to school, someone to turn to when emotionally troubled to avoid going deeper into depression, a place to meet friends every day. (Interestingly, both buildings also created a community space, a "club room" as it was called in one building.) The fabric of frequent contacts, a sense of security, and a philosophy of cooperation characterize these tenants' associations and promote communication and sharing of responsibilities. This structure is inseparable from styles of leadership and tenant attitudes. Yet it provides the situation to reinforce potentials for cooperation and accomplishment. Indigenous leaders emerged in the context of the network of preexisting social relationships found in a particular place.

Without the building level organization of the tenant cooperatives we doubt that we would have found the proportion of female leaders that we did.[9] The best organized cooperatives often worked outward from small networks of people with mutual interests, shared responsibilities and fates, and daily contact with neighbors and households. This outward networking, we speculate, counters tendencies to mimic bureaucratic leadership styles and landlord-tenant relationships.[10]

This style of organization may appear to those in positions of authority as inefficient because it sometimes avoids strict hierarchical chains of authority. In Brenda Doyle Farge's study of 122 women and 55 men in a Toronto cooperative where she examined seven categories of motives and gains, women's responses were almost twice as high as men's in two important categories. The women reported that co-ops produced social and community support, and were a way for them to learn and acquire skills.[11] Farge has concluded that co-ops provide women with "the happy experience of being both supported and encouraged." This type of ownership becomes a context in which women can become leaders in a way they cannot find in more patriarchal settings. Gerda R. Wekerle and Joan Simon's analysis of nonprofit housing cooperatives in Canada also reinforced these findings.[12] Co-ops attracted a higher proportion of single parents who were more likely to be female-headed. Poorer in income, women found a variety of gains in housing which did not require a down payment, whose costs did not rise as quickly as in the private market, and which provided a social space for empowerment. The survey data Wekerle and Simon reviewed substantiated the finding that one of the attractions of co-op living is to find a community. The co-op then expands "the definition of housing beyond shelter to encompass social support, services, and community enrichment."[13]

GENDER AND RACE

I F ISSUES of gender are still not routinely integrated into policy analysis, women leaders not as acknowledged as men are, there is even the knottier issue of gender and race. Clearly, in many of the buildings in which we interviewed, black men emerged as leaders also. In others, black women proved to be divisive. Neither black men or women leaders could handle every situation in the cooperatives. All too often it is easy to forget, and most never acknowledge, what it means in the first place to be nonwhite in this society and how that affects every incident. There is unrelenting discrimination on a daily basis, even for those of privilege.[14] Black women, in particular, have been attacked over and over again by whites, and the failure of the black family attributed to them. While black men are reduced to dependency by an economic system that either exploits or ignores them, black women have had to take up the slack in providing a stable daily life.

There is, however, another body of emerging work which ascribes to black women neither mythic nor deviant traits. Joanne M. Martin and Elmer P. Martin have traced the helping tradition in the black family and community and its connections to the extended family.[15] From Africa through periods of slavery, reconstruction, in rural and urban America, this tradition was connected to black churches, mutual aid societies, fraternal orders, women's clubs, unions, orphanages, old folks' homes and hospitals, schools, the protest movement, and race-consciousness organizations. Their thesis is at once interesting and provocative, with parts echoing our findings and our findings refuting some of their points. They argue that the helping tradition is no longer alive, a victim of the Depression, changes in competitive and monopoly capital, and frustrations and complexities of postindustrial life. They see the replacement of "fictive kinship, racial consciousness, and religious consciousness necessary for transferring the major values of the extended family to the wider community" with "individualistic dog-eat-dog, competitive orientation of the dominant urban society." In such a society, strangers are suspect. At the same time, they themselves point to ways in which the services and care blacks render to each other reduce the amount of time, money, and resources the greater society has to bestow on families and communities. Clearly, the roles played by the leaders we interviewed point to the older helping tradition merged with the integration of informal social work, and this is seen most prominently among women.

The stories of the strengths black women bring to bear have been told in other books which chronicle their incredible accomplishments, both those on whom the media focuses and lesser-known women.[16] Civil rights activist and musician Bernice Johnson Reagon once wrote about the shared "cultural autobiography" of black women:

> We understand that one of our responsibilities is to live and struggle so that there will be another generation of people. . . . The experiences and data that go into making up that identity [of children] come to the child carried by the personnel charged with the maintenance of the environment in which life begins and grows. In the Black community, this environment has historically been our responsibility. Whether it is from the mother or the grandmother or the aunt or the babysitter or the nursery, the first words that the child begins to speak, the first smells, the songs, the body stances, the tastes, come from the women part of the society.[17]

Her statement resonates in many of the stories we heard from men and women whom we interviewed.

The connection between gender and race also has a spatial component. A spatial area, limited within a city, can confirm people's identity in a positive way, but also act as an incubator in which discriminatory practices are carried out and compounded.

BEING BLACK IN HARLEM

IN EARLIER chapters we briefly traced the history of Harlem which led to this part of Manhattan becoming home to blacks, in both a literal and figurative sense. The making of Harlem passed through several different stages, at times hopeful such as in the 1920s and 1960s, but the aftermath of those periods brought even greater misery to countless households. The segregation of people and the dilapidation of buildings acted as a barometer which measured the lesser position of blacks in the broader economic and social worlds. There is no question that the majority of residents in the Harlem of the 1970s and 1980s were living in poverty. By chance, in buildings with and without architectural distinction, in different parts of Harlem, they found themselves victims of landlord abandonment in three out of five buildings. But although they chose to rent in one place over another, it is not accidental that in the larger picture the chances were high that they would find themselves in such circumstances. Race is a strong predictor for landlord abandonment; reports on the New York City rental inventory in 1982 and 1984 revealed there was a greater likelihood of living under conditions of abandonment if belonging to a minority.

Race came up in other ways in the interviews. Respondents spoke of it in relation to limited choices in housing location or places to travel to for recreation; as memories of a Harlem that was and expectations of what it could be or simply what happened to people living there; and of hurdles they had to overcome to successfully negotiate with the city over money for life-saving essentials such as boilers and roofs.

LIMITED CHOICES

THE PEOPLE we interviewed, particularly the older ones, often migrated from the South to New York at a time when segregation was at its zenith. There was no civil rights movement to sustain them in their journey North and celebrate their acts of personal courage. There was World War II though, and many of the older people's stories were similar; they had taken advantage of wartime jobs to improve their economic situation. One interview in the troubled co-op was with Mrs. Smythe who migrated from Guyana. Now housebound and confined to her wheelchair in an apartment overlooking 115th Street, she is surrounded by photographs of herself in other places. Interested in travel when she was ambulatory, she pointed to her skin and said that Canada was the only place where she could travel at one time. Asked about whether conditions for blacks in the United States had improved, her reply captured the situation for many as it was then and how it is now.

> For some, [it is] much much better because in my time when you see a black person at the bank he went to deposit money or withdraw. You didn't see him as a teller. . . . I have a friend, she's a RN from South Carolina and she came up here and they wouldn't take her because she

was black in the hospital. No, they didn't want her. But after the war broke out, they sent a call to her and she wouldn't go. She went in the factory instead.

In another example, she referred to the first black staff doctor at Harlem Hospital, who although trained, "couldn't go downtown to the hospital." Because he was black, "he had to stay in Harlem."

In one of the buildings now owned by a private landlord, Ethel, the retired chorus line dancer told us of barriers she faced when she began dancing:

> They would test girls, of course. . . . Have you heard of the color line? I went to the class, but the teacher couldn't guarantee me a job and you know why? Because they just didn't have girls in the line up, you have very few of them now, you know. The first thing is color. That made the difference

An optimist, and diplomatic, she went on to say that

> everything now is different. Any color can get a job now, doing whatever they want to do. We have no problems. All they need is the education.

Others told us of how they had to work as porters or dishwashers or domestics to get a job. In a few cases, the people we talked with had broken through some aspects of racial discrimination. Mr. Williams attended Columbia University when it was virtually all white. Mr. Bridely's two former wives had both been "firsts" in other ways. His first wife, who he was about to remarry, was the first black cosmologist in South Carolina; his second wife had a successful career as a musical comedy singer, traveling all over the world.

HARLEM OF HOPES: HARLEM OF SLIGHTS

SOME OF the people we interviewed had been the first blacks to move into their building; they never forgot that. What came across in the interviews was not an historical analysis of the speculation by white (and to a lesser degree black) developers who, not able to rent to whites, turned to a black market. Rather it was of pride associated with being the first to move in and that other more well-known blacks, usually entertainers, like singer Billy Eckstein and musical star Juanita Hall, had also lived there. Interviews in two successfully co-oped buildings, Mrs.

Michael's and Mrs. Knotts', brought this to light. Mrs. Hill, the elderly woman in Mrs. Knott's building, thought the Art Deco decorated building on 126th Street "was the first house built in Harlem that colored people . . . have." She was the second person to move in. That area of Harlem had been Finnish and they began to move out. It was a renter's market then: people received a free month's rent and she remembered some extras "for under her sink."

Others expressed the desire to move into a particular building and had been able to achieve that. Mrs. Lyons, for example, recalled:

> I used to pass this house before when I was rooming over on St. Nicholas Avenue. I had a friend down at 217, and I used to pass this house and looked in, and I said, oh I wish I could get me an apartment in there. . . . And my dream came true.

In another building, Mrs. Byron fondly recalled the lobby with its chairs and mirrors when she used to wait downstairs while her aunt went upstairs to get dresses made in someone's apartment.

For a place like Harlem, attachment operates in complex, often ambivalent ways. The history of Harlem like the individual histories of the people we spoke with reflects an amalgam of hope and segregation, based on racial discrimination, absence of economic choice, attachment to friends and neighbors, and determination to survive. Those we interviewed who spoke hopefully of their own personal lives and those of their children also saw a brighter future for their community. The various residents of the co-op on Convent Avenue were already in the process of passing down their own positive visions of place to their children and, more generally, to the next generation. This process was reflected in multiple ways: the leaders' children were staying and expressing the intention to stay; the young couple selected to fill the vacant apartment brought not only an infant daughter but also commitments to a cooperative vision; the co-op president was attempting to develop a day-care center as a first economic development venture and as an expression of care for the future of the community's children. Mrs. Michael spoke of her hopes in words that conveyed the memories she held on to as well as the strength of her vision:

> I believe this neighborhood will be like the old Harlem used to be. . . . The old Harlem was beautiful and you could go out at night. I could leave my doors open and could just go up on the roof, enjoy yourself, sit in the backyard, enjoy yourself and you weren't afraid . . . and everybody was friendly like and there were places to

go. . . . I just have that feeling about it, that it's gonna be that way again.

Different members of the board of Mrs. Michael's co-op tried to express the variety of ties they had to the building. Some focused on the other renovation going on in the area. Mrs. Harris, one older woman, told us that a friend of her son's had been on television showing the brownstone he had restored in the area.

Pride of place seemed also to include a sense of the importance of what they were doing. Mrs. Brent, the younger female board member, said that prior to moving into the building she had read of a court decision affecting the co-op. She referred to it as a landmark decision and remarked on how thrilled she felt to be moving into a building where people were taking control of their housing. On a more mundane level, residents told us that they had always fixed up their own apartments, that doing so was a mark of their own self-respect that could now be extended to the whole building. But even in this optimistic atmosphere, the dark side of Harlem's recent history defined the great amount of change still needed for Mrs. Michael's vision to be realized. When we asked her more about the old Harlem she remembered, she replied:

> You didn't have to worry then. They had dance halls, they had places that you could go, sit out, eat and enjoy yourself. Now you find a res-taurant every ten or more likely twenty blocks. You find a movie where? In the Bronx or on 86th Street.

In this building, fear of crime, a theme common in many of the non-co-op resident interviews, was acknowledged but minimized. Mrs. Brent's re-marks were typical. She described worrying about her teenage daughter's absence if she returned home to an empty apartment. But she qualified her anxiety as follows:

> I'm not frightened of the neighborhood. I am more uncomfortable if she tells me she is going places that I'm not familiar with. I think we've lived around here long enough, you know, to recognize the people in the neighborhood and I am pretty comfortable.[18]

The lives of other children were very affected by fear of crime and drugs in the wider neighborhood. Louise Carroll felt comfortable about 115th Street, her block, saying that everyone knew her young daughter but she wouldn't let her play downstairs by herself. Mr. Dawson, on St. Nicholas and 115th, spoke of never letting his children out of the house unless he was with them or they were in a supervised care situation until they were older teenagers. Another woman in Mrs. Michael's building on Convent Avenue spoke of the split shifts she and her husband worked so that at least one parent was available to pick their children up and be at home.

Limitations on physical mobility arose in part because of conditions in the community. Others of those we talked with looked back on the time when Harlem had been a safe community. Almost always they chose to describe the situation by saying "You could walk around on the streets then" or "You could go out at night and nobody would bother you." In these descriptions physical and social limits on mobility merged into the mugger's threat. Mrs. Pritchard, on West 142d Street, had stopped going to evening church meetings. She described her own strategies for avoiding trouble: never carry a pocket book, never go out at night, avoid areas with "boys on the street." Mrs. Smythe, on 115th Street, commented: "We old folks can't go out visiting so we visit on the phone. Old folks scared to walk the street even in the day so they're not coming out at night."

Harlem is a mix of different neighborhoods but there was always the sense of a Harlem of slights by respondents. There were references to smells of deterioration which were not restricted to residential buildings but mixed in with commercial uses, particularly at supermarkets. In their areas, older markets with narrow aisles often have grimy wooden floors that seemed to give off a smell even if the food was rated decent. Mrs. Lyons, the reluctant elderly leader of the tenant co-op she thought would have fared better under the pastor's tutelage, commented on the quality of shopping in her neighborhood: "You know how they do it in Harlem. They take the junk from the other stores and bring them here, but I'm still trying to survive."

Mrs. Howard, the woman in a community management building on 129th Street, who had left the South because of low pay, also commented on the smells in the nearby Chain Foods store, stating that "white stores don't smell." Mrs. James, on 114th Street, said that the quality of meat in neighborhood markets was not good. Those who could often went to particular places outside their immediate neighborhood; sometimes this was less than ten blocks away, other times about four miles away to midtown Manhattan. Mrs. Miller told us that she wouldn't buy most food in her neighborhood because of the poor quality and high prices, so she tried to buy when her son took her to his home twice a week. Some were resigned, as they were to their housing, and thought that there was no use in complaining because this was Harlem and it was "not the same as downtown." Their opinion about the quality of goods extended to clothes. Mrs. Sweeny, the mother of three children in the building where tenants were leery of allowing the family to rent, commented that opportunities for clothes buying in the neighborhood were not good and prices were too high.

There were other ways in which respondents felt the burden of being black and poor and disenfranchised. Mr. Taylor, in one of the buildings facing Jackie Robinson Park, objected to clogged sewers on his block which led to smells and rats in the courtyard of his building. Although he went to the Board of Health to report it, and they said they would send a man out, nothing was ever fixed. Terry Jones, on 129th Street, told us about the poor garbage collection, especially in the summer.

The most obvious example of perceived race discrimination was the reference to how quickly or slowly the city acted in turning buildings over to tenants. Mr. Bridely was explicit, stating, "If we were white we would have gotten the building earlier." He reported that they had tried to get the building six times. The tenants in his building had the support of the white establishment, a city councilman, a lawyer who later became a councilman, and the activist tenant-oriented Metropolitan Council on Housing. With the confidence of his experience as an organizer, his ongoing job with the postal office, Bridely conveyed his suspicions of racism to the administrators of the housing agency, complaining that they found "the least little thing" wrong. As we wrote earlier, they would respond, "No, no, no, don't feel that way." Mr. Bridely reported, "We would ask ourselves, 'What else can it be?'"

Mrs. Knotts expressed the interrelated ways in which race and income entered into the disposition of landlord-abandoned buildings, and what conclusions can be drawn from city policy.

> I was told downtown when we first took our building that the real estate agents wanted to see that program fail. They didn't want us to buy these buildings. The real estate men come by and charged the rents they wanted to charge. You see, the rents would have been astronomical. We couldn't have even lived here. Where would we go? And now they are trying to sell the building, that Koch and his plan about selling the brownstones. Except now the people in Harlem rent those brownstone houses. If they are up for sale, the people here. . . . There are a lot of blacks living out of the city that would love to come back if there was decent housing. They would love to come back here because even they have realized the importance of the transportation and everything.[19]

She estimated that the five room apartment in her building that the city required be sold for $9,500 could have sold from $65,000 up anywhere other than Harlem.[20] Younger co-op residents were sometimes suspicious that the events that led to abandonment and the programs the city developed to deal with it were all part of a grand design to "gentrify" Harlem. From their discussion, gentrify meant getting rid of black people.

CONCLUSIONS

G ENDER AND race need to be seen as central to the development of low-income housing policy. It is not only because of the make-up of the poverty population of which women and blacks and other persons of color make up a sizeable proportion. That is of course important and should command attention. While the numbers may lead policymakers initially, what is as important is to understand the cultural and racial autobiographies of people. There is a tendency for policymakers to think of people in traditional socioeconomic categories. There have been some efforts to transcend that and redefine the changing household, catching up with the reality of fewer nuclear families, more single parents and single people.[21] Even with that, the driving force has been the rising numbers of white nontraditional households. That blacks and other persons of color may benefit from that redefinition may not happen as a matter of course. To think fairly about gender and race it is also important to identify qualities associated with women, responsibilities they take on, and the different forms their leadership takes. Analyses of where people live need to be grounded in their reality, particularly if policymakers continue to be of different gender, income, and racial groups, unfamiliar with what blacks must do to achieve even a semblance of order in their lives.

There is another dimension that emerged from the interviews that also need to be integrated into the discussion of gender and race issues, and that is age, the factor we consider in the next chapter.

EIGHT

Getting Old

PERHAPS MORE straightforwardly than gender and race, the interviews revealed the incremental events and social awareness of getting old. This emerged when we asked people for their personal and residential histories. The periods of their lives were marked by their moves from one place to another, or having lived for so long in the same place, and by other people moving away or dying during the time the abandonment process occurred. Our sensitivity to age was heightened after we analyzed the first set of interviews in tenant-initiated cooperatives. We had not expected elderly residents to play such critical roles in saving and co-oping buildings. Earlier literature on limited equity co-ops had viewed the elderly as reluctant to participate since they had less time ahead of them to enjoy the benefits of work and sacrifices they made now.[1] Research on race and aging consistently reports black elderly to have more health problems, lower life satisfaction in many domains, and a more pessimistic evaluation of their present situation as compared to white elderly, not surprisingly since they also live in much worse economic circumstances.[2] Jacquelyn J. Jackson has looked at the situation for older black women in the United States, assessing the compounding of "economics, loneliness, mortality and isolationism."[3] Although Jackson's data draws from 1960 and 1970, her general conclusions are still relevant today; indeed given the perpetuation of low incomes and cuts in government assistance, it is reasonable to conclude that people are in worse situations today. Holden, Burkhauser, and Myers substantiate that although the well-being of the aged has increased over the past two decades, older women are characterized by their poverty.[4] In Jackson's work, the increasing age of black women was accompanied not only by heightened poverty but feelings of loneliness due to their living longer than black men.[5] Isolationism was heightened by the ways in which older black women are treated by the larger society. Jackson thought that there could be "countershifts" to all of these plights. In buildings where there were co-ops or struggling co-ops, the cooperative structure appeared to be just such a countershift. At a time of life when the family unit shrinks because of children leaving home and loved ones dying, the building activities can become a replacement.[6]

The first thing we learned from the elderly tenants was that stereotypes didn't fit. Their strengths, ingenuity and perseverence made critical contributions to the saving of the buildings. We realized that the cooperative structure provided security of tenure but also reflected something about the ways in which older people could act effectively. They could transform what is otherwise a terrifying and negative experience of losing their homes to a more affirmative statement. This can be seen in the remarks of Mrs. Knotts, a black woman leader at least 60-years-old in one successful cooperative. She saw fear as the motivating force behind seniors' efforts to co-op, and referred to the building as a "seniors' crutch." But she also expressed positive reasons seniors had for forming a cooperative:

> They are known there . . . they want to be able to say that this is mine, I own this apartment. Or they are going to say, "I live in a co-op apartment." . . . They want to say that the years they have worked up for show that they own something. . . . They can say "we own the building."

Even in Mrs. Lyons' co-op with high tenant conflict, the elderly president saw herself in a constructive way. She felt she was important to the survival of the building because of her abilities to keep peace. She could help others over the internal dissension with the same determined good sense with which she chased junkies away from the stoop.

Throughout the earlier chapters, the endurance, commitment, and skill of elderly co-op residents has been described. The ebullience and hope

characteristic of the elderly co-op residents, especially those who were
active, extended to their descriptions of their lives. Mr. Bridely talked
playfully about fixing up his apartment for his next wife after having stuc-
coed and painted years previously for his wife who had died. He laughed
about his friends' warnings not to kill off another wife. Mrs. Lyons, 70-
years-old, responded to the interviewers' disbelief in her age with the following exchange with doctors at the hospital where she was being treated:

> The doctor said "Are you really this age? You don't look. . . . Could
> you believe it? Guess how old this lady is. He said '55.' " Well I had on
> my clothes and I guess a little bit dressy, but he said "Jesus!" He looked
> up and said, "golly, how did you do it!" I said, "Hard work mister."

The accomplishments and sense of life so evident among elderly co-op
residents has been remarked on by those who have studied minority aging.
These older Harlem residents confirm the conclusions of those researchers
seeking to explain the low suicide rates among elderly blacks: "They have
never considered that life might not be worth living, nor can they conceive
of a situation or problem with which they, themselves, or with the help
of the Lord, cannot cope."[7] The leaders especially appear to be members
of the hardy survivors of a generation of blacks moving up North from the
South who brought vigor, excitement, and hope to their new homes, seeking better opportunities and able to withstand the discrimination and disappointments they often encountered.[8] Elderly renters' stories of their early
lives placed them clearly in the same cohort, but their sense of life seemed
finally to diminish under the strain of landlord abandonment and community
crisis.

It is possible that the older folks in the cooperatives began life with more
optimistic outlooks and greater energy. But we doubt that personality differences entirely explain the much more positive experience of older blacks
living in limited equity co-ops. Particularly in buildings sold to private landlords, tenants' lives were more restrictive, often physically housebound,
dependent on how involved they had been previously in other interests.
Their experience contrasted with those of elderly co-op residents on the
particular issues that studies have shown to be problems for black elderly:
loss of a feeling of usefulness and respect during retirement, time spent
sitting, thinking, sleeping, and doing nothing, loneliness, not enough to do,
not feeling needed, and not enough friends. Co-ops also provided settings
that decreased some of the concrete problems often faced by older blacks,
like poor housing, exposure to robbery, and fear of crime. Even some very
specific problems often reported by elderly blacks such as difficulty in walk-

Harlem, looking north from the northwest corner of Central Park at West 111th Street, the former Hotel Theresa and State Office Building at top, left of center

Harlem looking north from West 110th Street and Frederick Douglass Boulevard, St. Nicholas Park in background

Street scene on north side of 125th Street in front of historic Apollo Theater

Row of abandoned buildings on Frederick Douglass Boulevard

Restored houses on Strivers' Row, north side of West 138th Street

People relaxing in playground, west side of Lenox Avenue, between West 139th and 140th streets

Street scene on Manhattan Avenue just north of Morningside Park

80-year-old president of a newly purchased co-op on West 123rd Street, with her dog and children from the building

Mother of five cooking in her still unrenovated kitchen in a struggling co-op

Same resident gazing out of bedroom window at boarded up buildings on Lenox Avenue

Another resident of the Lenox Avenue building in her newly renovated apartment

Four women board members of a successful co-op on West 115th Street with man and young girl from building

Current officers of a successful co-op on West 113th Street, in the building's club room

A founding officer of that same building

Now retired president of successful co-op on Manhattan Avenue; he has been part of the tenants' association since 1946

Tenants organizing for co-op ownership in a building on Adam Clayton Powell Boulevard

ing up stairs were sometimes eliminated in co-ops because efforts were
made to move older people to lower floors when they had this trouble.[9]

OLD AND RENTING

HOUSING ECONOMIST George Sternlieb has referred to tenants who rent as "lifers." The expression accurately describes
some of the elderly people interviewed in buildings sold to landlords. With time on their hands, older tenants were painfully aware of
neighbors who had died or moved away and been replaced by strangers.
The following story, by Mrs. Carey in the 134-unit building on 139th Street,
is fairly common among elderly tenants in the private landlord-owned
buildings:

> I think I'm the oldest tenant now. Because most of them that I know of
> moved away or passed. Some of them [went] to different places to be
> with their family. . . . I think about going back home too . . .

Mrs. Jefferson, alert at 93-years-old, described why she would rather
move to a senior citizen building, even though where she lives is a de facto
senior citizen building:

> I have friends that are in the senior citizens' houses. And it's very very
> nice. They get good service and they look out for them. . . . Say for
> instance . . . in a real senior citizen house, they see to it that they have
> people that work in those houses . . . they have a dining room that
> they can get their meals . . . for fifty cents a meal. . . . I think it's
> like twice a week they have the doctor to come in to the ones that are
> not able to get out.

In that type of facility, she imagined a better social life with people her
own age.[10]

> You would have much more in common with people your own age than
> you would with younger people . . . it is hard for them to understand
> older people because you don't understand it until you reach there yourself.

Most elderly stayed away from younger tenants. Mrs. Queen, in one
of the buildings facing Jackie Robinson Park, explained why:

> There are a lot of new people but they don't always stay, about two
> years or something like that. They are mostly younger people, and I just
> don't bother with them.

Others talked of the loss of friends but did establish some new relationships with younger people. Mrs. Johnson, 57-years-old, complained of the behavior of tenants from other ethnic groups but she felt people on her floor would help each other:

> I'll tell you, on our floor here, I mean if I see anything with anybody . . . like she's got a husband that's sick and he's just out of the hospital . . . she and I and another girl across the way [who] works all the time; she is a young girl . . . and when she's there if anything happens that she can do, she'll offer too. Yes we stick together when we see something happening.

A minority of independent personalities found the situation in landlord-run buildings to their liking. In the same building where Mrs. Harry and several other elderly women spoke of loneliness and concern about crime in the neighborhood, Mr. Taylor, the older man who still kept up with baseball, occasionally coaching in the area, thought tenant relationships were fine. Some tenants get involved around particular holidays or events and he told us of one man who puts up Christmas decorations. But he viewed this kind of social involvement as something he did not want to be part of: "I don't mingle with them. I talk with them, but most of the time, I find my own friends."

The contrasts between the optimism of the co-op residents, especially the leaders, and the pessimism of most of the renters about their buildings and neighborhoods was not as strong for community management residents. For them, the more usual story was a turning away from emotional investment in the neighborhood. For the elderly, this involved a sense of futility and a narrowing sphere of efficacy. Younger residents on the other hand seemed satisfied with their housing in the main, but nothing connected them to the future of the area. Older residents perceived the younger ones as too wrapped up in their daily lives to care about anything beyond that. The few we managed to interview tended to confirm this image, with some exceptions. One woman in her mid-thirties tried to take time to decorate the ground floor hall of her building for holidays but her heavy work schedule and family obligations kept her away or busy most of the time. The absence of a structure of shared responsibility short-circuited the flow of place attachment from one generation to another that was so visible in the co-ops. Even those renters who were content with their situations, and even those few who maintained social relationships with a variety of tenants, viewed the future of their building and neighborhood passively.

The community management organizations that were regarded by tenants as responsive and effective were also the ones in which old and new tenants got along better. In these buildings, people did not necessarily have a great deal of contact, except with old friends or others on their floor, but trust in the community management's screening process led to a general feeling of security. In one community management building, only one of the older tenants was left, but she described her relationship with younger tenants positively: "They all treat me like I'm their mother or sister, or something. I like that."

In contrast, Mrs. George, an 83-year-old woman who had previously been active in forming a tenants' association, exemplified the way social life can become defused through the break-up of social networks even in well-run community management buildings. She disapproved of the new tenants who replaced her old allies who moved out:

> Quite a few of them that were living here [were active]. Some of them moved out, you know. Now they regret their move. After they see how the place is being rejuvenated. [But now] these are the laziest tenants here, and I'd rather not amalgamate myself with them. They're not too good.

When asked how the current tenants got into her building on St. Nicholas, she didn't know but speculated that it was either through advertising or because after they came they got the super to let in their friends. John Dawson, an older man once active in the same building, said all of his friends other than this woman and one other had moved out. Neither of them depended on people in the building to be concerned about their welfare. Dawson had children who looked in and sometimes lived with him as well. Mrs. George said: "All young people bother me. That's right." Yet at the same time, children of her friends would stop by and even stay with her when she needed help. She did admit that some concern existed among tenants:

> When we have a death everybody rallies and we give donations and we buy or either give them the money to their family. . . . If we know someone is sick, we would hear . . . if you would see so-and-so and they would say, well she's sick or she went in the hospital. That happens every now and then and we all get together. . . . But there are some things I know [are happening in the building] but I keep quiet because I'm scared.

Despite her objections to the people she was positive toward the idea of the building becoming a co-op, mainly because she wanted to keep her nicely renovated apartment. The older man also wanted to be involved in a cooperative.

Mrs. Pritchard, in one of the community management buildings on 142d Street, expressed a spirit of minimal mutual aid.

> Since I've been here . . . I've been keeping company with some of these people, we go to the same church, we see each other all the time. If it's something that I can do for you, I'll do it. If it's something they can do for me, they'll do it, and that's the spirit the people put in here.

Her attachment to the building focused on a sense of limited control. She had been active in a tenants' organization in her previous run-down building, stated her dislike for her current neighborhood, and made clear what she now tried to do as an individual.

> You can see the garbage and how they put it out there. If I had any say . . . it would be cleaned up. I've called and called and made a complaint about it over and over again. I called the Sanitation Department.

Her efforts served only to increase her sense of powerlessness.

> [They say] all right, we're gonna take care of it. That's their way of getting rid of you. . . . They have their hands full; they can't go around and clean up these buildings. That's all we can do is call in like we do. . . . And when I go down and see all that garbage, it really gets to me, and in the summer it's worse.

However, her apartment reflected her sense of security inside the building. At her own expense she had installed a brightly colored linoleum floor to match her furniture, all of which shone with polish. Matching crochet work that she made herself was spread around the room. She and another woman in a different building owned by the same community group were the only non-co-op owners interviewed who made such large investments in their apartments.

There were complaints and also contradictory opinions about any one community organization. Mrs. Howard perceived shortcomings with another community organization's performance as landlords. The organization hadn't done anything but raise rents.

> They didn't fix the walls, they didn't do nothing. They didn't give heat. . . . They raised my rent from $80 to $371 and now they cut it down to $130.20 and they wouldn't give me a stove, they wouldn't give me a refrigerator, and they got a white man who comes up here.

Mr. Fontaine, the past president of the tenants' association in this building, thought that the organization gave reasonable service. He blamed the building's condition on the new tenants who tore up the building. All but two of his old friends had moved. He no longer will be active, saying 80 years was too old for that. Nor did he trust the current tenants enough to want to work with them.

Community management buildings that had not undergone drastic deterioration during city ownership and that had not formed tenants' associations could be seen as approximating a paternalistic arrangement. Tenants exchanged some forms of aid with other tenants and looked to the organization to deal with larger problems. For example, Fiona James saw conditions in the neighborhood around 114th Street as improving because of activities of the community group:

> The landlords have repaired the buildings. . . . especially the last five years, they've put in a lot of new repairs and new construction, and it's better, I think, than it's been. . . . I think it's just part of Harlem . . . it looks like it's a little better than it was. . . . The landlord say . . . that things will be getting better on the block.

In another neighborhood, Mrs. Pritchard, on 142d Street, thought:

> The neighborhood has changed some. When I first came over here, nobody bothered nobody. You go on and mind your business, and I'll go on and mind my business, and everybody each to their own. . . . but since then there's been little bottles and things out in the streets, but not in here.

She described how she felt when she got inside the building, a countervailing attitude to the time when the building was abandoned.[11]

> You have nothing to fret about as far as the building is concerned. . . . Once you get in, well you're in. One thing I liked about the whole thing, when you get in that door downstairs, you didn't have to run or keep looking back.

Views then of the past and visions for the future varied even within the same building. The same individual might feel conflicted. Few expressed the pride in present activities that they had for past achievements. Many of the elderly renters in community managed and landlord-run buildings recalled with pride how hard they worked and the efforts they had made with their children and other young people to see that they grew up right.

While many remained proud of their own children, they seemed to view most young people as rather hopeless.[12]

The following excerpts from the interview with Fiona James reveal the contrast many Harlem residents came to feel between the more controllable, safer community of the past and the present.

> years ago. . . . If I see somebody hurting you on the street, I'm going to do something about it. If I see somebody on the street right now, I'd go home and call the cops. . . . When I first moved here years ago, and I saw kids out there on the street fighting. . . . I'd go there and tell them, no . . . your mother doesn't want you to do that. Go upstairs to your mother or something like that. They would listen and go.

Such efforts now, she felt would lead only to further trouble.

> But you can't do that no more. . . . they might turn on you. Or else if you went to their parents, they don't care one way or the other. . . . instead of being glad that you tell them about their kid, they don't want you to . . . because some of these parents are scared of their own kids, to tell you the truth.

At the same time, she had many ideas about how the community organization or churches could make an impact on the problems she saw with children.[13] She placed great emphasis on the development of a positive social life. She also thought the organization could do more for seniors. Neither her building nor the one next door, nor the neighborhood provided a "place where senior citizens could sit down and talk with each other." As a result, the senior's life was narrowly confined:

> The senior citizen has to stay in their house or go and visit somebody, or go to church on Sunday, come back and stay in the house the rest of the day. There's no place for them to go.

She thought there should be facilities

> like where my sister lives . . . or where she used to live . . . in the projects, they have places where the senior citizens can go down and they can sew . . . and some of them play a little cards . . . or something like that. That helps them, you know. They live longer too. Because they don't have to stay in their house or be afraid to go out all the time, or coming in at a certain time.

When asked if she would like to be active in getting something like that started, she said she would love to.

In another building that had deteriorated seriously before going into community management, and that had had some tenant activity to save the building, previously active tenants withdrew as the community group took over. Mrs. Jones, the older woman with a history as a volunteer organizer, had been able to make friends with the younger people who moved in on her floor and knew the history of everyone in every apartment in the building. Her knowledge of people has aided her in organizing the block in the past. The community management group had told the tenants in her building "to get a tenants' organization." She felt she should do this but was unable by herself.

> I could call a meeting, but I haven't been well enough to call a meeting yet, and my house isn't fit to call a meeting in. So I don't know who else's house I could ask to call a meeting in. . . . out in the hallway is too small. Well, I could get a place then if I could get enough people, I haven't had a chance and time.

She was torn between her personal obligations to her husband who was in the hospital and her granddaughter at another hospital. She had had "her hands full" and wasn't well herself. She knew from practice what the next steps should be, including the frustrations.

> They [the community organization] aren't fixing it [the building] and we're still living here. And if I could, I would tell everybody let's see if we can't find a house . . . and live decently. But where can you find a place to live decently where poor people pay the rent?

Nonetheless she looked forward to more organizing which would also be an opportunity for her to talk with younger tenants.[14]

PATHS TAKEN BY OLDER TENANTS

THE MIXTURE of people's personalities, conditions of their building, activities of a tenants' association, community organization, or private landlord influences the direction tenants may take. Some people reached a point when they felt they were too old, or facing illness or other personal troubles. Some evaluated the situation and were able to muster the energy to fight for themselves but were unable to do it for others. One older woman in Mr. Keen's building described her successful effort to obtain Section 8 and her obstinacy in staying put despite the landlords who:

make the rent as high as they can to try to get the senior citizens out
of the building. . . . Trying to get all of them out, but I won't get
out. . . . they can get more money for the apartments. If they get me
out, they can get more . . . for the apartment. That's the whole damn
issue.

Sometimes there was a mismatch between the spirits and efforts of people
and the physical conditions of a building. There seemed to be a lack of a
critical mass of concerned tenants.

Many of these points are reflected in the interviews in a landlord-owned
building. The Keens seemed in spirit much more like the older leaders in
the co-op buildings. They had in fact been active in a now disbanded tenants' association. The man told of his efforts to get the landlord to clean
the sidewalk:

I said, how about the sidewalk? The sidewalk hasn't been washed since
you took the house. Uhuh, I'm not washing no sidewalk (he says). I have
no hose to reach out there because the fellows in the block use the hose
to wash their cars.

Mr. Keen's first hand knowledge about the hose exposed the excuses of
the absentee landlord whom he told:

Now that's not true. . . . I said, I live here so you wouldn't
know. . . . nobody has ever used that hose to wash their cars since
I've been here because I'm the one that used the hose. When I get
finished with it, I put it back down in the cellar. I wouldn't let no one
use that hose to wash their car. . . . You wouldn't let a perfect stranger
go down in your basement, right?

Mr. Keen's wife was quick to establish that the building wasn't all that bad
and people would only stand for so much "because they will . . . call up
Mr. John Law." But her husband projected a future of decline for the building because of the landlord:

I don't know if they intend to sell this house, or walk away or not do
anything to the house. I don't know because what they are doing now,
they aren't doing nothing, nothing. . . . and the house will get worse
all the time, it will get worse all the time.

In some ways, Mr. Keen's actions are poignantly reminiscent of those of
Mr. Williams in the successful cooperative and Mr. Grayson in the building
that reverted to the city. He "just wanted to have something to do." It is
stressful when people like Mr. Keen try to improve their lives, and there

is both the uncertainty of knowing what the landlord is going to do and your own actions go unrecognized. For the elderly, this can compound the feelings of loss as they face the uncertainties of dying.

In the stories of elderly leaders in the successful co-ops and the struggling ones, we felt that there was a strong connection between the leaders' vitality in old age and their roles in the building. For most, leadership gave them socially productive work important to their community and they were proud of themselves for it. They were respected by the tenants of all ages, despite conflicts about building policies that did occur. Their visions of the future, drawing on their experiences of the past, sustained and animated the struggles of the tenants to control their buildings, and extend this control to the community.[15] Their determination and hard work energized younger people and heartened the other elderly in their buildings. They spoke most often of the future and little of the past.

When obstacles to realizing their dreams prevailed over the efforts of these elderly leaders, the effect on their sense of their place in the world and of themselves was strong. The Keens seemed to have reacted to their loss of control over the building by retreating from active engagement in the world around them. In the interview each talked a lot about the negative ways the world had changed since they first moved from the South to make their lives in New York. Mrs. Keen spoke of the way she worked her way up from a menial job in a department store to a better one. Such tales of hard work and the earning of rewards were frequent themes in the stories of elderly leaders. However, Mrs. Keen saw her own history as setting her apart from the young people of today. More successful leaders interpreted their histories as preludes to their successes in forming the co-op.

The tenor of the Keens' recounting of their lives had more in common with the stories told by older people in buildings that had never organized to fight negligent landlords or the city. Much like these older people, they also saw their neighborhood as in an irreversable spiral of decline. The Keens both laughed when the interviewer asked them about changes in the neighborhood and went on to tell him that he couldn't possibly imagine how much better, how "really beautiful," the neighborhood had been before he was born.

CONCLUSIONS

GENDER, RACE, and age each play a part in understanding the personal histories of the people we interviewed and their residential histories. Their life histories reveal the tangible integration of control over external conditions, group effort, and personality that make for empowerment or block it. Empowerment occurs through countless little acts that are rooted in everyday life and build up, each act adding another layer. Some of these roots extend back throughout the history of blacks' struggling for their civil rights. In this study, these long-accumulating experiences are sparked off by anger at being abandoned to live in deteriorating conditions. Their shared experiences lead black tenants to understand that the collective tenantry is suffering. Solving an individual problem comes to depend on solving the collective ones. In many cases, the sense of the collective emerges first. People then chose to "make a stand" in different ways. For some, they began to gnaw away at the legal issues, countering the rigidity of the bureaucracy, identifying people and programs who could assist them. Others took up mops and paint brushes. Some drew on knowledge from jobs they have held or hold now. Others plant flowers. Not everyone succeeds to the same degree; not everyone gets empowered.

Generational continuity in the black community is passed down through the collective pride mixed with experiences of discrimination. For elderly leaders and residents in tenant-run cooperatives, age became a positive rather than a demeaning state because they were able to reverse one kind of powerlessness, inability to control housing. They were called upon to remember how buildings looked and how proud they felt to have visited someone in the building where they now lived. The loss society faces when older people face abandonment but there is no assistance or structure to go beyond individual survival is revealed in the life of an elderly woman who was not a leader.

The older woman is Ethel, whom we have referred to before, the retired dancer who last worked at the once famous Roxie Theater. She was not an officer in a tenants' association; there wasn't even a tenants' association in her building, although some people tried to start one a while ago. Ethel exemplified the loss Harlem and New York as a whole suffers when poverty and public policy isolate people in their community. Their memories and attachment to place are strong; without it cities are hard pressed to keep their humanity.

As we spoke with her about the building she lived in, the history she recounted recalled not just pride in the physical past but also in the accomplishments of blacks who lived there:

> It was a beautiful building. Carpeting down the stairs, canopy to the street and the awnings were changed every year. I didn't know when I moved

in that it was named for one of the greatest entertainers, Florence
Mills. . . . She starred in Europe and in the big musicals downtown.
She was the biggest entertainer for a time, and she lived here. . . . The
leading people of Harlem lived here. . . . This is Sugar Hill.

The more recent history was marked by crime:

> I've been robbed several times. Most everyone has, you know. They
> come in to the place where the people are all sitting. . . . Even with
> the doors locked they get in downstairs. They get on the elevators and
> scare you half to death. This is the way it is. But not only here, all over.

Now animals were her trusted companions, and lent her security. She
reflected:

> Where would I want to go? In the better housing, no pets are al-
> lowed. . . . It's the same downtown, every now and then you read in
> the paper. . . . people going to court because the landlord is putting
> them out because they have pets . . . I guess there's no sense in me
> moving, taking a chance by not having a pet, so I'm just stuck here.

Despite her circumstances, she still felt connected to the city:

> I wouldn't want to live anywhere else in the world because this is the
> place where I would want to be. . . . I just love it here, I love New
> York and I get mad when I see the horrible things that are happening,
> and the terrible people that are living here, but that has nothing to do
> with New York.

She joins legions of older people on the streets, not as a homeless person but "just to break the monotony" gets on the bus, goes downtown.
She muses, "You'd think I'd just gotten off the boat. I go all over to make
me happy. . . . It's fabulous, this beautiful city." As we walked away from
the interview, we took some time to look at the flowers she had planted
across the street, around the base of a tree. She was full of life, planting
and tending a tiny public "garden" that brightened the neglected street.

Understanding the role of women, the connection to black history and
race pride, and the thinking of older people, led us to be more amazed at
the total disregard for the strengths and contributions of people like her
that characterizes almost all thinking about public policies affecting minority
and low-income populations. It seems particularly sad that politicians and
journalists fill the media with laments about the decay of the black community and the black family without considering deeply this other side.

Looking back over the transcripts, the waste of potential participants in the renewal of the black community prods us to look for ways to bring these human resources from the barred doors of their lonely apartments, to accelerate the gains in the successful cooperatives. In the next chapter we turn to a discussion of how policies can build on the strengths we uncovered, and directly address gender without bypassing race and age.

IV

A NEW RESPONSE

NINE

The Community-Household Model

THE PEOPLE we talked with provided better models of coping with adversity than their buildings did of housing. We saw that the huge reservoir of unused human energy and talent lying in waste in many poor communities will come to the surface when conditions allow for its emergence, even when physical circumstances are difficult. In this way, housing played a central role in the empowerment of some of the people we interviewed. It is the home that shelters and supports individuals and households and relates them to their neighbors and local resources. When people could stabilize their lives and those of their neighbors, when the benefits extended from individual to collective households, we saw the emergence of community-households. The goal of the community-household model is not simply to transform housing and neighborhoods, nor even whole cities; it is to facilitate the transformation that individuals, households, and communities seek for themselves.

We are not the first to note the importance of empowerment as a goal for actions taken to improve the conditions of poor communities. Julian Rappaport, a community psychologist, has defined empowerment as

both individual determination over one's own life, and democratic participation in the life of one's community, often through mediating structures
such as schools, neighborhoods, churches, and other voluntary organizations. Empowerment conveys both a psychological sense of personal
control or influence, and a concern with actual social influence, political
power and legal rights.[1]

The aspects of tenant-owned co-ops that struck us as most important for
the well-being of the residents relate to characteristics of empowerment.
Rappaport described empowering programs as collaborative, able to "free
self-corrective capacities," extending real responsibilities and power over
resources to participants, and sensitive to cultural diversity.[2]

Such interventions have a radiating impact such that effects on organizations also empower individuals and spill over into changes in other settings. Conversely, by respecting the powers and abilities of individuals,
such initiatives allow the strengths of individuals to promote positive changes
in a variety of settings and for other individuals. Opportunities for participation should be expanded as empowering interventions so that a variety
of people can be involved in ways congruent with their own autobiographies, their histories, cultures, and personalities. Rappaport also stated:
"Locally developed solutions are more empowering than single solutions
applied in a general way and applied in the form of prepackaged interventions."[3] Small settings provide more meaningful roles for members but they
must be large enough to obtain resources. His concluding statement echoes
the basic assumption of the community-household model: "Empowerment
is not a scarce resource which gets used-up, rather, once adopted as an
ideology, empowerment tends to expand resources."[4] To the extent that
the Alternative Management programs for landlord-abandoned buildings met
these criteria, they were indeed empowering to tenants. Where they fell
short, or situations such as building size did not support empowerment,
tenants reacted more passively, sometimes withdrawing into fatalism.

Harry C. Boyte described the process of empowerment as critical to
the success of the organizing efforts he investigated.[5] Communities Organized for Public Service (COPS) in San Antonio, Texas, provided his
clearest example. Many of the aspects of COPS that he associated with
empowerment echo the findings of our research. COPS succeeded in organizing the Mexican-American community to make effective demands on
the city government where many activist groups had failed before. The
early organizers drew on Saul Alinksy's philosophy of building power bases
among poor people and using them through confrontations with officials to

bring about changes. However, they added a new dimension of concern for what people wanted done and for the essential role of values in organizing and sustaining poor communities. The values stressed were those we heard from the co-op leaders in Harlem, commitment to community, religious values, and an emphasis on care. The deepest interests of poor and working class people in San Antonio as in Harlem were not in the more visible political issues like racial discrimination or police brutality, important as they are, but in the everyday persistent problems of home, family, neighborhood, and work: housing, utility rates, drainage, schools and so on. Ernie Cortes, one of the leaders of COPS, made another observation reflecting also the kind of linkage between household and community we see as central to the community-household model. He pointed out that the family was critical, the place where most people learn "the basics of relationships, reciprocity, nurturance, identity, habits, work, personal roots."[6] At the same time efforts to be effective in the broader world must be anchored in people's private lives. The family cannot exist for its own sake only. Boyte noted one other aspect of COPS that is similar to the tenants' associations in our study: "A striking feature of COPS is the strong leadership roles women have taken on—a rarity in both community organizing and also in Mexican-American organizations."[7] We think that the value base he advocates and the focus on problems of daily living contribute strongly to women's attraction to COPS and efficacy within it. It is similar to the examples of behavior of women in Harlem that convinced us of the need for a new paradigm.

BUILDING ON THE HOUSEHOLD OUTWARD: WOMEN'S ROLES

THE PERSPECTIVE on empowerment spelled out by Rappaport has a strong affinity with widely held female visions of the good society being elaborated by feminist psychologists and theorists. Carol Gilligan's groundbreaking work on women's moral vision emphasized the importance of connection and responsibility for others that is interwoven with women's pursuit of their own development.[8] Nel Noddings has also written that women approach moral problems quite differently from men by

> placing themselves as nearly as possible in concrete situations and assuming personal responsibility for the choices to be made. They define

themselves in terms of caring and work their way through moral problems from the position of one-caring. This position or attitude of caring
activates a complex structure of memories, feelings, and capacities. Further, the process of moral decision making that is founded on caring
requires a process of concretization rather than one of abstraction.[9]

Mary Field Belenky and her colleagues have found the same emphasis on
concrete situations in their study of women's ways of knowing.[10] They
rejected as immoral the application of abstract solutions to the problems
of real people.

Common threads that run through this body of feminist work include
women's feelings that they grow and gain satisfaction through their connections with others, that abstract, general approaches to problems fail to
provide solutions that respect the different needs and perspectives of all
the people involved. Women feel that communication, mutual commitment,
and shared action can lead to solutions that are more mutually beneficial
than those based on hierarchy or preestablished programs for behavior. In
our research, one of the most successful co-ops we studied was Connie
Byron's, led by four women. It well exemplifies these themes: communication among the leaders was constant, ways of involving all tenants had
been developed, responsibilities were shared maximally, and a multidirec-
tional flow of information established. More than this, the ethic of caring
for your neighbors extended from relationships among the board of directors through the actions of the committee system that looked after the
sick and elderly through willingness to bear the financial costs of sick, old
people unable to pay rent increases.

We depart from the work of feminist psychologists in that our research
and thinking links the strengths of female abilities to care for others, to
emphathize, and to work collectively to better their physical, social, and
economic conditions. We do not expect women to always demonstrate this
kind of connection and caring in their behavior. In addition, situations organized around individualistic principles can make such behavior ineffective
when it occurs. For these feminine strengths to surface and succeed in
transforming the lives of those involved, opportunities must exist, resources must be available, and the institutions of society must legitimate
and promote their actions, though not without struggle. It is beyond the
scope of this work to locate the origin of peculiarly female skills except by
referring to the traditions of domestic life women have long perpetuated.
It is quite possible that women's economic dependency and limited access

to power have contributed to these skills and in some cases hampered the upward mobility of individual women. But from the point of view of households, communities, and indeed the human community as a whole, the values and practices women have nurtured over the ages are essential.

In the previous chapters, we discussed the important roles women played in the formation of tenant-controlled co-ops and the similarity of organizing and running a co-op to domestic life. We believe that this base in domestic life contributes to the empowering quality of the successful co-ops we studied. In contrast to specialized housing or social service programs, these co-ops dealt with all the needs of people and households across the life span. Tasks, shared responsibilities, battles for control, nurturing, and socializing mixed in a not always easy combination similar to life within the household.

Domestic activities attempt to make up for the shortcomings of what the society offers us. Where housing and social services are of poor quality they require intensive investment of usually female labor and care to transform them into supports for life. To the extent that conditions in apartments of low-income people deteriorate, boilers break down, somebody in the building gets ill, or needs help shopping, someone must transform these conditions through acts of care and labor into useful goods and relationships. A great deal of time and effort goes into that management. Added to this is emotional work. Women find themselves managing the moods of others in the household, trying to soothe mates who may be worried about job security, job gratification, or getting a job, perhaps inadvertantly erecting barriers between members of the household in order to reduce stress on one or the other. There is no fixed formula, no relief, and no guarantee that an approach that works one time will do the trick the next. Similar emotional management is required to assuage anxieties about buying a share in a building, restructuring the rent, screening tenants, negotiating with the city, and handling dissension in the buildings.

Studies of poor and working-class households reveal a repeated pattern of women coping with adversity by intwining their activities in the household and the community.[11] Women in black communities have shouldered this burden with particular frequency, helped by the men in their community as economic fortunes would permit.[12] One aspect of women's work that explicitly links the household to a larger group is the "work of kinship."[13] Just as housework and the management of different household members' needs and emotions has its parallel in co-op organizing, so does the work of kinship. To the extent that holidays and celebrations are shared,

birthdays remembered, and in numerous little ways relationships reinforced, the co-op functions like an extended kin network. And as we have
seen this social glue is of great importance to the success of the co-ops.

This link with domestic life and a recognition of the particular contributions of women is missing from writings on community organizing and
empowerment. For us, these are the starting points of the community-
household model. The point of the community-household model is to provide guidelines for thinking about the development of social programs and
a structure that nurtures this nurturing rather than opposes it. Within the
community-household model, women would lead by asserting their values
and goals, not by subterfuge or denial of their strengths. Women's horizons
would expand, along with those of the others in their households and communities. To the extent that women can speak in another voice, it would
be heard in their communities and spoken in the policies and practices of
the society.[14]

CHARACTERISTICS OF THE COMMUNITY-HOUSEHOLD

W E DEVELOPED the community-household model through reflecting on the successes, failures, and problems of the co-ops
we studied and on the experiences of all the tenants interviewed. The goal of the model is empowerment. To achieve that, the model
can be seen as an expanding circle of connection and support, building on
the life of the household, but linking its strengths with those of tenants'
associations, neighborhoods, cities, and the nation. The critical ingredient
from a policy standpoint is the support of indigenous efforts and leaders
through programs structured to provide access to resources and skills they
need. The following seven characteristics in table 9.1 were developed to
formalize our view of the aspects of different levels of organization we see
as particularly important.

The most significant level to add to an understanding of how people's
lives are affected by circumstances not under their control is the realm of
the household.[15] Domestic skills within the home are a hidden resource
that often extends to the building level when a collective crisis occurs.
Actions at the household level are oftentimes ignored by policymakers because the concept of process as an organizing tool in developing a plan or
program is overlooked. When it is not overlooked, it is usually in relation
to programs aimed at individuals and not to building organizations. Participants in our study revealed a hybrid scale or organization that was critical

for their survival: the building as an extended household. At this scale, the skills women bring to the management of poverty can have the most effect by extending the strengths of domestic life in the remaking of community.

The second principle of the community-household is that prior social

---

TABLE 9.1
Principles of the Community-Household Model
by Level of Organization

	PRINCIPLES
Household	1. Domestic skills within the home, inclusive of budgeting, managing, and resolving conflicts, are applied to building and neighborhood conditions.
Building/ Block	2. Social relations between friends, neighbors, and relatives comprise a nonmonetary exchange of goods and services that acts as a first line of defense in times of housing crisis.
	3. Indigenous leaders emerge in response to crises, influencing organizational structure and participation; the structure that emerges for identifying priorities, allocating resources, making decisions, resolving conflicts, and planning for the future affects the possibility of community-households emerging.
Building/ Community	4. Positive memories of the building and community encourage people to organize for the future; the memories are passed on from one generation to the next. Attachment to place anchors people in their buildings and neighborhood and shores up commitment to working cooperatively for a supportive environment.
Community	5. By building outward from the resources and social and emotional ties of households and communities, links must be created to places and opportunities outside the immediate environment.
	6. Community resources such as churches, housing organizations, and technical assistance groups complement and supplement tenants' resources from the first stages of organizing against abandonment to formalizing tenants' associations to assuming self-management and cooperative ownership.
City	7. Public programs and laws connect emerging community-households to the resource allocation process of the broader society, determine their legal standing, and convey social legitimacy.

relations between friends, neighbors, and relatives in a building and on a block become a first line of defense in times of housing crisis. The third building level related principle is that indigenous leaders emerge in response to the crisis. This early response influences the type of organization and participation that emerges later on. Policymakers need to understand how social relations work beyond the building in a particular setting. For example, a planning study in New York of the Lower East Side, aimed at neighborhood revitalization *and* self-determination, distinguished between the urban block and the social block.[16] The urban block is an economic artifact which permitted real estate speculators to sell the maximum number of lots. The social block is the blockfronts on east-west streets between two avenues and includes the lots, buildings and people in those buildings facing that street. Zarza and Cohen wrote, "This is the basis on which most of the social and communication networks in the neighborhood are formed, and it provides the foundation for building a community movement."[17]

The fourth principle of the community-household concerns attachment to place. Acknowledging people's attachment to place means funding efforts to develop or highlight a sense of place.[18] Harlem as an entirety has a strong sense of place as the black capital in the United States. The fifth and sixth levels of the community-household are at the community level. The resources at the household and building levels need to be linked to places and opportunities outside the immediate environment, drawing on churches, housing organizations, and technical assistance groups. Finally, there should be connections to the city level, where the institutionalization of programs like TIL come in.

The city's programs we studied varied in the extent to which they reflected these principles. The co-op program had numerous features that contributed to empowerment, along with some that did not. The co-op form of ownership not only reinforces the importance of social relationship among residents; it also leaves open the opportunity for people, particularly women, to emerge as leaders who organize their home environments in ways more consonant with all their needs, not just the need for shelter. The committees formed in some co-ops provide examples of how this occurs. Many aspects of the social relations grew out of the resemblances to domestic life and provided the fabric out of which tenants could emerge as leaders. These factors, combined with the transfer of ownership to tenants, encouraged a focus on the positive aspects of tenants' attachment to the building and community. They were also a basis for rebuilding both.

In addition, the programmatic requirements for tenant interim lease buildings reinforce patterns of cooperation and commitment in several ways. First, without sufficient cooperation and commitment, tenants cannot enter the program and certainly, they cannot achieve the level of organization and consensus required to buy their building. In contrast to tenants' associations in other non-co-op buildings, daily decisions about the building are directly in the hands of the tenants. When tenants organized against a landlord, confrontation rather than shared responsibility set the agenda for the association. The cooperative form of ownership mandates a structure for tenant participation, even if it is primarily called into play when disagreements arise. As long as they live in the building, people cannot just decide that they will make their own decisions separately. Thus this type of ownership differs from single family or even condominium ownership. It differs from renting in that decisions about maintenance, capital investment, selling and renting of apartments, sale and maintenance costs, leadership and management rest with the tenants. If these are left to the leaders, tenants can still organize to change the leadership or to broaden participation through an existing structure. Regulations protect the rights of tenants who do not cooperate, particularly the elderly who can retain their apartments without joining the cooperative. The city's sale agreement limits the amount of profit that can be made on the resale of apartments. When it works smoothly, the availability of Section 8 and Senior Citizen Rent Increase Exemptions (SCRIE) facilitates cooperation by equalizing to some extent the tenants' ability to pay maintenance and operating costs. In 1984, 18,500 tenants throughout the city, also on public assistance, received Section 8 existing housing subsidy.[19] SCRIE applies to tenants 62 years and over by providing real estate tax credits to landlords whose tenants qualify; it does not reduce the proportion of income to rent that tenants pay. The limited availability of Section 8 will threaten the encouragement of new TILs. There are a number of proposals being discussed that may remedy this, including one that SCRIE be a model for direct assistance to low-income tenants.[20]

In other ways, the city's interim lease program limits the development of community-households. The required rent restructuring leads in many cases to splits in tenants' organizations between those willing and unwilling, able and unable, to pay the increases. The relatively little technical assistance provided to help tenants develop organizational structures and leadership skills places a burden on people already desperately fighting to save their stricken community. The limited amount of renovation and capital

investment mandated by the tenant interim lease program strains the resources of tenants while the program at the same time requires that buildings be brought up to code soon after purchase.

In addition, limited equity co-ops sold by the city formally address only
the provision of housing. Because of the actions of tenants in organizing
to save their housing, other needs of tenants for social and material support
are frequently met. However, the city's co-op program itself offers no assistance to households in meeting needs beyond shelter, no aid for example
in providing day care or other necessary facilities for children nor assistance in finding jobs, education, or special assistance for those with physical
impairments.[21] That in the course of working together, tenants informally
often take on the provision of such aid reflects the empowering qualities
of cooperative action. However, when the demands are too great for an
already crisis-ridden organization, no help is available, regardless of how
important the needs are for the individual and the community. Issues of
stress on leaders and non-leaders will be discussed further in chapter 10.
The problems to be discussed below of incorporating children into low-
income housing exemplify the shortcomings of housing programs that focus
on physical shelter alone. No one-stop programs exist to extend the cooperative control of vital resources beyond the provision of shelter. Only
if tenants are well enough organized do they then apply for grants, loans,
and other technical assistance.

The following section explores the ways the social life of tenants in landlord-abandoned buildings compensates for the limits of the programs. By
helping each other cope with the multiple crises brought on by threats to
their housing as well as the normal demands of life in a poor community,
there is a greater likelihood for empowerment to occur. This section traces
some of the ways the process of taking control of a building as a group
radiated out into other areas of life, both positively and negatively. This
level of analysis is crucial to understanding what is often missing in such
program planning and how programs intended to be empowering should
really function.

SOCIAL LIFE: A CRITICAL INGREDIENT OF THE COMMUNITY-HOUSEHOLD

S UPPORTIVE SOCIAL relationships are the ground out of which
cooperative efforts to take control over critical areas of people's
lives grow. Continuity between domestic organization and social life

was expressed in the informal neighboring that in the successful examples led to cooperatives.[22] The complexity of social relationships in cooperatives was missing in rental buildings where the landlord-tenant relationship set boundaries that were capable of being transcended but rarely were.

In most of the abandoned buildings studied, tenants knew each other because many had lived there for a long time. Elderly tenants usually had resided the longest. In buildings with a substantial number of old-timers, new people became a part of the network in the cooperative buildings more than in those operated by a community organization or a private landlord. Co-op tenants over and over again described the building as being like a family. In the rental buildings, the social networks of the older people frequently atrophied as death, illness, and the departure of residents for senior citizen housing and relatives' homes depleted the number of members. In previous chapters, characteristics of social relationships in different types of buildings were discussed in greater detail. The main point here concerns the differential courses of the development of these relationships during the process of abandonment and reclamation. When tenants, particularly women, used their social life as a basis around which to organize and take control of the building, informal relationships formed that created the basis for the development of a more formal structure.

The formation of tenant cooperatives began when leaders emerged and called on their friends to work with them. Mrs. Byron, for example, told of how Mrs. Wilkins talked to her and went around to a few other friends to get a core leadership group organized. Then again through speaking with her friends, and those friends speaking with their friends, Mrs. Wilkins brought together almost the whole building. The tenants listened to an experienced housing activist talk to them about taking over the building. This casual social network was transformed in the process of organizing into a system of leadership and committee activity encompassing all but one of the tenants. A club room for the building served as a place to go and meet friends. The sickness and courtesy committee sent cards to the sick, flowers to elderly mothers, and had parties at New Year's for those who might be alone. In Mr. Williams' description of the start of the cooperative there, he singled out the importance of his wife's activities, acknowledging her efforts in getting them as far as they did. It was she who looked after the social side of running the building and spurred him on:

> She had a greater view than we did for some time, so they [the women] had a big hand. . . . She [his wife] was interested because we had it almost like a social club. She was interested in like the little things, any

little thing that happened to go on in the building. If the super didn't do the right thing or if there was some small thing that was needed.

Likewise Mr. Bridely in another building described how:

> we organized. . . . we met in different apartments until we got set and we opened what we called a club room downstairs. . . . it was a junk basement, and we cleaned it out and organized it and met down there. We have been meeting down there ever since. Now we have a regular nice club room. We have parties and different things, and a kitchen.

They too have a committee to check on people who are sick, to send cards on special occasions, and to console the bereaved.

Differences in modes of tenant selection provided an important key as to how social life was more formally regulated. These differences also explained why younger tenants do or do not become involved with the older ones as a matter of course. In almost all the buildings, those who moved in prior to 1960 often did so because the relationships with people in the buildings. This practice continued in buildings that became cooperatives and less so in others. Of course those buildings with strong, long-standing tenants' associations exerted the most control. However, the one recently organized tenant-run building troubled by internal conflict, nonetheless, had a history of tenants being brought in through their kin and friendship relationships.

In almost every co-op, leaders and tenants told us "we are like a family here." To some extent the screening process insured such relationships. The tenants who do the screening become people the new tenants feel they can talk to; they are seen as a sort of sponsor. But the sense of belonging usually goes beyond this. Even new tenants spoke of having people to rely on and of friendships with tenants of different ages. As one new tenant in a co-op said, "I can go to anybody if I really needed them." It is not clear that people socialized more informally in co-ops; rather the co-op structure of association led to a sense of belonging and security. Sometimes co-op residents would say that they were not the type who visits. But they always went on to talk about a network of relationships they had in the building.

The vast majority of co-op tenants could describe most of the households in the building according to household composition, age, and often other aspects of their lifestyle. This rarely happened in rental buildings. The lack of tenant participation in tenant selection plus the absence of any formal organization that would support the maintenance of informal support structures usually led to dwindling social spheres. In landlord-owned buildings, tenants appeared most aware of this. The kind of social relationships tenants formed in rental buildings and their continuity depended primarily on chance factors. In the absence of more structure, the repeated crises and dislocations experienced by tenants as first landlords abandoned, then the city took over, and then the buildings were sold to a community group or new landlord, led many tenants to move. Many of those who remained withdrew feelings of investment in their building in the wake of many demonstrations of their inability to control the building's fate.

Some residents in community management reported stronger ties among tenants. Often tenants talked of having one or several very close friends, like the following tenant we quoted earlier:

> Now the four of us on this floor, we're just like that. . . . that one over there . . . me and her is closer than the others. We are like sisters.

Another women in a different community management building named her three best friends and described their method of interaction.

> The Harolds has my keys in case they don't hear me or something; then they will look in on me. I call the lady downstairs and she calls me. The gentleman upstairs, he keeps in touch by calling me and I call him. . . . We are our brothers' keepers. We have to look in on one another because we are at the age now when you don't know what will happen.

Her social life was more narrowly defined, oriented towards the needs they all might be likely to have as they grew older.

> If you're sick, we call the doctor, call the ambulance. That's all we can do. If you need a meal, we'll fix something and bring it to you. . . . I'll go to the store if you need something from the store, we'll bring that in for you.

There were other aspects of social life that revolved around sharing domestic responsibilities. As Carol Stack demonstrated, the reliance on sharing is a major value and method of coping with poverty for many black households. For example, Louise Carroll, the young woman in the cooperative building on 115th Street where so many elderly people lived, has a household organization and social life that suggests a similarity with findings in Stack's work. Louise remarked that when her husband wasn't home, the people next door prepared dinner for her and her daughter. They would go over regularly to have their meals with the neighbors. Her oldest daughter had gone down South to live with her grandmother when the mother had become pregnant with her younger child. Some residents in every co-op spoke of sharing their apartment with grown children, grandchildren, or other relatives when they were unable to find housing or live elsewhere. In one cooperative, Mrs. Byron spoke lovingly of the niece she had raised from babyhood as "my little girl." Several older single women living in co-ops, non-leaders, provided homes for their nieces and grandnieces for regular parts of the year. Many older women and one of the men had their grown children and those children's children living with them on and off.

The co-op may not only reflect the domestic organization of the black households we studied but a suggestive finding is that cooperatives may facilitate sharing. Two older people in community management buildings had such arrangements and no renters in landlord-owned buildings described such sharing. Possibly it occurred sometimes but was not mentioned because it may not be as acceptable a practice in a landlord-owned building, or perhaps the tenants represented less open styles of households, or, as they had gotten older, were more isolated from friends and relatives.

Nonetheless, there was some evidence of mutual aid among adults, even in the landlord-owned buildings. Many of the people interviewed appear to have chosen to remain involved with members of their households even when they became separated from them. Often in the course of describing their lives in their building, a person would remark that they had been living with a spouse at the time of some event. They would go on to say that they were separated now. But in a surprisingly large number of cases they would also describe continuing concern and mutual aid. Dorothy Monroe, the single mother in a community management building on 129th Street, said her child's father's family often took care of the child while she worked. A number of the older people interviewed spoke vaguely of still "getting along" with their former spouses.

A dramatic instance of such continuing relationships occurred when we were interviewing in one of the rental buildings on Bradhurst one day. We had the names of some of the older people in the building and were asking directions about entering the building from a group of tenants seated around the entrance. An older man, mistaking us for social workers, approached us to go immediately to see one of the residents. As it turned out, the woman we had inquired about was very ill. The man, her former husband who now lived in another apartment in the same building, explained that now that they were both older, they had to look out for each other even though they could not live together. While the information about such relationships was not extensive or systematic, it is suggestive that the open structure of the black households studied included not only taking in relatives and friends beyond the immediate family but also continuing to participate in relationships after couples broke up and went their separate ways. Carol Stack's work more systematically illuminated the networks of relationship in black households that can tie former mates together even after the couple dissolves and that provide options for those who need a home and help with the chores of daily living. We can only speculate that such an attitude reinforces the values and practices necessary to form more collective responses to crises like housing abandonment, and, in turn, cooperatives reinforce such responses.

But while informal social relationships form the bedrock of the co-ops we studied, they never existed independently of the other processes that affect housing and community development. When aspects of the larger support structure of organizations, programs, and community resources described in a previous chapter proved inadequate, social life could not always compensate nor lead to the formation of cooperatives. The problems many co-ops have in accepting female-headed households with children provide one example where the informal support and nurturing qualities exemplified by even successful cooperative leaders were stretched to the limits as they weighed the social cost to themselves and existing tenants.

In a household, all members are accepted and must do their part. Yet the fact that some members must necessarily be more dependent than productive finds acceptance because of the responsibility one generation feels for another within a family. This can be seen in the ways in which tenants in public housing projects are illegally providing homes for their children's children, while authorities look the other way. In a reversal of sorts, a sense of mutual responsibility characterized older co-op residents' attitudes toward other elderly and infirm who were their neighbors, but sometimes stopped short of including children. Whereas many elderly or sick people could still contribute to co-op activities, or at least not constitute a serious burden, children were not cooperatively involved in most co-ops and were often seen as drains on housing resources.

Only two of the most successful buildings, one where Mrs. Michael lived, and the one with the four women board members, actively welcomed children. The first of these buildings had just sold the only vacant apartment to a couple with a new baby. The husband, John Paynes, also brought desired accounting skills into the building. Other apartments had been sold to children of residents who had children of their own. In the other building one of two vacancies had been filled with a single mother and her young daughter.

More frequently, households without children were preferred. For example, in Mrs. Knotts' building, Mrs. Sweeny, the relatively new tenant with three children described her experiences in getting an apartment in an environment where there were few youngsters, most of them raised and gone a while ago:

> There was a question of how many children did I have. . . . at the time I only had two, two girls, and the rumor had got around that somebody wanted to move in with five children . . . and everybody was up in arms because it's basically a quiet building with people . . . who have been quiet in here for years.

No one confronted her directly, "They didn't come right out and say no because of the children, but I knew [it was] in the back of the landlord's mind [it was not yet in city ownership] and especially the tenants' minds." Nonetheless, an older woman whose apartment she and her family wanted to take over convinced everyone to allow her in. She had become a favorite with some of the older tenants, especially Mrs. Hill, providing companionship and assistance in shopping. They said, "She is a nice girl. She offered to do things to help other people."

One struggling leader in the building on Lenox Avenue was the most adamantly opposed to allowing children in the building. As president of the tenants' association, Mrs. Oilers stated, "I don't want anyone with five or six children because they will destroy the place." This woman had herself raised five children and still had a grandson living with her. Elba Jones, the treasurer in the same building reiterated:

> We screen our tenants . . . maybe somebody would recommend you but when you come, we ask a lot of questions. You have an application to fill out and then for the last five years, you have to give us where you've lived. We don't just take your word for it. We get in touch with the people and find out what kind of tenant you were.

The reasons for their screening were tied to the very strong opinions they held about repercussions from children of welfare families.

> We don't want a lot of welfare tenants. Welfare tenants tend to have a lot of kids. And the kids write on the wall or die trying. They put gum on the wall, they're going to break the plaster. They try to break the doors and other nutty and crazy things.

At the same time the president had brought the vice-president, a woman with twelve children, into the building from a welfare hotel.

The problem of the conflict between the needs households with children have for safe, decent housing that accommodates them and concern among tenants about damage and bad behavior will be addressed again later in recommendations for support systems. Here, it suffices to conclude by observing that, in all co-op buildings, the children who did live there were known to all. When parents worked, older tenants often looked after them. In every building, an older woman, usually on the ground floor, monitored the behavior of older children and teenagers. Several took it on themselves to chase away junkies from the door, as 70-year-old Mrs. Lyons in a ground floor apartment in the co-op on 115th Street described:

> There was a dope problem. They used to give me a scare over here and on the corner and in this building. . . . they broke the door. We got a new door that kept them out.

She was absolutely defiant toward them, having known many of the them when they were children growing up on the block.

> I knew most of them. They used to live down there. I'd catch them again and they would hear me open or unlocking the door, and they started running out the door. . . . I'd catch one, and not catch the other one.

Other tenants in her building did not follow her lead.

> You wouldn't believe this would you, that I was the only person in here who would say anything to them. . . . Let them hit me. I don't care. But they know better. None of them ever gave me any trouble.

She believed that this kind of attention and screening of tenants was needed to improve neighborhoods.

> People are so anxious to rent their places so that they don't screen people. I know you can screen people and sometimes you still make a mistake. But I think it takes a whole lot of screening now to make a very nice neighborhood; and after the neighborhood is good, everybody has to try to be nice and take care of it.

Despite the evidence of prejudice against children and especially large families, the most striking difference in the co-op residents' discussion of youth and that of the renting tenants was that the former were less preoccupied with the issue.[23] However, in all programs, parents of children still living in their homes were less satisfied. Similarly, in all the cooperatives but the struggling one, no tenant spoke of being victimized. The security and involvement tenants felt was reflected in their attachment to their buildings. The survey of 131 residents of buildings sold through the Alternative Management programs confirmed impressions gathered from the qualitative data. Tenants in the co-ops rated other tenants as more cooperative than in the community management buildings. Those in buildings sold to private landlords gave the lowest ratings. Retired and unemployed people in co-ops gave their living situation highest marks, followed by those in community management buildings. Employed people rated buildings in all programs about the same. This latter finding amplified the indication in the qualitative data that older people particularly value the social involvement offered by the co-op and suggests that the same is true for unemployed people. The fact that about 80 percent of the respondents were women may be relevant to this finding. The positive evaluation of their living situation spilled over into more positive ratings of the neighborhood for retired and unemployed co-op dwellers compared to all other groups.

The contrasts between the positive ratings of unemployed and retired people in co-ops with similar residents' ratings of rental buildings also point to the importance of place for this group. The dissatisfaction of parents with all buildings likewise raises concerns because they too have especially great needs for supportive ties to the immediate environment. The next section will look more closely at the ways in which place attachment plays a significant part in the formation of community-households, and the ways community-households shore up this attachment.

GENDER, RACE, AGE, AND PLACE ATTACHMENT

TENANTS IN buildings in the various Alternative Management programs of New York City were able to stay in their homes and neighborhoods. Others in landlord-abandoned buildings often did not have this choice. Indeed, Mrs. Oilers' story of attempting to stay in the building she previously lived in told of a common sequence of events: landlord neglect, landlord abandonment, decline in habitability of the building, tenants moving out, and then "consolidation" of remaining tenants into other city-owned buildings. Since another apartment of similar or better quality is provided, such relocations are seen by housing officials as little more than minor inconveniences or possibly as improvements in tenants' situations. Yet our interviews were full of indications that tenants felt otherwise about staying in their homes and neighborhoods.

In some of the worst buildings, tenants frequently expressed an emotional attachment to the area and the building despite the terrible physical conditions and threats of crime. Mrs. Miller, the elderly woman leader in one such building, spoke of the fact that her son was "on her back" to get her to move into his suburban Long Island home. But she resisted:

> I don't think much of it. . . . I'd be moving away from here. I'd be moving away from the people I see all the time. Plus where he lives is a residential neighborhood: there's no one, you know, well, you might as well say it's different as from daylight to dark from here to where he lives. . . . Everybody just gets up and goes to work in the morning. You don't see anyone. It's just totally different.

Mrs. Baylor, one of the leaders in a similarly dilapidated building that reverted to Central Management, reported feeling almost the same way:

> We had to almost relocate because it was so cold we couldn't hardly stand it here. So we were looking for an apartment and weren't able to find one. That was the only thing, and we went to Long Island and we started looking around. So my son said, "Mama, we'd better look for a house." So I said "okay." So we started looking for that. Then I started to think, you know how you do things when it comes to buying a house. So I said to myself, why am I coming all the way out here? I don't know anybody in the neighborhood. I don't drive. I'll be completely isolated. So I said no.

These two older black women expressed well what numerous studies by environmental psychologists and sociologists have found: women, lower-income people and minorities, and older people are more attached to the places where they live.[24] Many women invest more of themselves in personalizing their homes, they spend more time in them than men, and they gain more satisfaction from their homes.[25] In our study, many examples of the care women lavish on their homes and the gratification they get from the results of their work were evident: the pastel-tiled baths of the officers in Mrs. Oilers' co-op, the photo mural of a wilderness scene in the female park worker's living room, the bright red linoleum, couch, hand-made doilies and patterned wallpaper in an elderly woman's apartment, the numerous photographs and mementos and the comfortable corners where we sat in many of the co-op residents' apartments. That this positive concern for the physical environment spilled over into the building was obvious when we looked at the apartments these women co-op leaders renovated. Appliances were selected carefully with an eye to appearance and function as well as durability. Hard-to-find attractive tile-like linoleum was installed in kitchens and coordinated to the whole apartment's color scheme.

Lower income minority people frequently center their social lives more exclusively in the neighborhood and depend more for their survival on informal transactions in the area.[56] Racial minorities and some ethnic groups experience the dual pressure of positive attachment to the neighborhood and barriers of prejudice and discrimination that bar them from other areas.[27] Mrs. Miller and Mrs. Baylor expressed some of the positive associations in the quotes above. For some of the others we interviewed, their ties to the building were mainly of the latter kind. For example, the woman with twelve children that Mrs. Oilers found housing for would have preferred at this time in her life to live in senior citizen public housing. But her grandson lived with her and would not be allowed in such a facility. Her history of trying to find and keep housing for herself and her large family provided an example of the multiple discriminations and barriers faced by single mothers, large families, black people, poor people, women, and welfare recipients. Older people depend on their homes both as familiar physical environments they have organized to compensate for health or mobility problems they may have and as external memories of their lives and identities.[28] M. Powell Lawton identified a tendency for older people who cope well to increase the density of supports for their transactions with the environment and other people in their home environments. Mrs. Oilers' kitchen from which she ran the co-op, kept up with tenants' activities, and did battle with the city and contractors, stood as a clear example of this strategy. As we sat in her kitchen crammed with bills, reminders, cooking equipment, telephone, and co-op records, she talked with us, scanned her tasks for the day, answered calls about repairs, and answered the constantly ringing doorbell. Lawton singled out shared housing for the elderly as a supportive living environment. This was possible because of the density of their social relations in the building without going away from home. During interviews with most elderly tenants, we saw the density of their social relations to the building as neighbors dropped in and called repeatedly. The elderly leaders' tendencies to stay at home seems to have contributed positively to the functioning of the co-ops as they socialized, watched out for children, screened strangers, looked over workmen's shoulders, and otherwise took care of the interests of the co-op. Despite the problems of living in Harlem, older people like those in other elderly populations studied also liked the proximity to shopping and services and transportation available in a dense, urban area.[29]

The importance of being physically, socially and autobiographically "inside" one's home territory, noted by Graham D. Rowles in his study of

Appalachian elderly, was apparent in Harlem too. Eighty-four-year-old Mrs. Smythe laughed as she said she would not want to leave her apartment because her wheelchair knew its way around the corners. In apartment after apartment, older people showed us the photos of their grandchildren (their grands as they called them), children and relatives, of themselves as pretty young women, sons' trophies, and other tangible reminders of their histories and connections in the world. They told us how much they valued the friends in the building who looked in on them and were there in case of an emergency; one woman said a beautiful house wouldn't ever make up for leaving the companions she had. Our interviews in the previous chapters are full of examples of the feeling of being "inside" and the value older people placed on it.

Studies usually focus on the conditions that lead to different degrees of place attachment, or the consequences of the quality of dependence on, identification with, or attachment to place. The interviews we did with Harlem residents point out a neglected dimension of place attachment, the role it plays in people's contributions to maintaining and improving the quality of life in buildings and neighborhoods. A positive identification with place can occur only when people have some control over what goes on there. It depends also on individual and collective memories of the past and visions of the future woven together by durable, multifaceted social ties and activities centered in the neighborhood. Research has demonstrated that a combination of neighborhood social ties and signs that an area belongs to those who live there reduces crime and vandalism.[30] The reduction of crime in co-ops was a significant result of people taking control over their buildings and lives. Yet it is only a small part of the close connection between active, positive attachment to buildings and neighborhoods and the empowerment of individuals and groups who live there. Just as day-to-day social life can be overlooked in policy planning, so is attachment to place. However, our research shows that they are the warp and woof of individual and community empowerment.

Our study also confirms the negative effects of forceably severed attachments to place for women, low-income and minority people, and the elderly. Since most of the people we talked with were older, low-income, black, and female, the separate effects of these categories merged. Studies have shown that forced relocation of male-headed households leads to overcrowding and higher rent; for female-headed households it leads to the welfare rolls.[31]

Illness for people of all ages and increased mortality rates among the elderly frequently follow involuntary moves and moves in which people relocate from homes they value. Feeling and actually being sick are attached to less favored options.[32] In our interviews, we saw both sides of the coin, the leaders in their eighties apparently hardy and hopeful about the changes they are making, sometimes overcoming serious illnesses in the process, and the older people like the Keens who fought and lost, or those for whom life was out of control as one landlord followed another. These links between people and the places they live tie the physical well-being of one to that of the other, and the collective meaning of place to the individual's sense of self.

CONCLUSIONS

T HE LINKING of the individual to the collective, the physical to the social world, is the hallmark of community-households. Cooperative housing supports these linkages. Linkage policies of another sort were tried in three cities in the 1980s—Boston, San Francisco, and Santa Monica, California. These policies attempted to link development in downtown areas to communitywide goals, targeting employment, facilities, or services.[33] Some localities have experimented with taking a percentage of tax increment financing from redevelopment areas and applying it to social programs. The example of devoting a percentage of development costs to public arts programs is yet another way in which linkages are made to pay for one amenity through publicly assisted private projects. While some linkage policies have been successful, they are insufficient in depth and breadth. For future policies, we are suggesting linkage of another sort, tied to human development and empowerment, protecting existing social linkages that precede and need to at least accompany economic ones.

Absent these policies it is not surprising that social linkages have their origins in tenants or low-income people themselves. But as the TIL program shows, self-help is insufficient. In our research, we have begun to uncover the informal social economy and how it intwines and lays the foundation for successful co-oping, with the potential for emerging community-households. There have been few if any programs in the 1970s and 1980s that even mention the word empowerment. Certainly not the Alternative Management programs of New York City as they are currently structured. How far programs like TIL can be carried to encourage empowerment is reflected in our findings. Most important is how much deeper and further programs like these can go and what to do to encourage this; these issues are explored in the following chapters.

TEN

Structuring the Community-Household Model

I N CHAPTER 9 we set forth the connections between certains kinds of co-oping, empowerment, and the making of community-households. Our findings from our interviews and all that has been written documenting the feminization of poverty lead us to the conclusion that community-households cannot be encouraged or stabilized through narrowly conceived housing programs. People can rent or own, be a cooperator or not, and receive shelter and even security of tenure.[1] But if housing programs are to go beyond that, into certain forms of ownership, cooperatives are more conducive to empowerment, particularly for women.[2] This goal is also more likely to be realized when housing policies are expanded to include other needed services for low-income people, such as child care, home care for the elderly and disabled, and job opportunities. We are not suggesting services that are handed down to people by interchangeable workers in impersonal bureaucracies, but ones that engage people and make possible access to greater control over their living arrangements and to economic power. In this sense, the receiving of services should not include implicit or explicit censure of the individual or of the group to which the person belongs, such as black mothers,[3] but rather assistance in threading their way through institutional mazes that can be patronizing and racist. Richard S. Scobie in writing about "problem tenants" in public housing structures the service argument by differentiating between two views of public housing; on the one hand "as a public charity designed and operated as a minimum, stop-gap program for those in need," and on the other, "as one tool in a broader system of housing subsidies available as a public utility for *all* citizens" (our emphasis).

> Within the context of the first conception social services might function as a kind of peacekeeping activity designed primarily to eliminate or head off problems that might interfere with or complicate the traditional tasks of property management. On the other hand, if the second conception is dominant social services might be seen as an important amenity available to residents as part of a wide system of services and programs designed to create a richer and more supportive social environment.[4]

In his formulation, and ours, a variety of services becomes available as part of any "suitable living environment," for all income groups. Francis X. Russo and George Willis, who also tackle the issue of going beyond housing, define a "housing and urban environment services" system that "is concerned with the impact of people's environments on their lives, and the quality for most Americans is determined largely by the quality of the personal social services, health services, education services, and justice and public safety services available in their environments."[5] These services are usually provided at the local level.

Examples of what we call service-engagement rather than service delivery are the ways in which coordinators at the House of Ruth, a provider of a small emergency shelter and transitional housing in East Los Angeles, help homeless women become independent.[6] "Guests," who are without resources of any kind, arrive at the emergency shelter by word of mouth or referral. The shelter staff becomes the guest's support network, in a way another version of the extended household. The staff initially shops for food, prepares meals, negotiates with schools about children who may be in the district for only a short time, spars with the welfare bureaucracy to insure that checks arrive on time, handles problems with the Department of Children Services, provides transportation, and counsels guests about jobs and finding permanent housing. The staff does not take over the guest's life. Chores in the house, for example, are done collectively. As the women become more independent, and move into transitional housing, they take over the staff's roles, such as budgeting and buying food. By the example set by the staff, new ways are learned to navigate the education, welfare, and housing bureaucracies. This also happens in Chicago, where four staff women create the feeling of home and are role models in Housing Opportunities for Women (HOW), a transitional facility. A full-time program coordinator is responsible for facilitating household chores among guests.[7] The TIL and POMP programs were never conceived to do all this; as we indicated in earlier chapters, that the process of organizing low-income cooperatives can provide a structure for going beyond solitary housing issues is a function of tenants' personal resiliancy and their access to other resources.

Community management has another history; its legacy from the 1960s programs was a merger of housing and job creation, and it was thought by some bureaucrats that somehow this would lead to empowerment. One example of this thinking underlay the development and funding of a job for a "tenant relations specialist"; that is, groups could hire a tenant organizer to go door-to-door collecting rent, using that as a vehicle for assisting people to get other services and to form a limited-equity cooperative. The deputy commissioner in charge of the program at that time thought a position labeled organizer would not survive political scrutiny. Determining the effectiveness of a tenant relations specialist is beyond the scope of this book; clearly the issues go deeper than a change in name, but, also clearly, community groups being able to hire tenant relations specialists did not lead to a rise in the formation of cooperatives.

CMP has been consistently attacked by politicians for being too costly a housing program and for going beyond housing. Yet, there are benefits for those interested in seeing them. There were some existing community groups that were able to survive only because they had a CMP contract. There were new groups that were encouraged. In both instances, this meant a closer presence to the household level than a centralized housing bureaucracy. Other groups were able to leverage the CMP contract and become developers of new housing, health, and child care facilities. The ultimate impact on tenants is far more complicated to evaluate. To the extent that women find more leeway to emerge as leaders in cooperative rather than rental housing, that can be interpreted as CMP having lesser empowerment potential. There are other intervening factors. Many of the community management groups are headed by women; women form a substantial part of the staff. These women may also be residents in the buildings. Without additional research, we cannot draw firm conclusions about community management. Clearly, renters in community management buildings are not as satisfied and do not have as rich a social network as do tenants in cooperative buildings. Most critically, activities at the household level that stimulate the formation of community-households are bypassed, and, while community-households may emerge over time, their emergence will be more accidental.

The strengths of TIL buildings rest at the household level; the program brought tenants' initiatives to the surface. The tenant interim lease program acknowledged the abilities of low- and moderate-income people. The crisis accompanying housing abandonment opened up possibilities for taking control over their buildings. Some analysts view this as co-optation of tenants, particularly if subsidies are unavailable for rehabilitation, maintenance, and operations. This formulation denies the importance of tenants, many of them poor women with a myriad of responsibilities, in initiating a positive response to abandonment and choosing to co-op. Criticism of the program is almost always directed towards the inadequacy of rehabilitation of the building. When critics focus on the additional burdens that tenants bear, it is almost always in the context of inadequate funding. TIL holds more promise than imagined by its creators and its detractors, but the program has also created problems that deter the making of community-households.

IMPEDIMENTS TO FORMING
COMMUNITY-HOUSEHOLDS

THOSE WHO grudgingly support TIL, as well as those who say it could not have succeeded without tenants' involvement, may not have fully appreciated what that means. It became obvious from the interviews that the programs breed stress, and this was felt by leaders and non-leaders.[8] People like Mr. Keen felt inadequate and less productive in the landlord-run building, as did the man who coached baseball to local kids. They were "killing time," not happy in retirement. The baseball coach, when asked whether he like retirement, answered, "Who does?" It was not just the loss of money he felt but the loss of a work identity that had helped structure his life. The stress of others who were too fearful to let us come into their homes spoke of a life that was often very isolated. Some also suffered from poor health. Television sets seemed to be on continually, particularly in the homes of elderly living alone. Given our findings from the 131 interviews, that retired and elderly persons in co-ops were most satisfied than those in rental buildings, it is entirely plausible that a tenants' association could have reduced some stress brought on by isolation.

Particular forms of stress were felt by leaders who thought no one could replace them. Mrs. Miller, a leader in one of the struggling co-ops, spoke of her work as follows:

> I hate to think what would happen [if I left] because I can't. I hate to say it because it sounds like I'm patting myself on the back, which I'm not, but I can't see anyone here, if they are not doing now. I can't see anyone stepping forward and really taking hold and trying to keep things together and keep things going.

Mrs. Oilers, in another struggling co-op, put it more succinctly:

> Sometimes I get angry, then I say I'm going to give it up. Then they beg me, please don't, please don't. If you do, excuse me, what they said, we'd be up shit creek.

Mrs. Lyons' reaction to tenants who were less involved also reveals the strains of the job: "They can aggravate you to death. . . . You can't please anybody. If you're doing it right, it's not right; if you're doing it wrong, it's not right."

Even in co-ops with less conflict, the strain of leadership took its toll. Mrs. Michael remarked frequently on how tired the work made her, even as she planned ways for the co-op to launch economic development projects. Mrs. Knotts spoke of "sitting up here and fuming" about all the things the new leaders didn't accomplish after she was replaced. She recalled the constant knocks on the door, the middle of the night emergencies, the extra phone she had to install just for building work, and the disagreements among tenants that had made her physically ill when she had been president.[9] Mrs. Janes reported that she had been taking antidepressant medication and subsequently moved to the public housing project a few blocks from her old home. Mr. Fuller suffered a nervous breakdown while attempting to organize a building that reverted to Central Management. Years later, he was still trying to understand what he saw as his failure.

The responsibilities of fulfilling city requirements often weighed heavily on people. Carolyn and LouAnn described having to give up church work, hobbies like sewing, and even fixing meals for their families sometimes, to keep up with the demands of the building. One of them had headaches from trying to balance the books "the way that they [the city] want it to be done, not the way you want done." The two women were experimenting with doing it a little at a time, and then every other night.[10] Faced with the task of finding new doors, another leader was scanning the Yellow Pages in order to get estimates, unsure that was the best way to proceed.

Mrs. Lyons defined what she thought "know-how" was and how inadequate she felt:

> like making a contract for this particular job and for other particular jobs,
> and not have the building code, so that you won't feel like you're being
> ripped off on certain projects. . . . You have to know a lot about in-
> surance because you've got to go out there and get insurance. You got
> to know whether people are ripping you off, you got to know about in-
> surance profit, code of insurance or nothing.

The leaders were always "on call." During many of the interviews, a
repairman would ring the doorbell, tenants would telephone, others would
come to the leader's apartment to work on tasks they had to do. Mrs.
Miller's tiny, dark apartment held shelves of books on housing law and she
told of scouring *The New York Times* real estate pages for articles about
co-ops. Even in the building with the four women leaders and an active
committee structure, one of the leaders acknowledged that at times she
felt overworked and that nobody wanted to help them. However, interviews with leaders in that building contained the fewest references to being
overwhelmed and tired from work.

There was also stress in people's negotiations with the city. Regardless
of whether individual people at HPD extended themselves, we heard repeated frustrations about either trying to get particular repairs done or
even just getting the paint to redo an apartment themselves. In one of the
buildings that reverted to Central Managment, Mrs. Baylor and Mr. Grayson said they would rather be cold than ask the city for more oil. In their
words, it was "taxing on you" and "makes you feel like a beggar." One of
the most stressful situations in all the buildings revolved around the re-
tructuring of rents, an issue we discussed earlier.[11]

Rent collection also produces some stress. HPD's definition of a successful program is either co-oping (that is, getting buildings on the tax roll)
and/or a 100 percent rent roll collection—which is interpreted to mean
that tenants are satisfied or a group is doing its job. Successful rent collection, however, is a poor way to measure how people feel about their
housing, or to evaluate other aspects of their life. Paying rent on time may
be more of an ingrained social norm than an indicator of satisfaction. Indeed, we were repeatedly told that what distinguishes tenant-initiated co-
ops from the behavior of a previous and profit-motivated landlord is the
ability to tolerate late payment of rent, to establish a rapport between tenants in order that payment schedules may be worked out or assistance
given to finding subsidies, to place on-time rent paying within the broader

perspective of what else is happening in people's lives such as the pressure to buy presents at Christmas time.[12] Nonetheless, such understanding comes at the price of suffering the ill will of HPD and from the leaders' own recognition that rents are needed to pay expenses. In Louise's building, for example, there was some rancor from younger tenants about seniors getting a free ride. The seniors were neither willing to fill out the forms to obtain SCRIE—a relatively simple form—nor to let people from UHAB take the information from them, in both cases objecting to what they considered an invasion of their privacy. In another case, in Connie's building, a decision was reached about two people who were not willing to pay any increases, one a person sick with cancer, and the other very old. The tenant leaders felt that there was no way to resolve the issue other than to accept it somewhat philosophically. None of the people we interviewed looked forward to evicting anyone, and some like Carolyn and LouAnn remembered the difficulties of pressuring some people to move out.

Although unemployed and retired people felt more satisfied in cooperatives than non-co-ops, some non-leaders still felt the stress of becoming a cooperator. Mrs. Smythe had not anticipated buying a share in her building until some pressure was placed on her. She recalled: "I didn't figure that I should take that responsibility [to buy], but I was talked into it, about owning the apartment. . . . they told me that if I didn't, or the people, the tenants, the place will be sold and the rent will go up and all of that thing see, so I did it."

Another indirect source of stress may well be the underlying knowledge that respondents have of how the larger society views them. It is not just that they are in social categories that carry with them lesser status. Because they are women, black, or older, or any combination of these, they are considered incapable of managing a cooperative. One reason experts often give for favoring national housing policies emphasizing single family home ownership and landlord-owned rentals involves a belief that most people don't have the social and managerial skills to participate in a co-op. Nor, they assert, would most people want to do so. This argument is given even more weight when applied to poor people. The experts point out that leaders in such buildings have unusual and awe-inspiring faith and ability to make something out of almost nothing. Indeed, the leaders were special people. Even those who were struggling with the paperwork or fractious tenants, provided emotional support for other tenants at some level. The leaders were aware of some of the stress that they were under but found their efforts worth the investment. Some, like Mrs. Knotts, mobilized tenants and fortified herself by talking about her gains: "I really want my apartment and therefore all of you [tenants] are going to benefit because I am determined that we are going to get this house and I'm going to get my apartment, and you're going to get yours, so the enthusiasm was there." Others had visions that went beyond the shelter and were making plans to expand their scope of salvaging their neighborhood.

Those who organized to co-op their buildings took on additional stresses to achieve goals they valued. The enormity of the job of saving and managing buildings with no training and usually no experience often weighed heavily. Yet it was our impression that those involved in co-oping gained strength and support for the endeavor that helped them bear the stress. As we pointed out in chapter 6 they did not face their problems entirely alone but with the aid of numerous organizations and institutions. Thus their health and well-being usually were sustained.

But the research also documented that not all tenants' associations fit the model of a strong, heroic leader pulling along a whole building. Nor does it appear true that tenants not living in cooperatives lack leadership capacity. But those who suffered the most appeared to be those for whom the process of landlord abandonment led to successive dislocations in their lives. This lessened the control they had over their existence. Often the process involved the slow dissolution of the social worlds they knew as well as the more rapid decline in the quality of their homes, the lack of basic services like heat and hot water, and the increase in vulnerability to crime and vandalism. When these tenants' buildings were saved through Alternative Management rental programs, their housing improved but the quality of their lives, their hopes for the future, their ability to contribute to their communities usually did not improve commensurately.

How can programs, and in particular TIL, address these issues? Should there be specially trained staff in a housing agency like HPD, or in a technical assistance organization like UHAB, who facilitate responses to the types of problems we uncovered? To a degree, the help received through UHAB, and among some at HPD, is intwined with support for the tough job the tenants are undertaking. Those giving the support are frequently aware that they perform that function (some only after it is pointed out by outsiders) but may be uneasy about doing something that is not easily measured. Others accept that the business exchange also involves a personal exchange and view that as the "fun" or "human" part of their job. There is no explicit institutionalization of assistance that goes beyond the more technical issues of housing. Are there ways in which tenants and staff can be trained to be more effective socially and psychologically, to cope better with the stress brought about, first, by abandonment, and, second, by organizing cooperatives? In order to answer these questions, it is helpful to look briefly at the role training programs have played in housing.

DEFINING TRAINING PROGRAMS IN HOUSING

T RAINING PROGRAMS are a euphemism for a variety of different ent tasks: transforming tenant behavior into a sociable interchange with neighbors; working out budgets for the family and consistent rent payment; teaching tenants how to use equipment such as refrigerators, dishwashers, washing machines, and driers; preparing tenants for jobs, some related to housing development, management, and maintenance; developing ways to formalize cooperatives, such as learning bookkeeping, facilitating meetings, and establishing committees. There are also training programs aimed at leadership development which teach skills such as applying for nonprofit status; holding elections, running a meeting, and resolving conflicts; preparing funding proposals; building coalitions with related groups; and testifying at public hearings.

Training programs, particularly for low-income tenants, began to appear in public housing in the 1950s as the population shifted from poor unemployed whites to migrating blacks from the South. Emphasis was focused on resident training programs for alleged problem families in public housing.[13] Local housing authorities would hire caseworkers and management aides. Disruptive tenants were sought out, counseled and matched with available community services. Michelle Neugebauer, in an analysis of the relationship between housing and social services, wrote that programs were aimed at transforming attitudes toward housekeeping and childrearing. These included sewing, cooking, and child care, as well as counseling and referrals to other agencies. At the national level, emphasis was put on including social services in public housing. Attempts were made to coordinate efforts from the predecessor agencies to HUD (Housing and Home Finance Agency) and Health and Human Services (Health, Education and Welfare), an effort still being talked about today more than it is practiced.

With the 1960s, the case work approach to problem tenants came under attack for being paternalistic, an invasion of privacy of the tenants, and ineffective. A variety of different training interventions were created, in part motivated by the increasing problems and threats to the investment in multifamily existing stock.[14] From the tenants' perspectives, the training programs had a different orientation, one influenced by the civil rights movement and its call for self-determination. Perhaps the major program of this sort was the management training program initiated by the ineffectiveness of the St. Louis Housing Authority and tenants' actions in Cochran Gardens.

The organization of Cochran Gardens came in response to public abandonment but otherwise parallels tenants' responses to abandonment in Harlem. Two years after the St. Louis Housing Authority vacated Pruitt-Igoe in May 1974, its thirty-three buildings were demolished. The Authority wanted to tear down nearby Cochran Gardens next (it was the first project to be completed in 1953; Pruitt-Igoe was completed a year later). Early efforts to cope with the increasingly deteriorating buildings and the withdrawal of money, came from women leaders and the War on Poverty program. Mabel Cohen, an older women tenant hired by the poverty program as a "homemaker" to counsel families in public housing identified the leadership potential of one younger woman in particular, Bertha Gilkey. In 1969, the 20-year-old Bertha was elected chair of Cochran's tenants' association. She had grown up in the projects and, like tenants who remained in the buildings in Harlem, remembered it before "it had gone down."[15] Bertha recalls that, by the time conditions worsened, only a few were active in trying to change it, and people had "nothing but dreams." They started in small ways, and on something that had priority for them as women responsible for their families' clean clothes. They collectively tackled the vandalized door to the laundromat and pooled their resources to buy a lock for the door. Then they held fundraisers to raise money to buy paint for the graffiti ridden halls. Bertha recalls that "the elderly who couldn't paint prepared lunch, so they could feel like they were a part of it, too."[16]

The community they were rebuilding depended on certain rules of behavior—"no disruptions, fights, clothes hung outside, garbage, and so forth."[17] Renaming the building from 1121 North Seventh to Dr. Martin Luther King reflected a sense of pride. By the 1980s, the Cochran tenants' dreams were fulfilled to a great extent: grass replaced concrete, and a health clinic, a community center with different programs for each age group, and renovated buildings appeared. Job programs were developed, increasingly under tenant control—janitorial services, day care, health care, education, catering, nutrition, and housing management itself. Although the size and scale of Cochran Gardens—760 units in twelve buildings ranging from 6 to 7 to 12 stories—is quite different from landlord-abandoned buildings in New York City, the responses of the primarily women residents were very similar to the people we interviewed.

Technical assistance came through legal aid from local anti-poverty agencies who helped tenants enter into an annual contract with the housing authority to manage the property. The Ford Foundation allocated funds to St. Louis and then to other demonstration areas around the country. HUD replicated the program nationally through its funding of Tenant Management Corporations (TMCs). Robert Kolodny wrote that one of the critical ingredients to the success of such programs was proper training which meant "extensive long-term technical assistance from people who were well acquainted with public housing operations generally and housing management in particular." He elaborated:

> Short of magic, there is no way that a group of residents without experience in housing finance or the maintenance of mechanical systems or personnel management can run a large and relatively complex development unless they get training and on-the-job consultation. They are also likely to need continuing, if less intensive, aid periodically over time. Such aid is particularly needed where the TMCs [Tenant Management Corporations] begin to expand their scope, as they have in St. Louis, beyond straight real estate management.[18]

While it is undoubtedly true that self-help is insufficient, it is important to understand who is helping whom and what types of knowledge outside people bring that complements tenants' actions. Gilkey has become well-known throughout the country; she consults with tenants in other troubled housing authority projects. She has broad experience and is a model trainer. From the 1970s on, Gilkey has also been on the board of the National Congress of Neighborhood Women (NCNW) and has integrated their leadership training methods into her own work.

NCNW's concept of training focuses on empowering women. The National Congress is a community-based women's organization with a central office in Brooklyn, New York. Since 1974, under its auspices, a nationwide grassroots women's group has been formed. Its members are involved with housing, education, economic development, and employment at the local level. The Brooklyn group began with a neighborhood-based college-accredited program for local women returning to school, and has moved increasingly toward comprehensive community planning.

Its leadership training component evolved out of the women's movement, the previous community struggles people fought through the 1960s, and the needs and desires of poor and working class women in the Williamsburg and St. Nicholas neighborhoods of Brooklyn. The women wanted more education in order to be able to defend their neighborhoods from loss of services and gentrification. What evolved was a two-pronged goal for a college for neighborhood women, "education for community people and education for leadership."[19] Terry L. Haywoode, one of the teachers in the college wrote that, unlike conventional colleges where working class and poor people "are expected to shed the particular identities which link them to the families and communities of their youth and to develop the universalist frame of reference of middle-class culture. . . . The NCNW program was for people who would stay, for people who wanted to improve their lives by building their communities, not by leaving them."[20]

The program that developed was neither vocational nor leadership per se but "interdisciplinary, flexible, and problem-oriented" education.[21] The college's location in the community served as the central organizing element with the neighborhood itself a subject of study. The neighborhood provided the physical base for encouraging the education and leadership that took place as women transformed their ideas about themselves and the larger world. Class times were geared to family responsibilities; in turn family responsibilities were a subject of study. Sometimes more was needed. Counseling and peer support provided other mechanisms for helping the women over the tougher periods of self-doubt, family antagonisms, and the sheer difficulties encountered in managing family and school life. This kind of supportive network, although less formalized, was also found in the cooperatives with all-women boards among the tenants.

Since 1982, NCNW has been planning for a national institute that would bring people together to elaborate women's positions on a variety of issues, including housing, employment and economic development, health, child care, education, and community planning.[22] In the mid-1980s, NCNW attained United Nations status as a nongovernmental organization. In 1987, a four-day conference was held in Camden, New Jersey, an event that was part of the United Nations International Year of Shelter for the Homeless.[23] About 200 women, and some men, attended, from across the United States, as well as from Canada, Mexico, Great Britain, India, the Netherlands, and the Carribean.

The grass roots women's expertise has developed from firsthand experiences as well as from formal training. They have a commanding knowledge of the issues and a perspective that is often more pragmatic than that of some experts they recruit, and, like Bertha Gilkey, they are most effective in reaching similar groups of women. Rosemary Jackson, the new chair of the NCNW, from Camden, New Jersey, is representative of the ways in which leadership techniques are passed on from one person to another. Rosemary speaks eloquently about what she was able to learn from Bertha and others in NCNW, and her own work serves as a model for others. In describing her work in Camden, she often evokes the experiences at Cochran Gardens and of the women who wanted their homes and didn't see them as temporary, of residents who live in a neighborhood and care about it, unlike social service workers who leave at four o'clock and live "in another zip code."[24] In relating her experiences working with drug addicts, she reminded us of Mrs. Lyons who told us that she knew the drug addicts when they were little and wasn't afraid to chase them away. In Rosemary's case, the longtime knowing of people who had become drug addicts also didn't lead to a chasing away. In both cases, the women were responding to people whom they knew, had seen grow up, and remembered from a time when life was just opening up for them.

What people learn in NCNW from each other goes beyond a traditional issue area. For example, at the first meeting to elect a national board, a native American woman passionately protested the kind of food that had been prepared. She tied food to the respect people should have for the earth and for spiritual well-being. Clearly, her upbringing differed from others in the room who were able to learn from her in a supportive environment.

Jackson talks of how women leaders in NCNW offer hope to each other. The leadership technique used by NCNW in developing its network of low-income women depends on involving people in a personal and immediate way. This technique draws on peer counseling, consciousness raising, and the reevaluation counseling movement. Meetings begin by breaking into small groups and each participant responds to preset questions about herself in a prescribed period of time. People are not allowed to interrupt or be critical of others but are asked to listen to what each person is saying. This encourages participants to learn about differences and similarities among women of different racial, ethnic, and class backgrounds. With this insight, other women may be more clearly seen as allies, regardless of the differences. Empowerment is central to the NCNW planning and organizing model, and specific issues are viewed as means and not ends. For example, housing is not solely a commodity that improves material well-being but also a vehicle for empowerment if its development and management can be controlled by the women themselves.[25] An issue like gentrification of a community and displacement is tied to people's feelings of displacement when forced to leave countries with military regimes. These forms of displacement overlap, in the experience of uprooting from a national identity, a culture, or a place.

Before describing how NCNW's model might be applied to tenants in Harlem and to strengthening the community-household, or to any other

group of people responding to crisis in their everyday lives, it is instructive
to look at characteristics of training programs aimed at organizing cooperatives. They share, with the NCNW model, an emphasis on process.

EXAMPLES OF CO-OP TRAINING

WITH THE development of limited equity cooperatives in the 1970s,
a number of training programs were developed. In general, they
use a dual approach: first, addressing technical issues such as
bookkeeping and, second, understanding the process through which cooperatives are formed and function.

The technical aspects of housing management begin with bookkeeping.
In New York City, HPD has a contract with UHAB for offering classes
that include bookkeeping; the city's contract with the groups requires that
tenant leaders in TIL and CMP take these classes. Along with bookkeeping, tenants are exposed to practical suggestions about organizing a tenants' association, running good meetings, and keeping proper records.[26]
Common Space, a nonprofit corporation set up in 1977 in Minneapolis by
sixteen neighborhood groups to organize cooperatives, makes it clear that
organizing the tenants extends beyond the traditional use of the term training and into issues of control. Common Space's goals are "in effect, [to]
set up a viable small business and a 'government' operated by members
for their own benefit."[27] Common Space, like UHAB, also monitors the
cooperative's maintenance and business practices for the first few years of
the co-op's life. "These periodic reviews have shown us the value of the
organizing and training which precedes the coops' taking over the properties; business affairs are in order, and maintenance and upkeep remain
at high standards."[28]

The cooperative movement in Canada has been strongly supported by
the national government through the Canada Mortgage and Housing Corporation (CMHC). One of the most impressive projects is Milton Parc in
Montreal, whose cooperative structure links 2,000 people in 135 buildings
with 597 dwelling units in over twenty nonprofit groups in a six-block area.
The housing cooperatives range from 1 to 15 buildings, with from 7 to 32
units; the housing associations range from 1 to 24 buildings, with from 7
to 144 units. There are twenty commercial uses scattered throughout the
area. The building stock, much like Harlem's, constructed from brick and
limestone, dates from the late nineteenth century; some buildings were
originally rooming houses. Milton Parc was targeted as another gentrified

community when residents banded together in the early 1960s to protest the demolition of about 250 buildings and the construction of a hotel-residential-commercial complex. With the assistance of Montreal based agencies such as Heritage Montreal, which in turn set up an operating agency, CMHC, over a twenty-year period, acquired properties and then turned them over to the locally based group to run. The land is held collectively by the cooperatives and nonprofit groups; property cannot be used for speculative purposes or to make a profit. The housing, when available, is offered to low- and modest-income people who must agree to the same conditions. The rights of roomers have been protected by preventing conversion to larger apartments. The original equity was about $100 per share. In a booklet published in 1983 to commemorate Milton Parc, the principles and philosophy were embodied in the phrase "housing is not a market commodity."[29] In a section titled "New Social Relations," the structure was described.

> The co-operative movement in Milton Parc has more than an economic character. It is an attempt to build a richer and more people-oriented social life within an urban setting. . . .
>
> An umbrella organization representing all the groups provides continuity in dealing with areas of common interest. These include: managing the commercial properties, redistributing budget surpluses so as to keep rent increases down, defining and setting up community services, maintaining the laneways, and working out restrictions on future sales.[30]

The cooperative life-style is acknowledged as a learned one and built on neighboring.

> The housing cooperative is creating a new form of neighborhood. By offering networks for support and for the exchange of services it enables the solution of many problems. A new type of community is gradually being established and based on exchange and mutual aid.[31]

They endorse the idea that the cooperative is the creation of a new type of social space.

> The co-operative becomes a place for learning. Members learn how to chair meetings, draft minutes, keep books, maintain the properties and understand the renovation process. They thus learn to assume the responsibility for the administration of their properties and the development of the co-operative.[32]

The Canadian cooperative movement has developed a most impressive training program and series of manuals. Training by technical assistance groups takes place over a six-month to two-year period and can start when the cooperative may only be a gleam in someone's eye. In the case of a 153-unit cooperative housing project (one 11-story high-rise surrounded by low-rise garden apartments) in Mississauga, Ontario, about fifteen miles from the center of Toronto, people's involvement occurred after initial construction decisions were made but prior to occupancy.[33] Although there were differences among staff in the development agency responsible for building the project about when to start and the degree of involvement by potential residents, general meetings were held with a growing number of people. The group was "an ever-changing, ever-increasing number of people who had vastly varying amounts of experience in 'doing' this difficult process."[34] They met frequently and committees were formed on finance, recreation, day care, etc. The members decided the use of common spaces, how money should be allocated, how to make decisions, and remaining design decisions (construction decisions were made prior to the group forming) such as the set-up in the laundry room, and day care, and how the landscape should be done.

In general, there is a one- to three-year follow-up by technical assistance groups after the cooperative is occupied. The Canadian materials superbly discuss both the conceptual aspects of cooperatives and the tiniest details which contribute to a smooth running operation. Those details go beyond technical aspects to include tips on what materials are needed for a meeting, including a coffee urn and types of refreshments. Issues of seating position and personal space are noted. The manuals are organized around leadership, communications, problem solving, and decision making. Each of the areas is further broken down so that in a training discussion about leadership, examples are given of group roles organized around tasks (initiators, information givers, and information seekers) and maintenance (encouragers, harmonizers, and tension relievers), as well as anti-group roles (blockers, aggressors, and clowns). In the area of communication, interpersonal skills, group communication patterns, and communication of information is discussed. The manual describes effective sending of a message, classifying the message as containing content and feeling. Drawing on the psychology of group dynamics and using group exercises, they present a holistic approach to all aspects of co-op living. There is much more to learn from the Canadian experience and we will return to it in the last chapter.

Some techniques similar to those described above are used by the Voice of the People in Uptown (VOP) in Chicago where the goal is to create cooperative "management," not ownership. During a six- to eight-week course, babysitting and snacks are provided in a social atmosphere. The babysitting encourages the participation of "a lot of people [who are glad] to get rid of the kids for a couple hours."[35] People are organized into small groups with the chance to practice decision making. Because tenants are multi-ethnic and multi-cultural, and many do not speak English, classes are held in English and Spanish; the group is trying to figure out how to hold classes in Vietnamese and Laotian. For the present, whoever can speak the best English translates for the others.

These cooperatives value human potential in the formation of a "social" economy, where mutual services are achieved in a non-market, nonprofit based way.[36] How to connect issues of stress raised by even beneficial programs like TIL to the types of training programs that strengthen the social economy is discussed in the next section, followed by a discussion that links training with gender and empowerment.

TRAINING AT THE COMMUNITY LEVEL

THE EXACT kind of training selected will be affected by the particularities of the crisis,[37] the nature of the program, the amount of funds allocated, and the time period allocated for it. Most importantly, the training depends on the inclination and receptivity of "trainers" to acknowledge tenants' skills.

That acknowledgement needs to be extended to seeing the community where training takes place as a central ingredient. Some have referred to this as the social or life-space, in part rooted in the physical boundaries of a neighborhood, that provides both a location for training as well as a training ground.[38] In particular, for poor women, neighborhood and community play a much larger role in their adulthood. Both Alvin L. Schorr and Lewis Mumford recognized this in their writings, Schorr in illustrating the importance of the block level, as we discussed in earlier chapters, and Mumford in arguing for a "life-centered" neighborhood to replace the loss of three generations living together under one roof.[39]

Gerda R. Wekerle and Suzanne MacKenzie have written "that women's environmental needs emerge [as] a picture of an increasingly locally oriented population, defined largely by gender, for whom distance is not elastic: the elderly, single parents, and working women. For them, the neighborhood serves a critical function as a place for the delivery of essential services." But as our interviews reveal, the neighborhood is also an important base to connect with a larger geographic area. In our interviews, the place, Harlem, was important as a resource base. People continually reminded us of its location and the accessibility they felt this gave them to the broader community, even if they didn't travel around. As important were the leaders' attachment to their memories of Harlem, which they used to bolster and engage other tenants in their efforts. Echoing our findings are those of people at a national conference on families where the neighborhood was acknowledged as a place where informal aid occurred and support services were exchanged among residents. One participant had this to say about his neighborhood: "I like to think of it as one of the levels of systems in this society that I turn to for help, one of the primary sources of help for me and my family."[41]

We have seen how the community is connected to training in NCNW's neighborhood based college. A comparable model is drawn from UNESCO's experience in training "barefoot" architects, an idea appropriated from the Chinese model of "barefoot" doctors who provide basic health services in remote and rural areas with a simplified level of training sufficient to treat the most common health problems.[42] Similarly, the barefoot architect would deal with "major problems of marginal urban settlements or of villages . . . a variety of issues including roadways, water supply, and drainage as well as the construction of houses, and community buildings such as schools . . . able to guide local people in the introduction of simple technologies which enhance the use of locally available resources."[43] The underlying spirit informing this approach is that outside architects with centrally imposed plans and designs "are not the correct instruments for directly improving the built environment. Rather the main force for improving the built environment is the people themselves."[44] Based on the results of a UNESCO-sponsored workshop, three types of community people were identified as facilitators of development.

a. Community workers with some technical orientation, i.e., those who are able to mobilize community effort through leadership and example. This includes those who have a sufficient grasp of technical problems to seek appropriate assistance from local and external sources.
b. Technical persons who have little or no community or social orientation and who already possess one or more trade skills but have an adequate grasp of community problems to call upon appropriate assistance from local and outside sources.
c. Community leaders who whatever their orientation, are able to liaise

between government authorities and the people; who identify primarily with the community's interests; and who have a firm belief in the capacity of the people to help themselves.[45]

In diagram it would look like figure 10.1.

Community leaders

Community		*Technical*
knowledge		*knowledge*

Community   *Technician*
worker

FIGURE 10.1

It is easy to see how the leaders of the cooperatives in Harlem functioned as community leaders and workers, some with more technical knowledge than others. They were able to draw on their community knowledge and, with the availability of a funded program, and with technical assistance, transform their renter status into a cooperative one. Even in the non-co-op buildings, tenants possessed both knowledge and skills but were not involved with technicians from UHAB or community leaders who could have assisted them in reviewing various options. What is important is to recognize the history and location of the community, both of which help to shape the knowledge and increase the skills of people, and to integrate this into the content of training programs.

THE CONTENT OF TRAINING PROGRAMS

THE CONTENT of a training program can respond to multiple goals. When empowerment is a goal of community redevelopment, reducing stress is also desirable, and training may look to either a mental health or feminist model. The two are not mutually exclusive, although it is difficult to retain a feminist analysis within larger bureaucracies, and even workers in alternative agencies are faced with overall contradictions about the reasons for providing services in a welfare state.[46] Given the problems of a larger society, does it matter whether the content of a training program is explicitly gender based? We think it does, in part because of the unique ways women have of viewing their multiple responsibilities and their connections to the more intimate levels of everyday life. Women's roles are likely to pull them in many directions, and that pulling and struggling can easily be experienced as despair. This is not to say that men, and in particular black men, do not have equally difficult experiences. They are exposed to racism and find themselves in positions that are usually at odds with the roles associated with men, as breadwinners, as heads-of-household. Indeed, the roles black men and women are placed in need to be discussed in any training program.[47] How this is addressed has bearing on organizing men as well as women in the landlord-abandoned buildings. What may be illuminating is comparing the differences between a more traditional training approach and a gender related approach; this is discussed below.

William Brill and Associates were hired by the U.S. Department of Housing and Urban Development to prepare a training program for crisis intervention in public housing projects. There were three objectives to the Brill Associates' program: (1) increasing the capacity of residents and management staff to deal with crises; (2) encouraging leadership development in the community and a greater sense of community; and (3) increasing responsiveness and involvement of community services, including law enforcement agencies in the problems of public housing residents and staff. Two facilitators from Brill Associates, one a bilingual person with extensive housing background, the other with professional preparation and experience in crisis intervention, were to conduct training sessions attended by selected tenants and housing authority staff. It is not clear how the selection would be made, although the Brill document states that the criteria should be age, sex, race, and occupation. Some sessions were to be held with both tenants and housing authority staff, others separately. The facilitators "indicate the presence of crisis-states in themselves and others."[48] Crisis-states were defined to include a range of emotions from panic to helplessness, despair, isolation, inadequacy, and rage. The Brill report gives examples of life problems such as "family conflicts, death of a loved one, financial troubles, and difficulties around rearing children."

NCNW uses a different vocabulary and begins with the assumption that all women can become leaders and that all women leaders face difficulties in assuming leadership—"unemployment, low wages, sexism on the job or in the community or at home, lack of childcare, burn-out, feelings of isolation, frustration, or some other unknown reasons."[49] Their objective is to bring women together with "their peers to share experiences, feelings, ideas, strategies, skills and other resources in a supportive environment." Every woman's potential to be a leader and individual as well as group development is emphasized. NCNW suggests that there be two facilitators, two women, one who serves as group leader, the other as her assistant. Obviously, the more talented and experienced the facilitator, the richer the discussion. Intrinsic to their approach is that everyone in the group, every woman, has the potential to be a facilitator.

Brill's scenarios were designed to develop a "Stress Indicator" handout "to predict the potential effect of failure to resolve a major conflict in one's life."[50] The next step was to develop a "Severity Index," in order to "rank the potential outcome of unsolved problems in the lives of public housing residents."[51] Following this, ways were identified to resolve problems that arise. There is much in the Brill scenarios that is commendable but there are no explicit linkages to the special role gender plays in dealing with life crises. NCNW is more explicit about discussing the effect of various factors: gender, race, class, ethnicity, age, sexual orientation, and a variety of others such as physical handicaps, religion, politics, marital status.[52] They divide their training program into three main categories: personal issues, institutional issues, and developing resources and skills. Personal issues range from an intimate level to a household and community level. They suggest ways of discussing growing up, gender roles, changes in gender roles, self-image, relationship with one's own group, relationships with other groups, growing older, and violence. A range of institutions are examined: family, financial, public, church, education, media, and movements. Resources and skills relate to issues of power, goal setting, journal writing, women leaders, and controversial issues.

Table 10.1 presents NCNW's checklist for bringing a woman's perspective to community problems. There are four major areas: initiation and leadership, participation and control, benefits, and social change.[53]

In the buildings where we saw community-households emerging, and in the struggling cooperatives, women were central in all the tasks, active in participation and control over the process, benefiting from the process, and in moving from the household to the building level, positioning themselves to be open to social change. The actions that move that social change, or at best hold it in readiness for a larger social movement, are analyzed in the last chapter.

The tenant leaders we interviewed also developed a "stress indicator guide," albeit informally as seen in their awareness of individual tenants who needed more comfort than others, either about personal problems with children or buying a share in the building, or of other leaders who needed support and encouragement for their own problems. Whereas the end result in Brill does not appear to alter the fundamental power relationship between landlord and tenant, although it may well alleviate immediate problems, NCNW can help identify collective ways to fight the underlying issues creating the stress.

What is not emphasized in the NCNW checklist, however, is the relation of the community problem to either the physical location or the larger society. There is reference to "community relationships" but this is left undefined in the checklist. However, if we recall the NCNW college and the

---

TABLE 10.1
How to Bring a Woman's Perspective to Community Problems

Initiation and Leadership
1. Were women and men equally involved in the planning?
2. How many women were from the sponsoring agency?
3. How many women were from the community to be served?
4. Did women have leadership roles in the planning group?

Participation and Control
1. Do women participate in the direction of the project?
2. Are they women from the community as well as from the sponsoring agency?
3. Does the structuring of the program have some mechanism for getting feedback from the people served?
4. Do those served influence the direction of the program?

Benefits
1. Does the project benefit women directly? Indirectly? How?
2. Is there a procedure for identifying these benefits?
3. Is the project structured so that women who work on the project gain access to knowledge, resources, and the power structure in the community?
4. Do the women perceive the benefits as affecting key areas of their lives—such as family and community relationships, and work?

Social Change
1. Does this experience change women's role at home? In the community? At work?
2. Does this project increase women's options? Will she have more choices now?
3. Does the project cause hardships for the women involved—e.g., is it located too far from transit, shopping centers, day care centers?
4. Has the project anticipated these dislocations?

SOURCE: NCNW, *Guidelines for Women's Leadership Support Groups.*

dynamics between issues occurring in redeveloping the neighborhood and the support for the women who attended the classes, the community-household begins to define the community relationship. In a related vein, Ruth A. Brandwein examines different models of community organization that go further in clarifying this issue.[54] She traces one model to the Charity Organization Society (COS) and community chests and councils; the second to the settlement house movement. Women have been more involved in the second than the first.[55] Brandwein defines the differences in a particularly relevant way for understanding community-households: "The first is concerned with organizations in the community and the second is concerned with organizing the community."[56] She points out the tendency of women to work at the micro-level, in small agencies, organize in informal settings, and advocate for legislative and policy changes. Brandwein substantiates that women's approach to community organization—and as we see it embodied in NCNW and in the community-households—is different from men's and those differences need to be reflected in the content of any training program. Brandwein identifies the six characteristics of women's approach: androgyny,[57] wholism, synergy, a win-win power orientation, a web of relationships, and egalitarian relationships.[58] Each of these arises from a concept of behavior that rejects gender stereotyping and includes process *and* product orientations, believes that participation and involvement in decision making is nurturing *and* also makes for better decisions, looks for creative solutions where everyone is empowered, sees events not as isolated occurrences in a static period of time, and holds there are no permanent dominants and subordinates but factors which shift situationally in a search for resolution.[59]

Similarly Lisa Leghorn and Katherine Parker suggest that female values are more egalitarian than male values.[60] In their discussion of the economy of the world of women they suggest that power would not be based on biology, i.e., the patriarchal values associated with men, and public and private spheres would be integrated. "Public decisions would evolve from, be grounded in, and accountable to the community."[61] Rather than territories to be conquered, home and country would be respected places to be shared with guests who are made to "feel at home."

What is not evident in the NCNW checklist, Brandwein, or Leghorn and Parker, although hints are there, are the physical manifestations of the community-household. Whether there is a gender approach in design that parallels the administrative and organizing approaches discussed above is not as much of an unanswered question as it was in the 1960s and 1970s. A body of literature has developed and is still growing.[62] The work of Caroline

O. N. Moser and Sylvia Chant on training programs explicitly designed to integrate women in developing low-income housing projects and Joan Sprague's development primers for women are helpful guides. Moser and Chant, although directed toward improvements for people in developing countries, can easily be adapted to domestic situations. Their training manual sets forth the importance of women's participation in the execution of low-income housing projects, the different forms participation can take in different phases, the constraints which may limit participation including cultural variations and regional differences, and recommendations for methods and techniques to facilitate greater involvement of women. Sprague, an architect, with the assistance of a lawyer and a community reinvestment bank officer, formed the Women's Institute for Housing and Economic Development. The Institute develops training materials, holds workshops, and consults with grassroots women's organizations who are serving low-income women and their children. In the next section we highlight some examples from this literature that we think can foster community-households.

PHYSICAL MANIFESTATIONS OF
THE COMMUNITY-HOUSEHOLD

THERE ARE ways in which the built environment can support or discourage the formation of community-households. NCNW refers to dislocation problems because of poor access to transit, shopping centers, and day-care centers. But there are other problems in communities where landlord abandonment has occurred. It is not simply the absence of facilities but the absence of a tightly woven physical fabric. Often convenience stores have moved and public institutions like hospitals and health clinics have joined the movement out, usually preceded by private practitioners who are then replaced by "medicaid" mills. The people we interviewed reported that they shopped for groceries either completely outside of Harlem, near where they worked, or that a good supermarket was about ten blocks away. This of course varied with the neighborhood, but in general, tenants in those buildings around 116th Street had seen drugstores, supermarkets, and movie theaters closed. Mrs. Michael had told us of dance halls, restaurants, and more theaters that were no longer accessible unless you went "ten, more likely twenty blocks" to the Bronx or down to 86th Street. Traveling further distances is particularly difficult for the elderly. In Marjorie H. Cantor's study of 1,552 inner city elderly in New York City, services were located from three to ten blocks from a respondent's home, although facilities such as parks, restaurants, bars, movies, theaters, clubs, organizations, and employment could be twenty-one blocks or more.[63] Distances traveled for some functions varied by race. For example, although banking was primarily neighborhood based, "at a modal distance of from four to six blocks from home," black respondents had to travel further because there were "far fewer banks in the immediate neighborhood." There were also "somewhat" more blacks who traveled outside the neighborhood for doctors' visits.

Others have also looked at distance to travel for the elderly. Wekerle and MacKenzie,[64] for example, suggest that elderly women require basic services—a small grocery store or supermarket, a variety store, pharmacy, bank, and restaurant—within five blocks of their residence. M. Powell Lawton has written that next in importance to an old person's apartment or house was access to shops, medical care, police protection, family, neighbors, cultural activities, or even a senior center.[65] Similar findings from younger respondents are suggested by our survey of *MS.* readers.[66] In response to a question about desirable neighborhoods, some readers were quite specific about how far and how long it should take to reach a variety of activities. In one example, a respondent required that the home be situated about two blocks from a post office, photocopy, stationary and photo shops, quality library, bookstore, and computer store; five blocks from a grocery, health/exercise center, pool, liquor store, dry cleaner, pharmacy, J. C. Penny or the equivalent, hardware, children's store; ten blocks from babysitters of all ages, at least two clean parks, safe public and private schools, the sea or water; and twenty blocks to the unpredictable. In another example, the nearby desired services and stores included a doctor, dentist, gallery, cleaners, magazine store, and drugstore.

Whether in abandoned communities like much of Central Harlem where open space marks a demolished building, and is now a vacant lot or urban garden, or places where large-scale planning created vast and unused open space, planners and designers are beginning to proselytize about the virtues of infill buildings. For example, Lucien Kroll, a Belgium architect, "demodernized" a large-scale project in Alençon, France.[67] He added services like schools, kindergartens, and community facilities, along a curving path, in small buildings, filling the original open space between buildings. Parking lots were made smaller and decentralized, tied in to building entrances. Open spaces were also made smaller, and earth and trees used to break the large area into more intimate spaces. Similarly, in Boston, architects and planners in the Housing Authority developed a Main Street through one project, remodeling buildings with "private open space and individualized entries."[68]

Some projects are at the conceptual stage. Dolores Hayden, for example, in an influential article, suggests converting single family houses used for residential to social service.[69] Her vision was of groups of people cooperatively restructuring suburban blocks, facilitating the needs of different households, drawing support from each other and from the physical environment. Focusing on the elderly, Patrick H. Hare and Gail A. Price recommend that as people age in aging suburbs, social services, which are difficult to get to by increasingly immobile elderly, be dispersed in single family houses throughout the neighborhood.[70]

Hilda K. Ross' proposal for a new model for community mental health and the elderly takes the idea of the family and matches it with an area that defines a neighborhood family. Individuals define themselves psychologically and geographically by their neighborhood, and like the bonding values and relationships associated with family, develop a "surrogate family of 'brothers and sisters' to replace the ties of mutual succorance and concern remembered within the biological family." Physically, a resource center and meeting place are selected that are "realistic boundaries for community action, and a psychological 'home base' for supportive and outreach activities."[71]

Another formulation, more urban in scope, was Clara Fox's plan for instilling a sense of neighborhood in a 27-story high rise for 193 low- and middle-income families on the Upper West Side of Manhattan.[72] There, a first story neighborhood community center was proposed (and built) as a means of achieving social integration. The center's ground floor common space was designed to be large enough to meet the Board of Health's standards for a nursery school and to be operated jointly with areawide nonprofit cooperatives. A half-acre park was planned adjacent to the high rise, open to the public, with hopes that it would act as a village square, bringing community people together for open air concerts, dancing, etc. The laundry facility within the high rise was planned as a pleasant space to encourage socializing, at the ground floor level, and not stuck away in the basement.

Anne Vernez Moudon examines ways in which physical changes can be accompanied by administrative ones and views the family as the best social unit for maintaining, guarding, and taking over space without recourse to other organizational support.[73] For example, large condominium management units could "be divided into small, autonomous units with a small number of families. These condominium projects would become the equivalents of neighborhoods run by groups of residents. The neighborhood would then be further subdivided . . . into smaller territories . . . under the management of small groups of families."[74]

Some Swedish projects have been arranged physically and administratively so as to further encourage what we are calling community-households. An outstanding project is the 184 units of housing and services, Stolplykan, in Linköping. The Linköping model is of national interest in Sweden and there are various versions of it that are being tried.[75] Spurred by the passage of a new social welfare law and through the initiative of a group of seven women including a town architect and social welfare worker in Linköping, their proposal for collective housing was adopted. The buildings are linked together by an enclosed interior street at ground level, off of which are a day nursery, play center with small gym, woodworking shop, dining room; the "street" is a work of art with the faces of construction and maintenance people drawn on murals and freestanding sculpture. The trade-off for the common spaces was that the sizes of individual apartments were reduced by 10 percent but still remain spacious. The households are organized around "stairwell" communities, from five to ten apartments, who meet, discuss issues about the housing and generally foster a sense of community. Social psychologists have long been aware of the greater contacts made by residents who are at the entrance to stairs or an elevator.[76] Indeed, we found evidence of this in several of our interviews, although it was not always perceived as positive. The single parent who lived on the ground floor of a community management building felt that her privacy was being invaded. Her apartment is directly off the entrance and she thought she knew the face of everyone in the building. However, she felt that rather than this being an ideal place for social networking that it highlighted why buying a share in a limited equity co-op was less satisfactory than owning a single family house on its own piece of land. In other places where cooperatives had formed, there were women whose vantage point overlooking the street and the entrance was used as a way of maintaining control over who came into the building. Their role as guardians clearly gave them a sense of accomplishment.

CONCLUSIONS

IN PREVIOUS chapters we presented the setting and our findings, drawing conclusions from them that led us to formulate the community-household model. All along we have maintained that the TIL program, though far richer than even its supporters may think, was not purposely designed to foster community-households. Indeed, at times and in some important ways the TIL program itself breeds stress and strain for people already burdened because of their poverty. In this chapter we have suggested how to structure community-households through training programs that also include stress management and gender conscious discussions, and what a physical manifestation might look like were community-households to flourish.

One assumption we make is the importance of joining housing solutions to service solutions, and both being used to engage people in their own quest for empowerment, rather than providing units for a passive population. This is not the first time that the issue of shelter and services has been raised. The argument dates back to the early days of social reform movements for public housing when questions arose about whether a public housing authority should also be offering other types of services, like medical insurance, for example. The winning side, as it turned out in the short run, was that other public agencies—e.g., public health, schools, and libraries—should provide the service, on the site of the public housing. Since the 1960s, fiscal cutbacks have seen the erosion of those public offerings as various facilities were closed and programs eliminated. The attacks of public housing, and the long waiting lists—in New York City 175,000, almost as many as the 200,000 tenants—have placed a premium on city-owned property. Indeed, the inventory has been referred to as a second public housing. Both city-owned and public housing need to be analyzed as a piece of the whole, providing low-income units and services for a population that would otherwise be on the streets. Some of the ideas discussed here, particularly those for breaking down large-scale projects could be applied to the public housing units. The NCNW gender checklist could be used in both the public housing and city-owned inventory, regardless of whether a cooperative is being formed, or a tenants' association without ownership. Technical resources can be made available through extending the work of groups like UHAB, and hiring the more experienced co-op residents—some of whom like Connie squeeze time into an already crowded schedule to volunteer their organizing abilities on behalf of tenants in other buildings. All of this needs to be done within the context of connecting to local, state, and national initiatives that can begin to provide the funding and political muscle necessary to accomplish these changes. We turn in the final chapter to some current proposals that can help further these aims.

ELEVEN

Community-Households
in Society

F
OR ALL their accomplishments, these Harlem residents who managed to carve out a place of relative security and control in the midst of poverty face an uncertain future. At the personal level, many of them are old and sick, most lack adequate incomes and employment, some are trying to raise children in a time and location that offers little help and many obstacles. The events subsequent to the illnesses of Mr. Grayson and Mrs. Baylor and the eventual loss of tenant control of the building exemplify the pyramid of disasters that can easily befall tenants who individually and collectively have stretched their resources to the breaking point. The hazards and setbacks of life come with greater frequency to poor households. Tenants spoke of children suffering from nervous breakdowns and loss of employment. Husbands and wives left and died. Sons were murdered, others were imprisoned. Daughters and sons clearly on drugs wandered in and out of apartments, leaving their own children to be cared for by the elderly leaders of struggling co-ops. The enormous strength of the tenants who controlled their buildings is remarkable, but has its limits.

The interdependency that contributes to successful cooperation also leaves

217

people vulnerable to the fragility of lives lived in poverty. Their vulnerability is multiplied because they are not surrounded by the cushions of income, job security, pensions, medical benefits, personal insurance, friends and relatives with less pressure on their lives, and housing that operates well with little personal investment. The cooperative feeling that is essential to the ongoing life of the building will begin to vary as old tenants die and new ones replace them. The structure may remain intact but the personal ties will change, and this will invariably affect not only decisions but the informal processes that enter into the decision making—who talks to whom, who trusts whom, etc.

The buildings in which these low-income people make their homes echo the same vulnerabilities: age, a history of lack of care, insufficient financial support, dangers from the surrounding community. Tenants in even the most successful co-ops worried about the numerous capital outlays still required to get buildings up to reasonable standards. As they struggle to achieve these improvements, normal wear and tear lead to more repairs. Rises in maintenance costs, insurance costs, property taxes which they have to pay as soon as transfer of ownership is completed, as well as emergencies such as a fire or embezzlement, all can push buildings over the thin financial margin in which they operate. In the eight years of the Reagan administration, the tenants of these buildings most likely lost real income as housing costs escalated. Access to loans will usually be poor while at the same time the burden of additional interest on debts may be excessive. All of these conditions are accompanied by specific governmental policies at different levels that often weaken the buildings' likelihood of survival as good housing for low-income people. For example, since the study was completed, New York City has begun to enforce its "60 percent–40 percent" resale agreement whereby the city must be paid 40 percent of the amount an apartment is sold for. (Before and after this agreement, there are time restrictions on when the unit may be sold. Unless the co-op board imposes higher restrictions, the tenant will receive upon sale the original $250 purchase price, the amount of special assessments paid, the amount spent for capital improvements to the unit, and, depending on board approval, a percentage of the balance of the sales price.) Since many buildings use resale of apartments as a way to cover improvements that go beyond the capacity of the rent roll, or to build up the usually small reserve funds, the effect has been negative in several ways. Co-ops must sell to higher income people in order to get anything out of the resale. This pressures those tenants committed to keeping prices down for other low-income tenants. At the same time the market in some areas drives prices up, reducing the absolute numbers of city-owned properties available for low-income people. All of this is exacerbated by the previous eight years of parsimonious federal policy for low-income housing. Available government support dropped from $33.7 billion in 1981 to $10.2 billion in 1987.[1] On balance, the buildings end up with little needed money from the sales and the cost of housing is edged up. As a side effect of the situation, some tenants feel that their ownership of the building is not real but actually subject to changing political winds in city government. (Others among them, even shareholders, think their ownership is not real because it is a share in an apartment building.) The phasing out of Section 8 rent subsidies poses another threat to buildings in the long run as the income of tenants would have to carry all costs, an impossible situation for many existing tenants.

The point is not that low-income co-ops do not work. Our research shows that they do and they are preferred by the most vulnerable to rental housing alternatives. The problem is the more fundamental one: low-income people in our society lack security and the necessary supports of life. Poor, old, and unemployed tenants, many of them women, in limited equity co-ops have managed to claim for themselves, through their own efforts and the successful use of the limited social resources they can locate, housing that they control and which they largely find very satisfactory. This is unusual and the forces of the society that make it unusual do not let up when they take title. This chapter addresses the possibilities of linking the struggles of these tenants to gain and keep decent housing that they themselves control with the struggles of low-income people throughout the nation for resources and self-determination. What is at stake is the need to rethink the relationship between the intimate levels of the household and the importance of the neighborhood, and this in turn relates to the value attached to each.

HOUSEHOLDS, NEIGHBORHOODS, AND CAPITAL

A STANDARD analysis about the linkage between households, neighborhoods, and capital is as follows. In our economic system, businesses and institutions survive and flourish if they continue to accumulate more and more capital. Such a system has to have winners and losers. The people who suffered through landlord abandonment of their housing and went on to take control or at least to survive did not escape being in the loser category. Their legitimate economic place in the society is to sell their labor, usually at underpaid work. The other illegitimate options include crime and social dependency, the first fraught with risk, moral pain, and social stigma, the second, low paying, unreliable, and also stigmatizing. Most had worked at the hardest and lowest paid jobs, nurses aides, factory workers, domestics, building supers, mechanics, and the like. These histories put them at risk.

Yet as individuals, households, and collectives, they fought to gain not only basic needs but control over their lives.[2] They want economic security for themselves and their households, to live in a place that provides adequate shelter, nurturing social relationships, control over daily life, and access to a supportive, familiar community. These everyday goals conflict at times with the goals of the industries and institutions that employ them or provide benefits and that use their communities or want to use them in the future. These industries and institutions are structured so that they shift employees and locations to make the most profit. They need workers who have the more highly prized skills at the times they need them and for the lowest prices. At the same time, they seek to locate in environments that provide access to a suitably skilled work force, at the best cost, and in places equipped with the transportation, housing, markets, and other resources that will support their businesses and work force. During the period from the late 1960s through 1980s, these mostly black, working-class tenants often lost out in many ways. They described losing jobs and employers going out of business. New York City, like other northeastern cities, has been steadily losing manufacturing jobs. New jobs have been geared to a skilled work force with more than high school degrees or are low-paying service jobs. The predicament of the people we interviewed in landlord-abandoned buildings indicates the flight of capital from their neighborhoods, as do their descriptions of the closing of local businesses and the neglect of public services in their communities.

Yet investors of capital need to keep their options open. Places that are not necessarily good locations for business and people who are not good candidates for employment may nonetheless be needed or desirable in the future.[3] Even if a particular population or place is not attractive in this generation, the efforts of people to survive and adapt to economic conditions might produce a competitive investment environment in the future. Thus while the survival of the particular residents of Harlem in the 1980s might be irrelevant to most investors of capital, their collective efforts to survive may contribute to the regeneration of an economically productive community. Indeed, the very act of poor people in creating an "island" can be interpreted as part of a larger strategy to stabilize particularly attractive neighborhoods.[4] This is reflected in Robert K. Davis' remarks; Davis is deputy commissioner at HPD in the Office of Rent and Housing Maintenance. He spoke about the 2,300 units sold to tenants and nonprofits through DAMP and the anticipated 2,500 more that were about to be sold in the three community boards. To Davis' mind, these sales and the ninety-seven brownstones sold since 1985—sixty-seven to residents of Central and West Harlem—are "real anti-gentrification measures that go a long way toward stabilizing the neighborhood and giving residents a feeling of pride."[5]

Although it is beyond the scope of this book to document the extent to which gentrification is occurring in Harlem, signs suggest that a regeneration may be in the offing. To what extent this will benefit Harlem's low-income residents is unanswerable at this stage. Several events occurred as we completed this book. The Mayor proposed turning over the majority of the city-owned stock in Harlem to private developers to produce market rate housing. A new 600-unit building of apartments constructed by the New York City Partnership, a private-public joint venture, opened within two blocks of the successful co-op on Manhattan Avenue. Meanwhile, the Harlem Urban Development Corporation (HUDC), an arm of the State's Urban Development Corporation, "is trying to obtain financing for Harlem on the Hudson, a huge complex of apartments, theaters and stores that is planned along the riverfront near 125th Street."[6] An American businessman, A. St. George B. Duke, who is scouting sites in Harlem for the Japanese government and investors, fuels the rumors by reporting that he doesn't think his clients would be spending so much time if they weren't serious about their interest. Donald Cogsville of HUDC is optimistic that Japanese investors will be major backers of his agency's proposed waterfront development.

Community Board 9 which includes the area for the proposed redevelopment has not endorsed the project until it receives more information. A ten-year-old idea for an international trade center has been proposed in Community Board 10, for 125th Street and Lenox Avenue, to house representatives from Africa, the Caribbean, and the South Pacific, as well as offices for the Port Authority of New York and New Jersey, and the state and federal government. New York's Governor Cuomo has persuaded the Port Authority to endorse the trade center project and commit $50 million. An area in East Harlem in Community Board 11 is all but designated for an economic development zone.

In their efforts to survive and control their lives, the households of the tenants in co-ops pooled some of their economic resources and a lot of their labor to maintain and improve their buildings. In doing so, they strengthened themselves as individuals, first by avoiding poor housing or homelessness, and, second, by gaining skills, knowledge, and an increased sense of their own abilities. They created homes for working and unemployed people, for the elderly and parents, especially single mothers and their children, that offered safety, security, social support, and affordability. These tenants, who sometimes did not lead the fight for co-oping, were able to get their lives together in different ways, sometimes return to school, sometimes make it through psychological depressions, sometimes return to live in Harlem when they would otherwise have moved out of New York in search of better conditions. It seems very likely that the co-ops provide an environment that supports people in finding and keeping jobs and raising children who can find jobs.[7] The same can be said of rental buildings that were recycled through Alternative Management programs to house low-income people. The co-ops illustrate a further point, however, that is, the extent to which individuals and households managing to survive against unemployment and disinvestment can, by taking control of some resources, have the effect of changing the future conditions of capital investment. The next question concerns the effect of such success on the people, their offspring, and other similar households.

For the most part, these low-income Harlem tenants were more satisfied, with housing conditions, management, and the control they had over their housing in co-ops than in rental buildings. Most often, social support networks were more extensive in co-ops, and people felt more secure in the present and optimistic about the future.[8] The more successful the co-op, the stronger the pattern. The 1983 survey by the Division of Alternative Management of New York City's Housing Development and Preservation Agency revealed similar co-op success in all the boroughs of New York having DAMP co-ops and rental buildings. Although Kolodny and Lawson studied only co-ops, their conclusions were also congruent.[9] The Harlem co-op residents also brought out other dimensions of co-op life: the dense network of support that allowed older people to function in their homes and the opportunities for female leadership that arose in the co-ops.

The DAMP programs succeeded in preventing the proportion of those living in landlord-abandoned housing who could not have found alternative dwellings from becoming homeless. The tenant co-ops and community managed buildings secured ownership of land by low-income people or groups seeking to protect the interest of low-income people. Whether the buildings will continue to shelter low-income people depends on issues not yet decided, at a local, state, and national level, and are political as well as economic in nature. Will adequate rent subsidies be available, can costs be kept to affordable levels, can the buildings meet repair and capital investment demands? Will changes in the financial allocations and rules and practices governing the DAMP programs continue to allow very low-income buildings to become co-ops? Will they allow the time, learning, and building of cooperation needed for co-ops to go beyond the provision of mere shelter? Will money be available to support the technical assistance so vital to co-op development? Other threats arise from the very success to which the co-ops contributed, economic revitalization. If the housing market strengthens, can co-ops in general resist the financial enticements of higher purchase prices and maintenance costs? Will future low-income limited equity co-ops be unable to compete with market pressures to sell the land and buildings at market rates?

Questions like these are beginning to prompt responses from a variety of sources and alternative structures are beginning to appear.[10] One of the most promising ideas, one that would protect poor and working-class tenants, is a collectivizing of individual cooperative buildings into a Mutual Housing Association (MHA).

MUTUAL HOUSING ASSOCIATIONS

N EW YORK City's limited equity cooperatives operate as separate corporations. Therefore, each building must handle all the maintenance, managerial, and financial tasks required. Not only are single building co-ops too small to benefit from economies of scale, they also tend to absorb all the energies of the residents, leaving little time or enthusiasm for the development of new co-ops to serve other low-income people. Even when some residents, usually ex-leaders, evidenced an interest in extending the skills they learned in this direction, no mechanisms have been in place to connect them with those in need of housing or programs that would be necessary for the development of new co-ops.

One long-standing alternative has been the Community Management Program where nonprofits could act as an umbrella organization for multiple co-ops. While community-managed rentals should in principle be moving toward cooperative ownership, and perhaps might draw on the skills of the larger organization, this study suggests they function more like rental properties. There are very few co-ops that move through the CMP program and the community groups act more or less like benevolent landlords.

In the exception, when an individual building is co-oped within a community management contract, there is little evidence that the community management group retains any of the tasks connected with running the building.[11]

There is a relatively new proposal that indicates that an alternative form to the singly organized co-op is the mutual housing associations springing up in New York and elsewhere. Mutual Housing Associations vary greatly in their exact form and purposes. They have in common an effort to participate in the development and management of new housing based on cooperative control by members aimed at providing affordable, high-quality housing for low-income people. The definition of who can be a member and how they are elected is critical to the nature of the association. Generally members include residents, prospective residents, and representatives of organizations with housing development expertise, as well as community leaders. The relationship between the MHA and the residents of existing buildings also differentiates types of MHAs. Sometimes the MHA works very much like an individual TIL housing cooperative except that several buildings are involved. For instance, Route 2, a federation of low-income, limited equity co-ops in the Echo Park–Silver Lake district of Los Angeles, grew out of the resistance of low-income renters and homeowners to being displaced from their housing owned by CALTRANS. This State transportation agency had first acquired the housing, displacing one group of residents, to build a freeway. When the project was dropped, CALTRANS began to attempt to sell off the housing, as well as neglect services. Residents organized to buy the housing themselves. Through a series of actions including a rent strike, residents were able to purchase the single and multifamily dwellings. Tenants in the scattered dwellings along the old designated route (although dispersed, the dwellings are relatively close to each other, some, but not all, adjacent) organized as five cooperatives to form a federation of co-ops charged with policy decisions affecting all units and with many management functions. The federation also began to develop one new co-op. Much like tenants in landlord-abandoned buildings, the federation members fought with governmental agencies to gain and retain direct control over its actions. Co-ops are represented on the federation board and open membership meetings are held.[12] In New York City, a group of squatters organized by ACORN (Association of Community Organizations for Reform Now) took over city-owned buildings in the East New York section of Brooklyn. They formed the Mutual Housing Association of New York and, through sweat equity, community support, and negotiations with the city, are attempting to rehabilitate the buildings for residents.[13]

Other MHAs are initiated primarily by sponsoring organizations that involve potential residents as they develop housing sites and plans. For example, the Neighborhood Reinvestment Corporation is a national nonprofit organization with a recent mandate to fund demonstration mutual housing associations. One project has been completed in Baltimore and another is beginning in New York's Lower East Side.[14] Several community groups that have had contracts with DAMP for community managed housing in New York, including one represented in this study, are considering forming MHAs. To further protect housing from speculation, some MHAs form land trusts that hold property titles. MHAs or co-ops then lease the property and own their own buildings. This arrangement adds a second layer of protection to retain the land for use rather than speculative exchange.

MHAs may be one ingredient in solving some of the problems of financial vulnerability and management overload experienced by co-ops. The extent to which they result in housing that involves residents in empowering experiences and that leads to more control over their lives depends on the way organizing is done and the role of co-op education and training, as discussed in chapter 10.

Self-Help Works, a new organization in New York initiated with participation from UHAB, brings together existing tenant housing co-operatives to work collectively on solving their problems. Resale policies are being reviewed by the board. Avenues for borrowing are being analyzed, including a Self-Help Works Credit Union. The group has established a fire liability insurance program, as well as a program of pre-paid legal assistance.[15] Co-ops can obtain architectural assistance through the organization. The goal of Self-Help Works is to maintain monthly costs and assure affordability. Organizers believe it changes the outlook of residents and connects them with channels of political activism from which they might otherwise remain isolated.

Whether this approach will be encouraged or not is as yet unknown. Mutual Housing Associations and entities like it are not what the report of the New York City Commission on the Year 2000 is advancing.[16] In "New York Ascendant," optimism is voiced about national legislation for more public housing. One recommendation is that city-owned property be placed in a special division within the Housing Authority and whenever possible, returned to the private sector and nonprofit groups. The report expresses approval for existing Local Development Corporations (LDCs, often used interchangeably with CDCs, Community Development Corporations), and urges a systematic search for every neighborhood for "local managers, beginning with the neighborhood's own LDC." There is also no mention of tenants' groups. In response, Manhattan Borough President David Dinkins, while he agrees with the setting up of a special division with the New York City Housing Authority, calls the report to task because only one-quarter of newly constructed or rehabilitated housing in the Mayor's ten-year plan will be within the monetary reach of low-income families.[17] In addition, Dinkins' comments point out the year-after-year underfunding or many of the DAMP programs.

An alternative position is that of advocacy groups brought together by the Association of Neighborhood and Housing Development under the umbrella of the Housing Justice Campaign. The Campaign includes tenants' associations, nonprofit community groups, labor unions, religious institutions, and civic organizations. They have coalesced around the disposal of the vacant city-owned buildings, a large number of which are in Harlem. Indicative of the city's emphasis on the private market, this stock was moved out of the Office of Property Management (the parent division for DAMP and Central Management) and into a new bureaucratic home, HPD's Office of Development. In response to the change in disposition strategies (according to ANHD's executive director, Bonnie Brower, changes that began with an emphasis on sales around 1980 and 1981, and a turning away from an earlier position of viewing the city-owned inventory as a second source of public housing), the Housing Justice Campaign adopted a seven-point policy that rests on an economically integrated mix of homeless, low- and moderate-income people with annual incomes below $25,000. Emphasis on disposition is to strengthen control among non-speculative owners and not the private sector.

Our emphasis on connecting households and encouraging community-households may best be realized by a structure like Self-Help Works.

COMMUNITY-HOUSEHOLDS AND POWER

SELF-HELP Works represents an especially important direction for low-income tenants in New York because it may be capable of not only linking them together to obtain services but also to influence crucial political decisions. While the TIL Coalition and ANHD in New York have attempted, sometimes successfully, to marshal political power to fight city decisions that would weaken the program for low-income tenants— as in the retention of the $250 per equity share for forming a co-op—the dependence on voluntary activity in the TIL Coalition with limited paid staff burdens already burdened leadership. Additionally a service and training component should induce participation from less politicized co-op leaders and residents. In Canada, it has been the banding together of low- and moderate-income housing cooperatives to influence government policy that has salvaged their development and assistance programs. Technical assistance groups play a major role in organizing tenants through their programs for cooperative education, as was described in the last chapter. The Cooperative Housing Foundation of Canada coordinates much of the lobbying, watchdog and organizing efforts required to keep the Canadian programs viable. In addition, it develops cooperative housing services. One of these is an adult education program for volunteers in housing management and other cooperative housing skills that results in a certificate. It has organized bulk purchase arrangements, a discounted insurance package, and recently a high-risk, front-end loan fund. It is a membership organization representing about 80 percent of the low- and moderate-income co-ops in Canada as well as most technical assistance organizations. The organization of regional federations has been especially important in developing the strong political clout the group has. For instance, in a recent fight with a conservative federal government, the federations walked out on negotiations with the government rather than compromise their commitment to mixed-income programs. The government took the line that only the very neediest should have access to housing subsidized by government funds. The result of the action was that the co-op program is now the only Canadian housing program supporting the development of mixed-income housing.[18]

This is not to say that Canada has solved all the housing problems for lower income people or that cooperatives have worked well for everyone. While there are more cooperatives today than in 1974, at that time one analyst simply didn't think that co-ops could even comprise a third force of housing between the private sector which doesn't produce for a low-income population and a public sector that some people in cooperatives are ineligible for because of their higher income.[19] Others have suggested that cooperatives be seen less romantically and that cooperation should be viewed as "an experience in capitalism rather than fellowship," and that this could lead to less posturing and a deeper understanding of how to live together creatively. Nonetheless, the co-op movement in Canada with its adherence to process in any one cooperative and "cooperation among cooperatives" represents an enormously advanced step in comparison to the United States.[20]

In the United States, even in New York City with its high proportion of housing co-ops, the Canadian kind of political organization has not developed. The existence of over 220 limited equity co-ops suggests the impact such political organization could have on local and citywide politics. New York and the nation face problems in organizing that have been difficult for low-income people to overcome. Chief among them is the problem of multiple racial and ethnic populations failing to form political coalitions. This study has shown a positive side of ethnic enclaves: their ability to reinforce trust and cooperation in the organization and management of low-income housing cooperatives. Housing co-ops deal with the most intimate environments of daily life. The physical form of much of the multifamily housing as well as the participation in important daily life decisions of housing co-op members create many ways in which residents intervene in each other's lives. Thus, the shared assumptions of a common cultural heritage and a racially linked past of oppression smooth the process of negotiating interdependence. The success of Harlem residents in saving their homes and building strength in their community deserves to be known. It goes counter to the negative stereotypes of blacks that fill the media and often serve as rationales for punitive housing and welfare policies.

However, to defend the interests of low-income people, coalitions across racial and ethnic lines must be formed. It is possible that the absence of a strong coalition of limited equity co-ops and community managed buildings, which would ideally include also tenants of buildings owned and managed by the city (the Central Management inventory), reflects the general weakness of cross-racial, low-income population coalitions in New York and the attendant weak influence of minorities in city politics.[21] In any event, it is a challenge that must be faced if low-income people are to gain and hold access to affordable housing that they themselves control. The Route 2 cooperative housing federation in Los Angeles offers a possible model of how such multicultural organizing can be successful.[22] The NCNW training program discussed in the last chapter also addresses how to think about multiracial, multiethnic organizing. A fledgling organization of tenants in public housing projects in Los Angeles may also be important to follow insofar as it can lead to a greater understanding of how to overcome spatial dispersion and create a coalition of multicultural groups. The experiences of the Chicago-based Voice of the People in Uptown (VOP) can also inform this discussion. Dovie Thurman, a former VOP tenant organizer, spoke of learning to understand the background of Asian tenants. When one woman spoke in her native Laotian language about how she wished she could speak English, Thurman said, "It brought tears to my eyes because there was feeling! I felt what she wanted to say."[23]

Co-op housing is not the only form of housing through which low-income people can gain homes and some measure of control over their lives. The

Cochran Gardens' experience of organizing public housing tenants is one example of a similar process and similar outcomes in public housing. Just as multi-cultural organizing is essential if poor and working-class people are to achieve their goals, so is it necessary to link residents in housing structures that arise from different funding mechanisms. Rosemary Jackson in Camden, New Jersey, talks of organizing that crosses over from public into private housing. The National Low Income Housing Coalition provides an important resource in this direction.[24]

There is another "crossover" that is necessary to mention, i.e., the world of people who are developmentally disabled and the nondisabled. The disabled share with the elderly and people of color negative images and low expectations by the larger society. While we can only mention this in passing, Canada's Prairie Housing Cooperative and Sweden's extended neighboring projects provide ways to think about meeting people's special needs in a supportive community setting.[25] The concept is simple—as with the examples described earlier about homeless providers. Small numbers of people live together either collectively, or in separate houses, where care can be provided both formally and informally. In Prairie Housing, no more than two people with handicaps live in the same household; houses are dispersed throughout the community; neighbors are recruited to live in the co-op and form connections; the handicapped people are involved in decision making; people with handicaps have equal security of tenure. In Sweden, at the Lambohov estates in Linköping, four households living in separate units look after a fifth; there is also a policy of "normalization," where elderly people live in their own apartment building but are connected to younger people in other buildings through physical means (walkways, corridors) and programs that take place in the common areas.

Often the legitimate demand for more units and programs that serve the very neediest first pits one group of the excluded against another and swamps the equally legitimate demand that poor and working-class people control that housing. Just as policymakers often err in separating production of units from availability of services, providing units without control can foster a more passive population. Indeed, it is possible that the empowering aspects of housing control are as important in forming a lasting coalition of low-income people who fight for their needs. In particular, reflecting on the Canadian experiences, a more active consideration of the role of limited equity co-ops in a national housing strategy, including the empowering possibilities of the form, could benefit the housing agenda a coalition can pursue. A proposed national omnibus housing program makes limited equity co-ops part of a centerpiece for "social" ownership, production, financing, and managing of housing.[26] The "social" sector would take housing out of the realm of speculative investment; housing would be seen as a service, as it is in many European and developing countries, valued for its use, where everyone is entitled to that service. A version of this program has been introduced into the House of Representatives by Ron Dellums of Berkeley, California.

Harlem residents' struggles for housing and self-determination shed light on the abilities of severely disenfranchised people. These circumstances, for these women and men, led to actions on their own behalf that often lead to the achievement of these goals. This in itself is a rare phenomenon. Their stories hold clues to the kinds of problems and conditions in which such organizing arises. Policies based largely on the image of weakness, laziness, incompetence, amorality, and hopelessness can never really improve the lives of poor and powerless people. Likewise, community activists must connect with the enduring strength and rootedness we found among these often elderly and female black leaders. Because they were in many ways such unlikely leaders, and because they focused first on improving the most tangible and debilitating aspects of their situations rather than on redistribution of political power, they can easily be overlooked by the white majority or stereotyped.[27] Rhetaugh Graves Dumas' analysis of the leadership roles of more middle-class black men and women highlights similar ways that the leaders in our study have been viewed.[28] It was not only that the women, and men, we interviewed were working at the level of the building, but that the situation for them was like that of the "mass of black women in America" Dumas writes of, exposed to events

> that tax the physical and emotional stamina of these women, undermine their authority, compromise their competence, limit the power that they might conceivably exercise, and thus limit their opportunities for rewards and mobility in the organization—not to mention the impact of these on job satisfaction.[29]

Furthermore, their styles of leadership and the small worlds in which they operate can isolate them or put them at odds with politically active groups that try to speak for their communities.[30] At the same time, these activists and organizations that function at the community and citywide levels are critically important resources for these very local leaders.

While the actual experience of tenants in forming limited equity co-ops also reveals the ways in which the context did *not* support further empowerment, certain aspects of the experience offer guidelines to successful approaches. Shared control over essential parts of life is the cornerstone for empowerment. Harry C. Boyte has made a similar observation. Poor and relatively powerless people become involved in changing their conditions when political movements and groups address their basic daily needs and most strongly held values. Approaches that emphasize one single issue at the expense of others and that eschew mundane accomplishments in favor of more dramatic ones cannot gain widespread support in communities where daily survival requires so much effort. Our research adds an analysis of the critical role existing social relationships and commitment to home and community play in fostering active participation in social change. Many forces in modern life fragment social ties in the interest of achieving specific goals such as employment, education, and better housing. Yet the sharing of and making of place bonds people to each other and a common future in a unique way. While policies that assist income, housing access, child care, health care, and employment can in principle be developed, the particular household has to bring all these together in time and space and compensate through noneconomic activities for the shortcoming of these services. Housing co-ops provide a promising starting point from which to integrate and maximize the value of other services. Because the elderly, women, and children center their lives closer to home, housing centered programs have a much greater chance of involving them, and of their involving others.

Cooperatively organized endeavors of different kinds should be explored more thoroughly as means of empowering as well as serving low-income people. The real level of control a person can have over life in this society correlates highly with disposable income. The development of a co-op sector could be an alternative to the prospect that large numbers of people will be able to exert less and less control over the services and work on which they depend. While low-income people may have no other options, even those in the middle might find this an attractive alternative. How many middle-income people can expect to age in social worlds characterized by the supportive, interesting, and productive relationships and activities of the elderly co-op tenants? Wekerle has documented the value residents of housing cooperatives organized by women place on the supportive communities they develop, a value on par with the affordabilty of housing and alternative to homelessness the co-ops offer.[31]

At both the state and federal level, legislation that has passed and other legislation being proposed provide hopeful signs for increasing the number of cooperatives. At the state level, California Senator David Roberti's Housing and Homeless Act authorized a $300 million general obligation bond issue in November 1988. The $15 million Family Housing Demonstration Program of that act will offer incentives to private developers to build multi-unit rental or cooperative housing with job training and child-care services.

A $150 million general obligation bond issue will be placed on the 1990 ballot. At the national level, Representative Joseph Kennedy II has introduced the Community Housing Partnership Act, which will provide $10 million to support expenses and training for the staff of nonprofit community based organizations, and for the administration of education, counseling, and organizing programs for tenants eligible for affordable housing. It also proposes to provide $500 million in grants to subsidize the development of affordable rental housing and home ownership. The Committee for Creative Non-Violence (CCNV), Coalition for the Homeless, and the Union of the Homeless worked together to develop a bill for affordable housing that includes funding for child care and job counseling services. Representative Barney Frank of Massachusetts has introduced a version of this bill. The proposed national omnibus housing program referred to earlier has been introduced into the House of Representatives.[32]

As we have shown in chapter 2, it is clear that society has been moving towards a polarization of "haves" and "have nots." There is a steady stream of research that documents the difficulties black men have in finding employment, the feminization of poverty, and sorrowful conditions for children of poor people. The visibility of homelessness which has spurred the recent and proposed legislation is an ever-present reminder of these divisions. The current political context is not going to change without the participation and emerging although usually "hidden" leadership of the "have nots."

At least two different types of strategies have been attempted to reduce the gap between micro- and macro-analyses, and between what happens in people's everyday lives and national or state, or even local, legislation. One strategy is to begin at the national level and develop programs that are responsive to grass roots organizations. Such a strategy typified the 1960s' programs. Unavoidably, a strategy of this sort depends on bureaucratization and stultifies the energies exhibited at the local level. A second strategy places additional resources at the level of collective households. Although less tried and less known, there are some prototypes for implementing the second strategy.

FROM THE HOUSEHOLD TO THE COMMUNITY TO THE NATION

CRISIS OF some sorts, whether it is in housing conditions (abandonment), economic conditions (plant closings, movement of corporations), environmental impacts (oil spills, toxic waste dumps), can be countered by grass roots organizing. Resistance and efforts to change the situation become visible through protests to a landlord, corporation, and/or government agency. The individual protestor and the protestation gains momentum and legitimacy through working in ever-widening circles outward, as we have seen, from the household through building-level organizations. There are forces that encourage linkage between the household and grass roots to national organizing: the women's movement, the environmental movement, unemployed workers' councils, and voter registration campaigns extend beyond one household, neighborhood, community, and city and provide a countercontext from the mainstream political environment. Each begins to have its own structure, sometimes surfacing as third party political campaigns. For example, in Newark, New Jersey, former mayor Kenneth Gibson initially ran on such a ticket. Barry Commoner's and then Jesse Jackson's leadership in organizing the Rainbow Coalition legitimated the types of issues we have been discussing by influencing the mainstream Democratic Party.

Existing nonprofits, sometimes foundations, other times religious institutions, all with ties to national-level structures, link the household/building level to the broader community. Excellent examples of this are seen in professional groupings such as the national network of Legal Aid offices and issue groupings such as the National Low Income Housing Coalition.

In New York City, the Association of Neighborhood and Housing Development provides linkages between community organizations, the city, and the state. Another local example is the Legal Aid Foundation in Los Angeles. Legal Aid funds a community economic development section headed by Gilda Haas, a recognized housing and organizing expert. Haas has been working with public housing tenants to build the kind of leadership exhibited in Cochran Gardens in St. Louis and in the TIL buildings in Harlem. She works with individual public housing resident associations, and, in coalition building among residents in different housing projects. One particular issue illustrates the ways in which organizing occurs horizontally across community groups, as well as among the Legal Aid lawyers: Mayor Tom Bradley's announcement that the $750 million cap or limit on the Community Redevelopment Agency (CRA) would be raised, and proceeds from tax increment financing applied to affordable housing and the homeless.[33] The Mayor's housing coordinator, with CRA staff, has been developing a plan that would distribute the $5 billion, half for affordable housing, located throughout the city, and half for infrastructure (streets, parking, some child care) that would be tied into an ongoing downtown revitalization effort. Haas has facilitated the organizing of a group of grass roots organizations and technical nonprofits in the city, called Housing L.A. Housing L.A.

formed a subcommittee on the cap with the idea of educating themselves so as to pass this information to the community, and *from the community*, a position on how the anticipated funds should be spent will be forged. Elected and appointed public officials turned out at an open forum called by a coalition of groups; the issue has been debated on the floor of the City Council. Reminiscent of what Boyte reported about Communities Organized for Public Services (COPS) in San Antonio, Texas, Haas and others believe that what will emerge will be a more comprehensive statement of needs that goes beyond housing and places it in the context of daily life, with a concern expressed for schools, security, health, etc. Simultaneously, Legal Aid lawyers are organizing to educate themselves about legal strategies to raise the cap. Homeless health care advocates are also becoming involved. It is too soon to assess this effort but greater communication between groups has already occurred, and Housing L.A. has made its presence felt in an antidemolition ordinance as well as in support of the location of a low-income project in an area of the city where residents were in opposition.

International Women's Year provides a near-perfect prototype for moving issues from the micro- to the macro-level. Local and state meetings were held to identify issues and elect representatives to a national congress in Houston in 1977. Local groups formed around the conference event and participation drew from individuals and existing organizations. State agendas were developed. At the national conference, twenty-six resolutions were passed; while there may be little to show materially, an important document became available as a tool around which to organize. Mainstream women's organizations such as the National Organization of Women (NOW) and political candidates such as Geraldine Ferraro and Patricia Schroeder, and Shirley Chisholm before them, have put forth the spirit and substance if not the exact resolutions passed at International Women's Year. Linkage between macro- and micro- is seen also in the Brooklyn based National Congress of Neighborhood Women, which evolved from a local community group to a national organization with a grass roots advisory board.

Often an organization becomes personified in particular leaders. The evolution from the household outward is forgotten. Yet the strength of the leadership of those who move this agenda from the household to the national level lies in its fidelity to the base. Jan Peterson of the National Congress of Neighborhood Women, Bertha Gilkey of Cochran Gardens, Rosemary Jackson of Camden, Kimi Gray of Kenilworth-Parkside public housing in Washington, D.C., Lois Gibbs of Love Canal, and Claudia Moore of Nickerson Gardens (a public housing complex in Los Angeles) work, often successfully, to make this link to larger political forces and a broader agenda.

Bottom-up and top-down strategies are not mutually exclusive. However, top-down approaches have been more frequently tried and have yet to galvanize those most affected. The moral imperative of the 1960s' War on Poverty was its initial emphasis on "maximum feasible participation," and on bypassing traditional groupings controlled by city hall political machines. Model Cities was to have involved residents in their own wishes and hopes for their communities. When the original mandate for participation was narrowed, traditional and even the newly created bureaucracies got mired in paperwork. The coordinated effort to plan for housing and human services remained largely uncoordinated and with no control over other housing programs such as urban renewal. Funding was insufficient and the War on Poverty was lost before it even got off the ground. Just as the Depression tempered and, for some, changed forever the hopes and expectations wrought by the Harlem Renaissance, the War on Poverty had only marginal success.

What is needed now is not just the skirmish that the War on Poverty turned out to be but a full-fledged commitment to build on non-market values in order that a valued society for people of color, poor and working-class people, and other vulnerable populations can prosper. The 1980s' unrest, symbolized by the protests and demonstrations by students of color on campuses around the country, is symptomatic of the problems facing the country in the coming decades. Indeed, these demonstrations are more portentious. Unlike the 1960s when there was a spirit of optimism and belief that change could occur against a backdrop of a growth economy, racial and economic groups have been polarized. In order to create change, what has long been regarded as valueless must be turned upside down, and this needs to start with an understanding of how the dominant society treats poor people and how the ordinary housework of everyday life fits into a new formulation.

THE ROLE OF VALUES

THE PRESSURE to value only what can be turned into profit is enormous in a country like the United States. Yet, there are pockets in every community, in every city of the nation, where people survive and cope because of the ways in which they help each other. Earlier we discussed how social relations are the first line of defense for poor people, and how the successful buildings functioned like an extended kin network. This can be traced to valuing collectivity, and was expressed best by the four women we interviewed who told us, "We are not trying to be landlords. The only thing we are trying to do is just make sure that money comes into the building, that we are able to be self-sufficient so we are able to have a home." Then one of the women expanded on what it will take and what can happen. "[If] we don't put nothing into it, then it won't be anything, but if we all work and put something into it, then we can have a mansion, a palace." The building itself was only the first step. It may seem contradictory for us to interpret Connie's evocation of a mansion and a palace as reflecting the motivation of the tenantry, but the leaders were motivated in part because of this version and they were not talking about personal aggrandizement.

Charles Hampden-Turner, who has critically analyzed Community Development Corporations, is informative about this when he clarifies the role values play in the psycho-social development of poor people.[34] Hampden-Turner began with values such as those we found, from the perspective of the poor themselves, and extended that to the need to be self-sufficient through economic development. His warnings concern the imposition of dominant values of a society that can disturb the survival strategies of a poor community, which most often rest on interconnections with other poor people.

> Often the dominant "helper" will see "traditional" values as impediments to the modernization process, rather than vital yet fragile skeins of social continuity. Take an "obviously" anti-developmental norm—the idea that persons should not desire too much wealth or too many worldly possessions, since these are foredoomed to frustration. In fact, such a value may be a thread by which the sanity of a poor community hangs. Given the danger of expectation outrunning productivity, only a preference for human bonds over material gain may stand between a community and an epidemic of corruption or a Gadarene rush to sell out one's own community to the Man.[35]

Hampden-Turner argued that CDCs should build on "shared neighborhood values," and go beyond the purely economic definition of surplus value so "that the neighborhood organization and its members experience themselves as the origins of wealth and value."[36] As we have said, the neighborhoods, and by inference its values, are the domain of women although not exclusively. In discussing the realization of value that provides for "a kind of human innovation,"[37] Hampden-Turner talked of

> Production that has a social purpose beyond itself, and beyond mere consumption, [which] could do much to transform America's social and cultural climate. In origination lies emancipation—and a shortcut to power. For all the victims of our society have at least one potentially valuable piece of expertise—they know the system's failures, from underneath, where the fissures are obvious and the oppressions crude and undisguised by gentility. In motivation and awareness they have a head start in devising remedies.[38]

What he went on to say about jobs generated through building on neighborhood corporations and shared values is particularly pertinent to our findings; these shared values can create a "high quality role structure," and "permit poor people to fill positions of skill, variety, mobility and importance, roles which stand in marked contrast to those of welfare recipient, dependent child, problem family, hard-core jobless, and high-risk, target area resident."[39] Hampden-Turner discussed ways in which competence builds within people, and how CDCs can contribute toward that by organizing "inside" viewpoints. This is also compatible with our earlier discussion about place attachment.[40]

CDCs need to be distinguished from cooperatives and Mutual Housing Associations; although Hampden-Turner's prescriptions can be applied to the making of community-households within CDCs, we are suggesting that the values he talks about are more likely to be realized in cooperatives and Mutual Housing Associations.[41] Cooperatives by their very nature have to be based on a sharing of responsibilities and rewards, regardless of whether the underlying reason for joining is altruistic or not. By valuing cooperatives, placing them in the forefront of a national housing policy, a necessary first step is taken that redirects social relations and power in a more explicitly equal way. There is enormous pressure on community development corporations to succeed as a business. As the business ethic dominates, so too does an organization grow, a hierarchical leadership becomes established, then entrenched, and inevitably there is further distancing from the household level. The further development occurs from the household the less attention is paid to the lives of the people affected. Attention turns away from the nurturing of people to the production of things and money. Status becomes attached to these outcomes rather than to the daily work of maintaining life.

For many reasons, the most devalued work in our society has taken place at the household level, with housework. Without a change in thinking about housework, the kinds of linkages we are talking about are unlikely to occur. It was only in the 1960s and 1970s that research and political strategies began to emerge about the value of housework. Although there were movements around home economics at the turn of the century, and the kitchen as the "work zone" for the wife, that was largely the result of a conservative agenda whose goal was to idealize and confine the role of the wife to the home. When middle- and upper-class women did come out of the home, it was to apply their "homemaking" function to the munici- pality.[42] In the 1960s, Betty Friedan, in her now famous *The Feminist Mystique*,[43] talked about the disease with no name that afflicts full-time housewives and of how housework expands to fill up the day. Ann Oakley, in her work, legitimated the study of housework as a category of research and an issue worth understanding that sociologists had long ignored.[44] Other sociologists like Jo Ann Vanek were updating time budget studies of earlier decades.[45] Many people were aghast at the findings, amazed that so much time was devoted to personal and household upkeep and to child rearing. The portrait of housework and the conditions under which it took place began to take shape: privatized, not social work; products for use for the family, not the market; no wages, no routinized time off for vacations; inidirectly controlled hours and work processes; content changes in re- sponse to changing technology; often coexistence with waged work, inside and outside the house.[46] Later studies by people like Ruth Ann Cowan[47] and Susan Strasser[48] were persuasive in demystifying the impact of house- hold technology, that in fact, they did not reduce the time spent doing housework. In Italy, England, France, and the United States, a tumultuous debate arose from Marxists and feminists—including feminist socialists, radical feminists, and mainstream feminists—about how to conceptualize household or domestic labor.[49] Was housework part of the production sphere, and if not, where did it fit, what was its value? Maxine Molyneux ques- tioned the comparability of the value of housework in a country like Italy, with its longer history as an agricultural society where women's work was an intrinsic part of production, to the world of multinational corporations that operate in the United States and other more rapidly industrially de- veloped countries. The debates around this issue were linked to 1960s organizing in New York City where Carolyn Reed among others helped organize "household technicians," the vast "army" of servants and do- mestics. In recent years, there has been an International Campaign for

Wages for Housework, a rallying cry for organizing housewives. The home is seen as a "social factory."[50] Boycotts have been called of butcher shops and supermarkets for selling inferior and or high-priced goods. Dario Fo, the Italian avant-garde playwright, captured the battles in one of his plays, and subsequently novels and movies depicted the travails of a housewife sometimes "mad." Juanita Krebs, a former Secretary of Commerce and an economist, was among the first to set forth how much a housewife was worth by relating the anecdote of a widower paying a salary to a house-keeper, only to marry her and thus save his money.[51] The uncounted value of housework is also reflected in the lives of some of the women we interviewed who were domestics, hired to do the same kind of housework and child care that they received no wage for in their own homes.[52] Krebs and other economists calculated how much annual earnings a housewife would have, were her labor to be counted. In 1970, for example, if all women were paid for housework, the total would be between $500 and $650 billion annually; this would be more than half of the Gross National Product (GNP).[53] The Wages for Housework campaign has also argued that women's work in the house should be included in developing the Gross National Product of a country. In 1975, the women in Iceland went on strike, carrying banners that said, "When women stop, everything stops," illustrating that women's work was crucial to the economy.[54] Suzie Fleming has summarized the effort to get housework on the political agenda in Great Britain and the United States (with some attention to events in Canada).[55] Fleming writes that by 1980, "the United Nations had produced figures estimating that women do two-thirds of the world's work, receive only 10 per cent of world income and own less than 1 per cent of world assets."[56] Issues concerning the value of housework exist in developed and developing nations, revealing the universality of unpaid work in the home. Socialist societies have come in for their share of criticism as well. Lisa Leghorn and Katherine Parker have pointed out that at the most fundamental level, in the home, work has not been redistributed equally between men and women. They have written, "Even the most libertarian socialism is thus only a partial solution, unless women and female values are in the forefront of building a new economic model involving total redistribution of society's resources."[57]

Against this background, and with rising interest in the informal economy as a reflection of tight job markets and massive firings, housework has continued to be re-evaluated. Ray E. Pahl suggests that if married men are still referred to as the "chief earner," his wife should be known as the "chief worker." By devaluing and ignoring housework, attention focuses on "the individual earner rather than the household as the basic economic unit."[58] William M. Nicholls and William A. Dyson's work looks at the intersection of the domestic sector and the community/mediating sector in their field studies of Canadian families.[59] Their findings are of an emerging informal economy that is structured through cooperative social and economic networks and self-reliance. David P. Ross and Peter J. Usher have developed a classification system of informal economic structures that also includes small business enterprises, collectives and cooperatives, and household activity.[60]

Unwittingly Roger Starr, a former housing commissioner in New York City, has a contribution to make to this debate about the value of housework as it applied to women in the buildings (called tenements in his work) where we interviewed. Writing about early efforts to salvage these buildings, Starr comments that "the maintenance of the tenement house was inscribed on the back of the janitor's wife," for while the janitor was out at his other job needed to support the family, it was the wife "who scrubbed the stairs on her knees, swept the halls, and tried to keep the airshaft free of garbage. . . . tried to collect the rents and terrify the fractious children of tenants into reasonably decorous behavior. When the janitor's wife rose from her knees, the economics of tenement house operation disappeared."[61] She also had to take care of her own cleaning, child care, budgeting, and food preparation. There is a major difference between the women we interviewed and Starr's depiction. The people we interviewed had a triple day, many of them working at or newly retired from outside wage labor, responsible for their own household's maintenance and well-being, and taking on the added responsibilities of the building's maintenance and tenants' well-being.

As important as is the valuing of housework to our findings, we agree with those theorists who argue that focusing only on housework, done within privatized spaces like the home, is insufficient.[62] It would not have been enough for us only to find out from the people we interviewed about their burdens inside their own apartments. Indeed, the nature of landlord abandonment is that it collectivizes individual experiences that might otherwise be unconnected. If Connie doesn't get heat, neither do other members of her household, nor do her neighbors; if there is no electricity to light dim hallways, it affects everyone. We share with Hilary Rose[63] and Temma Kaplan[64] an interpretation of social struggles that grow out of the living space. The struggles we have reported here are experienced by what we call community-households.[65]

CONCLUSIONS

I T MIGHT be asked why a government that overwhelmingly supports private market forces would even consider the fostering of community-households, much less facilitating connections between the micro- and macro-levels. Why would a government that routinely ignores housework in calculating its GNP, value it in efforts that bring landlord-abandoned buildings from the brink of uninhabitability to use? Some may argue that government involvement is motivated by co-optation of discordant tenants; others that government funding is minimal and that a state responsibility is being transferred to poor people who are being asked to shoulder a burden not of their own making. If funds are made available to these people, then, it is simply to tide them over, to leave them with a meaningless form of ownership and control since they do not have access to the resources of the greater society.

It is true that without major structural change, and absent the presence of a well-organized movement inside and outside communities of people of color, the best that can be expected from the government may be additional funding. But that funding can go further and deeper when people's own strengths and skills are allowed to flourish as in the emerging community-households. We think people are poised to enter into stronger political coalitions that extend outside their buildings. This type of organizing will take time to put in place and will probably suffer setbacks as people's individual lives respond to micro- and macro-changes of the economy. But our work has also shown that even when people like elderly black women are discounted in a society, they can assert themselves. There cannot be empowerment by proxy and that is why any policy that involves housing and services has to begin with the valuing of housework itself at the most basic level of organization. Many of the people we spoke with hold out hopes for the remaking of households into community-households. If we are a nation that is truly committed to its democratic principles, then we need to begin to listen to the voices of people, of the women as well as the men, in neighborhoods that the majority abandons unless it can make a profit but where others make their homes.

APPENDIXES

APPENDIX A
Program Characteristics of CMP, POMP, and TIL

	CMP
Goals	enable tenants and community members to become more involved in maintenance and day-to-day management responsibilities
	develop a new form of building ownership as tenant-owned cooperatives or nonprofit community-based rental
	develop competent, local nonprofit housing organization to provide effective decentralized management and maintenance capacity in multiple dwellings
	provide competent, locally based nonprofit management; locally based groups to manage 100–350 units of city-owned housing
	extend useful life of building
	stabilize living conditions
	improve living conditions
	treatment substantially contribute to block and neighborhood improvement
Type and Extent of Assistance	assist in restructuring rents (60% of tenants must accept for entry to program)
	CMP staff regularly inspects all buildings
	weatherize building

POMP	TIL
stabilize conditions	assist tenants' association in developing economically self-sufficient buildings, improved housing services, and their own property management skills
aim at firms for which 200–300 units of city-owned housing is no more than two-thirds their workload (typically smaller firms with some base in neighborhoods experiencing abandonment)	tenants agree to pay rent at level to cover maintenance and operating expenses
provide responsible, effective management	
review disclosure questionnaires (screen prospective landlords)	DAMP survey to show repairs can be made with rent roll plus limited Community Development Block Grant funds.
	weatherized building
solicit information about firm from government agencies, Community Planning Boards, local organizations	evaluate monthly report documenting rents, collected rent arrears, management expenses
POMP staff visits firm's buildings, interviews tenants	
POMP staff negotiates each building's operation and maintenance budgets	
POMP staff details inspection and evaluates building's rent rolls and expenses	

APPENDIX A (*Continued*)
Program Characteristics of CMP, POMP, and TIL

	CMP
Level of Repairs and/or Rehabilitation	funds intensive maintenance to moderate rehabilitation
Responsibility for Repairs and/or Rehabilitation	DAMP Technical Services; Community Management Groups; Community Management Groups contract out
Average Repair/ Renovation Cost	$16,500 (1985) ($12,450 in 1983)
Source of Funds	Community Development Block Grant; Section 8
Funds Cover	Staff; repairs and in some cases moderate rehabilitation
Management Fee	$17.50/occupied unit/month; $8.75/vacant unit/month for 1 year; thereafter 11% of rent roll
Sales Time Frame (As per DAMP Constraints)	3 years (2 in some cases) (can be 6 years or more in practice)
Training Programs	Community Management Group Subagreement with tenants where cooperative is being formed

NOTES: CMP = Community Management Program; POMP = Private Ownership and Management; TIL = Tenant Interim Lease.

SOURCE: New York City Department of Housing Preservation and Development, "The *In Rem* Housing Program," First through Sixth Annual Reports, 1978–1984.

POMP	TIL
POMP staff inspects buildings for first 6 months' repairs; see Source of Funds	Typically one or two major systems (e.g., plumbing, wiring, windows, heating)
Private real estate firm; Construction Management	DAMP Technical Services; Construction Management; Tenants
$5,500 (1985) ($4,000 in 1981)	$4,000–5,000 (1985) ($2,500 in 1981)
Community Development covers difference between rent roll and building's maintenance and operating expenses for first 6 months of contract, and cost of repairs	Community Development Block Grant
Maintenance and operating expenses and repairs for first 6 months	Minimum repairs, typically one or two major systems (e.g., plumbing, wiring, windows, heating)
$17.50/occupied unit/month for 6 months; $8.75 per vacant unit/month for 6 months; 10% after 6 months	Up to 8% of collected rent roll
1 year	11-month lease, after which lease can be renewed (actual time frame runs to several years)
	UHAB, tenant officers required to attend training course on property management and accounting

"Goals" vary historically by program, and perhaps none more than CMP. For a complete history, see Sullivan et al., *Analysis and Assessment of the Alternative Management Programs for New York City's In Rem Properties,* and Leavitt, "A Neighborhood Housing Strategy for Community Board 9."

APPENDIX B.1
Sales of Division of Alternative Management Buildings 1979–1983

Fiscal Year	Buildings	Units
1979	0	0
1980	5	85
1981	50	1,630
1982	112	2,263
1983	104	3,049
Total:	271	7,027

SOURCE: New York City Department of Housing Preservation and Development.

APPENDIX B.2
Sales of Three Major Alternative Management Programs,
Leasing (TIL +7A), Community Management (CMP),
Private Ownership and Management (POMP) 1979–1983

	YEAR					
	BUILDINGS/UNITS					
Program	1979	1980	1981	1982	1983	Total
Leasing	0	5/85	10/254	46/1,027	50/1,521	111/2,887
CMP	0	0	8/102	44/721	18/306	70/1,129
POMP	0	0	9/516	6/222	22/964	37/1,702

SOURCE: New York City Department of Housing Preservation and Development.

APPENDIX C
Interview Schedule

I. Building Residential History
   1. Could you tell us when you moved into the building?
   2. Why did you move into this building?
   3. Did you know anyone when you moved in?
   4. How did you find this building?
   5. What led up to the landlord's abandoning the building?
   6. Could you describe the conditions in the building then?
   7. How has the building changed since the landlord abandoned it? What were conditions like under city ownership? How has it changed since the tenants (new landlord or community group) took over?

II. Personal History Related to Past Residential History
   1. Were you from New York originally?
   2. Why did you move to New York?
   3. Where did you first live?
   4. What did you do?
   5. What jobs did you have over the years?
   6. Where were you living during this period?
   7. Do you have any pension from those jobs? Probe for periods of unemployment.
   8. Where did you go to school? For how long?
   9. Are you married? Have you ever been married? Probe for marital history and children.
   10. Who was living in this household when you moved in?
   11. How has the household changed since you moved in?

III. Personal History Related to Current Residential History
   1. Does anyone live regularly in the household with you now?
   2. Where do your relatives live? Probe for locations.
   3. How often do you see sisters, brothers, children, other relatives?
   4. Do your relatives come to visit you here?
   5. How often do you speak to your relatives on the telephone?
   6. If children, talk about child care.
      a. How old are your children?
      b. When they were small (or now) did you have any child care help?
      c. Did your children spend time in the homes of neighbors in the building where you lived? (Probe for different circumstances in different residences.)
      d. Do you let your children (did you let them) play downstairs in the street, or go out alone? Why/why not?
   7. Whether children or not, how does this building work for children?

APPENDIX C (*continued*)
Interview Schedule

IV. Tenants' Association History
1. Is there a tenants' association? (If not, has there ever been one?)
2. How did the tenants' association come to be organized? (Probe about prior tenant groups that came together.)
3a. How are decisions made in the building? (Probe for board of directors).
3b. What does the tenants' association do?
4. Do you participate in decision making in the building? How?
5. Do you vote for officers in the building?
6. Are you, or have you been, on the board of directors? Could you describe what you did, or do. (If never on board, probe whether person wants to be.)
7. How often does the board meet?
8. How often are there tenant meetings?
9. How do you find out about tenant meetings?
10. Do you attend tenant meetings? How often? (Probe for other activities.)
11. How active are other tenants in the building? (Probe for differences between men and women; people with children; people confined to their apartments; retired people; elderly people.)
12. Do you participate in any committees? In what way?
13. Have you ever been contacted by any committee? Describe.
14. What other activities is the association active in in the community? In the city?
15. What other activities are you involved in, in the community, now in the city?
16. What about church organizations and activities?

V. Repair History
1. What work has been done on the building before sale? Since?
2. Has the city done any work?
3. What work is left for the city to do in the future?
4. How have repairs been done in the building? (Probe for contractor, tenants, respondent's participation.)
5. What work has been done on your apartment?
6. Who paid for the work on your apartment?
7. What work do you think needs to be done in the building?
8. What role do you think the city should have played in repairs? What role should the tenants have played?
9. In retrospect, what role do you think the city should have played in repairs? What role should the tenants have played?

APPENDIX C (*continued*)
Interview Schedule

VI. Building Profile
1. How many units are in the building?
2. How many units are vacant? (Probe for condition of units.)
3. How many vacancies were there in the building when it was first managed by tenants? (Probe for conditions.)
4. How many units have been sold?
5. Were all the apartments sold at the same time and to tenants living in the building?
6. Is there any Section 8, or Senior Citizen Rent Increase Exemption (SCRIE)?
7. Do you have Section 8, or SCRIE? (Probe for procedure through which tenant received.)
8. What do you think will happen to this building in the next five years?

VII. Rental Policy/Sales Policy
1. How do people find out about vacancies in the building?
2. Is there a screening committee?
3. If new tenant, did you go through a screening committee? Describe.
4. Does the building have any policy on renting/selling to families with children?
5. What is your opinion about renting to families with children?
6. What type of tenant does the tenants' association look for?
7. There is a lot of controversy over the $250-per-unit sales price. Do you think that is a reasonable price? Why/why not?
8. If sold building, was your apartment sold at $250?

VIII. Ownership Related to Housing Satisfaction
1. Have you ever owned your own housing before?
2. If bought, what differences has it made to you, owning compared to renting?
3. What are the best (and worst) things about owning a share in the building?
4. How does owning a share in the building compare to owning a single family house?
5. What are the best (and worst) things about living in this apartment?
6. Have you ever considered moving? When? Where? Would you consider moving now? When? Where? Does owning make a difference in your thoughts about moving?

IX. Neighborhood Use and Satisfaction
1. How long have you lived in this neighborhood?
2. What are the best (and worst) things about living in this neighborhood?

APPENDIX C (*continued*)
Interview Schedule

---

    3. We are interested in the way people use their neighborhood. For example, do you use the neighborhood to do grocery shopping, buy clothes, buy furniture? Do you use the neighborhood to attend church, medical facilities, schools, senior citizen center, day-care center, parks?

    4. How has this neighborhood changed since you moved here?

    5. What do you think will happen to this neighborhood in the next five years?

  X. Personal History/Time/Social Relations

    1. We are interested in how much time people spend on their work in the building in relation to everything else.

      a. Do you spend time on the building? (Probe if not clear from previous answers.)

      b. Does the time spent on the building put pressure on your household responsibilities, time you spend with your family, free time? In what way?

      c. How much time do you spend with other people in the building on the building's affairs?

      d. How much time do you spend visiting with other people in the building?

      e. Do you have any good friends in the building? How many?

      f. How often do you see them? (Probe for telephone contact.)

      g. What kinds of activities do you and your friends do together?

      h. Do your friends help with any of the following?
         –child care
         –food shopping
         –emergencies
         –sickness
         –anything else

      i. Do you help with any of the above?

      j. Do other people in the building help with any of the above?

  XI. Health Related Issues

    1. Is there anyone in this building who is having or has had health problems? How has this been handled?

    2. What would you do if someone in the building has a serious illness?

    3. What would you do if you had a serious illness?

  XII. Income Related Issues

    1. What is the income range of people in the building?

    2. Does anyone have trouble paying their rent on time? If so, is there a policy the tenants' association has?

APPENDIX C (*continued*)
Interview Schedule

3. If you had trouble paying your rent, what would you do?
4. Some people think owning an apartment gives you more control over other parts of your life, like knowing what your housing is going to cost. What do you think?

NOTES

1. HOUSING ABANDONMENT: A CRISIS FOR COMMUNITIES AND HOUSEHOLDS

1. All tenants were in programs of the City's Housing Preservation and Development (HPD) Agency. The tenants interviewed were in buildings administered by the Division of Alternative Management Programs (DAMP). By 1983, the Division of Alternative Management Programs had sold 128 buildings. Sixty buildings were selected for the city's survey. The buildings sampled were a stratified random sample chosen to reflect the proportion of buildings sold through each program proportionately distributed by borough. (DAMP buildings had been sold in Manhattan, the Bronx, and Brooklyn.) About 10 percent of the tenants of selected buildings were interviewed, resulting in the sample size of 131.

The 88 tenants selected for face-to-face interviews by us were drawn from sold buildings in Manhattan. At the time the study was conducted, there were only three community groups in Harlem that had community management contracts and only two private landlords had contracts. We interviewed tenants and community managers in each of the three groups, and tenants in buildings owned by the two landlords.

2. Alvin L. Schorr, *Slums and Social Insecurity.*

3. See Peter Marcuse, "Abandonment, Gentrification, and Displacement," pp. 153–177.

4. Samuel G. Freedman, "Harlem and the Speculators," pp. 1, 19. The impact of rent control on abandonment has been a much debated topic and is covered in other books. For a discussion of the point of view reflected in this book, see Peter Marcuse, *Housing Abandonment*. He found that even in cities without rent control, abandonment occurs. Others have made the point that even were tenants' rents to be raised, they would not be able to pay the increase because of their low incomes. For a different point of view about rent control, see Peter Salins, *The Ecology of Housing Destruction: Economic Effects of Public Intervention in the Housing Market* (New York: New York University Press, 1980).

5. A pilot study by an intern in DAMP in 1981–82 of 28 distressed properties in the Bronx, handled by three banks, suggested different foreclosure criteria, "but the principal impetus in the case of the banks studied was community pressure. Prior to the development of knowledgeable and active community groups, the outright 'dumping' of mortgages through mortgage sales was widespread." Mortgage sales to investors were usually on properties in better condition than foreclosed sales (an average price of $185 per unit, $10,000 per building on mortgage sales compared to $1,391 per unit, $79,301 per building on foreclosed sales). One common bank practice has been to demand full payment of the mortgage balance from owners after two months of default. Only after working with the owner and determining whether there is any further interest in managing the property will the bank foreclose. Meanwhile, another bank may defer winter payments and collect the money at a later and more profitable time. After foreclosure, one bank tried to sell the building to "one of the few legitimate buyers of distressed properties studied, the superintendent and his son who acted as handyman, [who had] requested and bought the building." In another case, the bank sold the building to a nonprofit community organization and the original tenants' association was going to be the on-site manager. In other buildings, the buyer, whether it is the superintendent or an unknown entity, fails. At that point a building can become completely vacated and demolished, partially uninhabitable, and remaining tenants are withholding rents. Another bank's practice was to let the building become city-owned if there were no buyers and the former owner had lost interest. In this case, the bank "will only foreclose if the neighborhood is good (no abandoned buildings on the block), if the tenants are good (no sign of drugs, no graffiti, no major vandalism, rent roll up to date) and if the building is in good condition." Another bank has tried to avoid foreclosure by negotiating conflicts between the owner, tenants, and nonprofit community group in the area. A bank may also demand high payments from a new owner.

6. Local Law 45, enacted in 1976, and put into effect in 1977, was intended to increase tax revenue by reducing the amount of time a property could be in tax arrears, from three years to one year. Under the earlier law, in fact, properties were sometimes in arrears for more than five years. Parcels are taken in borough "sweeps," notices sent to owners after the Finance Department files the actions with the county clerk. The owners may still redeem their properties, either paying the arrears in one sum or over a four-to-eight year period. Even after foreclosure the owner has up to four months to redeem the property, and up to two years if the city agrees. Another taking can occur through New York Statute Article

19-A. Tax delinquency is not the only cause for transferring title from the landlord to the city. Transfer can also occur when the owner has not asked for rent for at least three consecutive months and has not taken action to be paid, or when there is a danger to tenants' life, health or safety because of failure to make repairs, supply janitorial services, buy fuel or other needed supplies, or pay utility bills.

7. All the programs referred to are under the City's Housing Preservation and Development Agency. About one-third of all foreclosed and occupied property is under DAMP; the remainder is under Central Management.

8. Robert Kolodny, assisted by Marjorie Gellerman, *Self Help in the Inner City.*

9. Ronald Lawson, *Owners of Last Resort: An Assessment of New York City's Early Low Income Housing Cooperatives* (New York: New York City Department of Housing Preservation and Development, Office of Program and Management Analysis, 1983).

10. The limited equity cooperative is a financing technique whereby a small amount of equity is required from prospective cooperators. In New York City, the sum of $250 reflects the average sales price at auctions of foreclosed property in the early to mid-seventies. In New York City, elderly people 62 years of age and over can stay in a co-oped building without buying a share. The Human Resources Administration will buy a share for people on public assistance; however, the share is owned by the city agency. In some other cities, limited equity cooperatives require a payment of $750 to $1,500.

11. Funding was aided by Allan Weiner, as area officer of the local U.S. Department of Housing and Urban Development (HUD), whose previous tenure as Deputy Commissioner at HPD (then HDA) familiarized him with receivership and community management programs. HUD had to grant a waiver to release Community Development Block Grant (CDBG) money for the Division of Alternative Management Programs because they were outside the scope of authorized activities. Community Development money was available for these programs as of September 1979.

12. Hispanic or Hispanic origin is used instead of Latino and Latina because of references to data in government documents that favor the former.

13. The concept of the community-household is similar to that of municipal housekeeping found in work by Jacqueline Leavitt, "Women As Municipal Housekeepers," Columbia University Division of Urban Planning Working Paper, 1979; Dolores Hayden, *The Grand Domestic Revolution: A History of Feminist Designs for American Homes, Neighborhoods, and Cities* (Cambridge, Mass.: MIT Press, 1981); Marilyn Gittel and Teresa Schtob, "Changing Women's Roles in Political Volunteerism and Reform of the City," *SIGNS: Journal of Women in Culture and Society* (Spring 1980), 5:S67–S78.

2. THE SETTING AND THE PEOPLE

1. Gilbert Osofsky, *Harlem: The Making of a Ghetto.*
2. Herbert G. Gutman, *The Black Family in Slavery and Freedom.*

3. To geographers and urban planners, developers and speculators, Harlem as a place lies northward from 96th Street on the east and Central Park and 110th Street on the west to about 178th Street, in Manhattan. The eastern and western boundaries fluctuate: East Harlem is primarily inhabited by persons of Hispanic origin in a section that goes from Fifth Avenue to the East and Harlem Rivers (although at times a smaller area from Lexington to the rivers is considered East Harlem); on the west the border is the Hudson, with its eastern borders Edgecombe, Bradhurst, and Morningside avenues (again, a smaller area between West 110th and 125th streets, from Morningside to Eighth avenues is often referred to as West Harlem). Central Harlem has been referred to from north of Central Park (110th) and from Morningside Drive and St. Nicholas Avenue on the west to Fifth Avenue and the rivers on the east.

4. Osofsky, *Harlem: The Making of a Ghetto,* p. 127.

5. Margaret Perry, *Silence to the Drums,* p. 5.

6. Ibid., p. 5.

7. Nathan Irvin Huggins, *Harlem Renaissance,* p. 303.

8. Gutman, p. 453.

9. Huggins, *Harlem Renaissance,* p. 4.

10. Ibid., p. 4.

11. Commission on the Harlem Riot of March 19, 1935, *Mass Violence in America: The Complete Report of Mayor La Guardia's Commission on the Harlem Riot of March 19, 1935* (New York: Arno Press and *The New York Times,* 1969).

12. D. J. Capeci, Jr., "The Harlem Riot of 1943."

13. Jervis Anderson, *Harlem, the Great Black Way,* p. 346.

14. Allon Schoener, *Harlem on My Mind,* p. 135.

15. Ibid., p. 137.

16. Ibid., p. 138.

17. Ann Petry, *The Street.* In *No Crystal Stair,* p. 13, Gloria Wade-Gayles states the relationship of the social sciences to fiction very aptly:

"My examination of black women's literature does not suggest that fiction can substitute for a history of black women in real life. Fiction never equals fact, but it mirrors fact and in a profound way is "an interpretation and compilation of history, anthropology, sociology, psychology, and a host of other areas" that puts us in touch with the sound and sense of real life."

In trying to understand the human meaning of the statistics we unearthed, we found the writings of novelists frequently helpful. In this spirit, we incorporate quotations that particularly express the lived experience of poverty, inadequate housing, and a shortage of housing options.

18. Petry, *The Street,* p. 7.

19. Ibid., p. 7.

20. Rosa Guy, *Bird At My Window.*

21. Ibid., p. 179.

22. Sonia Sanchez, "Bubba," *Homegirls & Handgrenades,* pp. 56–58.

23. Richard Schaffer and Neil Smith, "The Gentrification of Harlem?" p. 359. Schaffer and Smith cite four constraints and limitations to gentrification: the supply of gentrifiers, the negative image of Central Harlem, the building size and zoning

limitations, and the supply of private mortgage financing. By analyzing the number of applications in a city-sponsored lottery who sought city-owned brownstones and the relation between rehabilitation costs and income, they concluded that it was unlikely that there will be any long-term gentrification by blacks, even from outside of Harlem. They reason that the auction had flaws. Eighty percent of 2,500 applications for twelve brownstones in 1982 were received. Eligible households would be those earning at least $20,000 a year. However, the estimated rehabilitation costs for a medium-sized townhouse were over $125,000, and this requires a household earning at least $55,000. An examination of the 1980 census data revealed that only 262 households in Central Harlem had incomes over $50,000, and there were less than 8,000 high-income families citywide. They concluded, "the process could begin as Black gentrification, but that any wholesale rehabilitation of Central Harlem properties would necessarily involve a considerable influx of middle and upper class whites." At the same time, they did not believe that whites will easily move into the area. They wrote:

"To the vast majority of middle-class whites, Central Harlem is perceived as a dangerous place. However accurate this image might be, it is also perceived as a Black-defined geographical space in the city, and therefore by this fact alone, threatening. Thus it is impossible to disentangle white middle-class fear from racist perceptions about the area. The reality of Central Harlem is quite different from the ideological image and yet the image is a trenchant one, and will remain so for years to come. It is probably the most immediate barrier to white in-migration."

For a discussion of another neighborhood and its transformation from white to low-income black and working poor, the latter through the church-based Nehemiah plan to provide home ownership, see Sharon Zukin and Gilda Zwerman, "Housing for the Working Poor: A Historical View of Jews and Blacks in Brownsville," *New York Affairs* (Winter 1986) 9:3–18.

24. Board 9 has a total of 258 buildings with a little more than 4,100 occupied and vacant units under Central Management and 35 DAMP buildings with 1,001 units. In Board 10, about 1,200 buildings with almost 18,000 occupied and vacant units were in Central Management, and 53 buildings with 1,184 units in DAMP.

25. Ruth A. Rae, "The Facade is Fake: Perceptions of the Occupied Look Program," unpublished paper prepared for second year Ph.D. requirement, Environmental Psychology Program, The City University of New York, The Graduate Center, August 6, 1986 draft. Rae interviewed 30 Brooklyn homeowners randomly selected from a list of Sterling Place Block Association members, and sampled half from each side of two blocks facing each other. "The aim of this [Occupied Look] Program is to make abandoned buildings look better, and it assumes that this will positively improve the morale of neighborhood residents, deter vandalism and break-ins to the building and attract investment to the area." A key finding was that "some respondents saw the decals as a sign or symbol that someone was paying attention to a previously 'abandoned' building."

26. New York City Human Resources Administration, Office of Policy and Economic Research, "District Resource Statement: An Analysis of Expenditures and Services by Community District, Manhattan, Actual Fiscal year 1985, Planned Fiscal Year 1986," Manhattan Community Board Districts 9, 10, and 11. Where other

figures are available, boundary lines are different. For example, there is data by U.S. postal zipcodes, but boundary lines are either overlapping or cover a substantially different area.

27. The early interviews in tenant initiated cooperatives (tenant interim lease or TIL) included blacks, whites, and Hispanics, with some residents of all three ethnic backgrounds living in Harlem. After conducting about thirty interviews divided almost equally among the three groups, differences among them seemed apparent. Since neither of the authors spoke fluent Spanish, we felt that our grounded approach to research would be compromised if we attempted to include a large number of Spanish speaking people in the sample. Therefore the decision to concentrate on English speakers was made. As we read over and over the transcripts from the predominantly white buildings and those from buildings with mainly black tenants, we made the further decision to limit ourselves to buildings with a majority of black tenants. All of the seven white TIL residents we interviewed could be considered the "voluntary poor," students, artists, and young entrepreneurs just starting out. All had expectations of higher earnings in the future. Looking at the interviews with black TIL tenants, we also began to see an important link between the history of Harlem as a black community and black tenants' experiences of abandonment. Black cultural patterns concerning women's roles and status also appeared germane to our findings. These factors combined with the extremely few buildings in Harlem tenanted chiefly by whites led us to focus our energies on understanding the experience of black Harlem residents.

28. We asked permission to tape interviews and were granted it in all cases. We stressed that at any time the participants could ask us to turn off the recorder. Frequently tenants would do so when they were talking about interpersonal problems, especially when they wanted to say unflattering things about other tenants. This information was not used in our analysis, nor did it seem particularly significant for the purpose of the study. Tenants spoke of conflicts in tenants' associations in more general terms for the record. Often, and after we had packed up the tape recorder, as we put on our coats and prepared to leave an apartment, the tenant volunteered some information or we asked another question. Frequently, as soon as we had left the apartment, we would record the material. Tapes were transcribed verbatim.

29. The limitations of funding forced us to focus on interviewing older people. While we believe that their central roles in the co-ops we studied warranted this comparison, the fact that we only interviewed a few younger people in the Community Management and Private Ownership and Management Program buildings limits the variety of experiences study participants shared with us.

30. The authors conducted all interviews themselves, usually together, although, on a few occasions when one or the other was unavailable, a white female graduate student filled in. Interviews lasted from forty-five minutes to two hours, with most taking about an hour and a half. Theresa Kilbane and Ed Moses of UHAB helped us identify most of our original contacts. Within HPD, the Division of Alternative Management Programs, Kevin Alter, Bruce Dale, Richard Heitler, Michael Simon, Bill Smith, and Joan Wallstein also provided names and addresses, as well as other information. Steve Kotick and Eileen White also of DAMP were very

helpful in providing us with information about the buildings. All our sources approved our using their names in introductions.

31. For respondents in buildings where the tenants had co-oped, all held or had held office in the tenants' association that ran the co-op. An officer could be the president, vice-president, secretary, or treasurer.

32. Nicholas Nelson was then a doctoral student at The Graduate Center, the City University of New York. Working under the supervision of Susan Saegert, Nelson interviewed tenants in Community Management and POMP buildings. He was generous in his time and energy, and provided us with an important perspective about the validity of our findings. To attempt to keep the open-ended interviews somewhat comparable and to assess differences, Saegert listened to the tapes from his interviews and discussed them with him. Twice, the interviewer and the authors conducted interviews with the same participants allowing a more telling check on differences in material elicited. The topics covered and the information provided were identical with one exception. In both interviews with the black interviewer, the participants were more open about their beliefs that the negative conditions of their buildings and neighborhoods can be attributed to racism. Their language was also a little less "polite."

33. Interviews were conducted in the same manner and covered the same topics. The program where tenants could purchase a share in the building was described for those unfamiliar with it, and participants were asked what they thought of such a program.

34. Jacqueline Leavitt, "A Neighborhood Housing Strategy for Community Board 9"; Daniel Zarza and Harriet Cohen, *Loisiada: Strategies for Neighborhood Revitalization.*

35. Michael A. Stegman, *Housing in New York: Study of a City, 1982.*

36. Michael A. Stegman, with Doug Hillstrom, *Housing in New York: Study of a City, 1984*, p. 234.

37. Robert Kolodny, assisted by Marjorie Gellerman, *Self Help in the Inner City;* Ronald Lawson, *Owners of Last Resort: An Assessment of New York City's Early Low Income Housing Cooperatives* (New York: The New York City Department of Housing Preservation and Development, Office of Program and Management Analysis, 1983).

38. Jacqueline Leavitt and Susan Saegert, *The Tenants Report: A Study of DAMP Buildings After Sale.* The survey contained no questions about the period prior to city ownership nor any information about the process of organizing and managing buildings. Therefore, we have used it primarily as a comparison to the qualitative data addressing current conditions in buildings sold through different programs.

39. These demographics are similar to those reported by Kolodny and Lawson, adjusted for inflation.

3. TENANT COOPERATIVES

1. The struggles of tenants in predominately Hispanic and white tenanted buildings bear some similarities to those described below. All had become coop-

eratively owned by the time we interviewed the tenants. All had encountered problems with the city in their efforts to co-op. For several, the rent restructuring required had posed a threat to cooperation but solutions were found. Tenants in one of three Hispanic buildings and in three of the four white buildings went on rent strike against the landlord.

However in other ways the buildings were quite different. Tenants in all of the white buildings saw the financial benefits of ownership. In two of the buildings, it appeared that some of the white tenants moved in in order to be able to buy in the event of city ownership. The tone of their responses differed from those in the black and Hispanic interviews. White tenants more often spoke of financial motivation or the value of the property. Hispanic and black tenants spoke of saving their homes and of the difficulty of finding decent other housing. For example one white male leader in a co-op described getting involved as follows:

"I moved here basically for greed. A couple of friends of mine had lucked into a building. The city had gotten into the business of selling buildings around the end of the sixties and these two guys got together, pooled their resources, bought into a 10-unit building, fixed up the apartment, sold it at what seemed like a reasonable profit . . . and one took off to California, the other moved out to Long Island. Bingo, wonderful, I'll do the same thing."

He then went on to say, however, that he found out that the hard work and cooperation involved made him attached to the place and the people and that he no longer wanted to leave. He also described how the building had skewed its rents so that the elderly could stay.

In another building, Anne Marie, a white female leader responded to the question about whether any tenants are trying to make a profit, in the following way:

"I would think maybe half or a quarter. . . . But I think most of us are really young. None of us have a lot of money. Maybe two people have a potential large income right now at this point, one recently had one because she's an older woman, so she's been working for a while. But most of us are under 30, maybe even under 25, very few people much older than that . . . so not a lot of people have money so it's . . . nice because now we all have homes. We feel like we have a stake in something that's nice, that's big, that's important, that we can use to our advantage. And why not? Why should other people have the opportunity and not us? And since we've worked so hard for it, we've put in a lot of money. We put in most of the money, got very little money from the city."

Many of the people in this building, which is on the upper West Side near Columbia University and other educational institutions, were students, musicians, and visual artists. There is one black single parent, Joanne, with two sons living in the building. She was trying to take care of them and herself, held a part-time job in order to be available to her children when they came home from school, and was in the process of applying for assistance from various programs, including Section 8 and social services. Both the single parent and the leaders we talked with told us of the support the building was giving her. The white female leader said:

"Well she's basically doing it. The only way we're helping her is just understanding her problem and trying to be sympathetic, being supportive emotionally I guess. Giving her letters that she needs."

They were also understanding when she had trouble paying the rent (at the time of the interview, she was three months behind). The superintendent helped her by doing some work in her apartment. But in other ways, she was at a disadvantage. The tenants in the building had recently switched policy on repairs in the apartment: instead of the association paying for repairs, each tenant assumed responsibility with entitlement to a $750 rebate for paint and plaster, the rebate to be paid out in $50 a month installments. This placed a greater hardship on Joanne's meager earnings.

Interviews in all the white buildings revealed this mix of pragmatic individualistic motivations and a growing commitment to the co-op, an increasing interest in helping others as well as themselves. In the subsequent development of the co-ops, both motives continued. Bitter fights about selling prices and profits arose in at least one case. The Hispanic buildings differed from the successful co-ops in ways that made them more similar to the struggling ones described in the next chapter. These similarities will be discussed in that chapter.

2. The demographics of leadership may differ among ethnic groups. For example, among the Hispanics we interviewed, middle-aged and younger men more often held leadership positions. In one Hispanic occupied building, a group of women had recently been elected to the board as officers. However, the leadership that existed during the struggle to buy the building had come from men. The newly elected women had eventually come to think that the male leader was taking too much responsibility and that it should be shared. In two of the three predominantly white buildings, young women had been key organizers and leaders. These possible ethnic differences are suggestive, but should be examined in more extensive research among different groups.

3. See Ann Petry, *The Street.* Lutie, the protagonist, takes a live-in job in Connecticut after other failed attempts by her and her husband to earn a living. Her husband then takes up with another woman and Lutie and her son must live with her father. That too proves untenable, forcing her to search for an apartment, an episode which leads to further tragedy for her and her son.

4. Sometimes other forms are used to circumvent closure to the money economy. Aubrey W. Bonnett writes of rotating credit associations, not limited to black immigrants, often formed out of the "informal aspects of bureaucracy" where people worked. He offers the case of Phyllis, a nurse's aide at a Brooklyn Hospital. Over lunch in the hospital cafeteria, she was told of the organizing of a "box" (fund).

"Phyllis was told that the size of the fund was $450. She was expected to pay $15 a week to the organizer, who also had fourteen other members. The box was to last for approximately five months, and Phyllis was told when she could expect to receive her $450 fund. Phyllis got her money in four weeks even though she was a relative newcomer. She was told that she was expected to have her $15 sent or taken to Mrs. H's home every Sunday and that she could not, under any circumstances, be late or stop her schedule of payments." (Aubrey W. Bonnett, "Volunteerism among West Indian Immigrants," p. 121.)

5. This theme of informal aid as a precursor and requirement of cooperative ownership emerged in all our interviews. Although we have too few interviews with Hispanic and white cooperative owners to analyze their differences, we will

note the clear similarities throughout the rest of the book. For example, Carlos, one Hispanic male leader described why he chose his building: "When I came over here, I knew all the people since living over there (Santa Domingo), and that's very important to the building because you try to get together with people you know."

6. We found this pattern of deterioration of service in a number of interviews. One of the predominantly white buildings had also gone through a decline in services as the "good" landlord died and was replaced by less involved and responsible kin. The pattern occurred also in buildings to be discussed in later chapters.

7. This point was also made by Kolodny, assisted by Marjorie Gellerman, in his 1973 study of New York City's first low-income co-ops, *Self Help in the Inner City*.

8. Whereas Carolyn and LouAnn tried to do a little bit of bookkeeping each night, Anne Marie seemed to have an easier time integrating the work into her life. Some of that may be attributed to the more flexible jobs outside the building that Anne Marie had. She was studying to be an opera singer, and earned money as a governess; from time to time her father supported her studies. At other times, she had reduced her monthly rent by renting out rooms in her apartment. LouAnn in contrast worked at a nursing home all day, then had to combine her responsibilities as a wife and officer into the remaining evening hours of the day. Whereas the elderly black women spoke of being exhausted and having to do things the city's way, younger people did not. Anne Marie's bookkeeping schedule was facilitated by adjusting her singing practice accordingly.

Michael Stansky, the current building manager in Anne Marie's building, answered in a similar way. A musician, his building work varied from day to day. He arranged the twenty hours of work over the week. He and Anne Marie also shared a more casual way of assessing the building's workload. Although he was overwhelmed with his managerial duties the first week he began that job, the situation changed afterwards. Part of their assessment would seem to flow more naturally from people whose upbringing was possibly less chaotic and somewhat more privileged, and whose personal histories included relatives who might be more likely to rehabilitate old buildings. They integrated the building work into their own lives, in much the same way as the black men and women leaders did, but with what seemed like considerably less hassle.

9. This quotation reports the tenant leaders' perceptions. In fact, the landlord had no legal right to dispose of his building when it was in tax arrears if the city had already taken it over. If the arrangement was made prior to the city taking possession, the new owners, that is the tenants, would have had to pay back taxes owed as well as formally arrange for the transfer of title.

10. This was expressed by Brian Sullivan, Robert Schur, Howard Burchman and Meadows/Woll, "Analysis and Assessment of the Alternative Management Programs for New York City's In Rem Properties." The authors wrote that the city was so unprepared for the onslaught of abandoned properties that it was looking for ways in which to reduce their inventory.

11. This theme emerged in the predominantly white and Hispanic buildings also.

Yet the kind of family that was meant seemed to vary with ethnicity, just as blood related families tend to differ in different subcultures. Tenants in the white buildings were younger and saw their ties as close, but they did not use the phrase "like a family" to the same extent. Hispanic tenants however did often refer to relations in the building as similar to familial ties. For at least some male leaders the building was like a patriarchal family. One leader described the way in which the building was like a family as follows:

"When the father gives an order you got to listen to the father. If there is something that you go to ask to the father, why then everybody listens. That's why everybody gets together and explains to them what is going to happen if we will buy the building. I explained to them too what is going to happen if we don't buy the building. That's why we got to agree on this and it is better that we buy our building because we could lose our house. That's why we have it exactly the way it is now."

He then said he didn't really know who the father was, that it was just an example. However, the majority of his comments suggested he felt both the responsibility and the authority to act as father of the family. His descriptions of frequent parties and get-togethers also had the tone of an account of family parties. Another Hispanic male leader spoke of the burdens he felt as head of the co-op, saying he had never expected to "be a landlord." He also went on to explain that most of the women in the co-op were not "prepared" to be leaders. He stated that he didn't know if they had the capacity, but they just didn't have the education. Again, the paternalistic theme was clear.

A leader in another Hispanic building, Mr. Rameros, responded in a somewhat similar tone.

"We got so many women involved in the matters of the building, but no one wants to get involved directly on the Board of Directors. . . . They are welcome but I'm trying to say this. Many are women involved with other problems but no one wants to be on the board."

It may be that the reason for that is found in an older woman's remarks. In front of the male leader, she said:

"When I went to the meeting, Mr. Rameros talked, talked, talked, said everything and I said nothing. Mr. Rameros explained this, and explained that, said this this way, and the other way. Mr. Rameros explained everything, but anyway the people are happy."

There may also be other reasons. Rameros thought that many of the men in the building work in taxis during the night, and that the women are taking care of the children. Nonetheless, more women than men show up for the meetings.

In the small 8-unit building over a pharmacy, which Carlos organized, seven of the eight co-operators were from Santo Domingo and the eighth from Nicaragua. For one woman who was going to be 50 when we interviewed her, suffers from heart disease, and has had to quit working, the building functions like a family. While we were there, people were coming in and out of her apartment. She told us that she never locked her door during the day. The only time she locked it was when she went to bed at ten o'clock. Her 23-year-old son lives with her. If she needs help from anyone else, she can knock on the floor or the wall and someone comes to help.

12. See May Engler and Roberta R. Spohn, "The Elderly in New York City: Demographic Characteristics," pp. 65–66:

"Since 1972 New York City has attempted to protect the elderly from increases in rent through the Senior Citizen Rent Increase Exemption Program. In 1983, 71,330 renter households 62 years or older paid no rent increases if their income was $8,000 or less after taxes and their rent was one-third or more of their income. The program cost the city $44.9 million in lost real-estate taxes in 1982. While the program protects aged renters from increases, it does not reduce their rent to one-third of income. If they are paying 40 or 50 percent of income prior to eligibility for the program, they will continue to pay the same high proportion for rent. Those with low income, therefore, require a Section 8-type subsidy where the maximum rent would be no more than 30 percent of income. The Rent Increase Exemption Program has protected the elderly from subsistence living during these years of inflation, but it is no substitute for an expanded, federally supported rent subsidy program which would limit rents to no more than one-third of income."

13. There are several buildings where first floor residents are referred to as "watchers." This occurred in buildings regardless of their racial and ethnic make-up.

14. Although Rameros had only lived in his building for about three years when he was interviewed, and did not have a longtime history of neighborliness, he described a benevolent policy regarding late rent payments. Perhaps he even had his own situation in mind when he was disabled in a work related injury.

"If for example, a husband is ill and can't work, and they come to him and they speak to him and they can't pay the rent for two or three months because he is in the hospital or whatever, they work out an arrangement where they pay a little bit at a time and perhaps pay up those three months rent loss over eight months. But they have to come to him and make an arrangement and they have to pay. They have to pay some amount to show good faith, that it isn't a matter of just not wanting to pay rent, but there's a real situation there that causes them to at this point not to be able to pay."

He reported that he had made arrangements like these with tenants in three or four apartments, and that it was working out well:

"There was a time when they couldn't pay, but now they are caught up, and the landlord wouldn't have allowed something like that. Their landlord would have put them in the streets."

15. In the 25-unit building near Columbia University, Martin Kelly expressed a desire to start activities that would repay the community for its support of the tenants' efforts. He wanted the building to open a tool co-op.

"I keep badgering them about taking a percentage of the income and putting it aside, and they keep saying, yeah, yeah, yeah, yeah, yeah, yeah, we are going to do it."

Martin thought it would be a service offered through the churches. When asked about why one should be started, he said:

"I think it's important that we do it because we've got a lot of help from the community. You know, we didn't get monetary help but we got a lot of support from the community, a lot. Even in some cases positive feedback, but also we knew and we still know that if it had come to a knock down, drag-out fight in any one of the stages that we went through that the various tenants' organizations would have common cause with us and come down and fight with us."

16. *Marie Laureano, the Tri-United Tenants' Association, Ruth Skinner and Rose Reves* v. *Edward I. Koch, as Mayor of the City of New York, et al.*, Index No. 12629/82, #103 of 7/23/82.

Following Laureano, during a three-year period when the lawsuit was pending and a compromise plan was being worked out where the city would receive 40 percent of the share of any profit realized, Alternative Management sold 77 buildings a year. Since 1981, 502 buildings with 13,110 apartments were sold, three-quarters of which were to cooperative corporations.

17. Anne Marie, the white female leader in the building near Columbia University, shared some of Louise's feelings and, spoke positively of what she was learning:

"There's a certain amount of exactness involved. I like the treasury [her role as treasurer] because I wanted to be treasurer because I wanted to learn about money and bookkeeping and paying bills and that sort of, the exact thing I have to do. Whereas Terry [the president] had to make the phone calls and do the political stuff and write letters and get grants and get the, buying the building which I always thought was more difficult, nebulous you know, where she found that exciting. But I like just having to collect the rent, fill out the books, you know, do that."

18. When we knocked at her door, she was in the midst of looking through the Yellow Pages to find a door supplier. This was similar to the interview with Mrs. Michael who had been up in the very early hours attending to a broken boiler and was simultaneously interviewing boiler repairmen as we interviewed her. In the co-op tenanted primarily by whites, a board member described ongoing relations with contractors which were similar in all the buildings.

"Unless you're here breathing over contractors' necks they don't do jobs right at all. So we learned a really stiff penalty because we had a man who was doing the roof walk out on us after only 40 percent was done. We paid him pretty close to 80 percent. So we learned. We learned not to give out. . . . Now a third at the beginning, a third after half is done, and a third after it's all done."

19. In analyzing tenants' responses in one of the predominantly white buildings, it became clear that the need for low rents was often tied to careers. Many of the people in leadership positions were young musicians. When asked what was the relationship between your career and the building, the 23-year-old building manager, Michael Stansky, responded:

"This building is the center of my life at the present time. If I lived somewhere else and had to pay more rent and didn't have the security of knowing that I'd never be kicked out, and that if worse came to worse I could make some money off the apartment, I'd probably be typing for some company just to get by. Actually, that type of work goes against the grain, and I would probably have to move out of New York and look for an orchestra job. If it weren't for this apartment, I probably wouldn't even be here. It's so great for me because what I really want to do is to be creative and do something unique. . . . That fact that I have this apartment, that the rent will stay low, that I can't be kicked out really enables me to do what I want. That's why this building is the most important thing that has happened to me in the last couple of years."

20. Kolodny, assisted by Marjorie Gellerman, *Self Help in the Inner City;* Lawson, ed., with Mark Naison, *The Tenant Movement in New York City, 1904–1984.*

4. STRUGGLING CO-OPS

1. Many Hispanic tenants we interviewed also described physical disabilities and chronic illnesses that prevented them from working in paying jobs.

2. All four of the predominantly Hispanic tenanted buildings had also reached a serious level of physical deterioration prior to co-oping. Tenants described holes in their walls and ceilings, no services, rats, and other signs of landlord negligence.

3. Mrs. Oilers' building, like some others, had commercial uses on the ground or first floor. Income from these uses were helpful in reducing the amount of maintenance and operating costs. Some commercial uses seemed more prosperous than others. An example of what seemed like a thriving moving company was located in the predominantly white building near Columbia University. In many ways, the commercial use there is an example of how activities in the building can be expanded into the neighborhood, creating resources, similar to the hopes that Connie has for her building. According to a white female leader, the moving company was a family business, and employed one of the other leaders in the building. In addition, the moving company had begun to fix up the storefront. Because it was open on Sundays she also thought it made the building much safer.

4. This was the one case among black respondents where we did not interview in the building. Fuller was no longer living in the building. We felt his story, beginning with the fact that he had deliberately moved into the building in order to organize it, was worth telling. In a related way, Stephen E. Barton lived in a city-owned building that became part of an urban homesteading program and the subject of an analysis by him. While we do not know whether Barton moved in with the explicit idea of testing theory, he became co-chair of the Tenants' Union, an organization of squatters and original tenants whose efforts, Barton wrote, saved two buildings in 1975. Subsequently Barton wrote, "The Urban Housing Problem: Marxist Theory and Community Organizing," *The Review of Radical Political Economics* (Winter 1977), 9:16–30. Barton distinguished between a "community economy" and a "domestic economy." The former extended beyond individual or family activities to involve more substantial numbers of people. (pp. 24–25).

5. Other tenants believed that the officers used some building funds for the bathroom renovations, thus leading to a strain in tenant relationships.

6. City documents were contradictory for this building. One city record listed items contracted for and totaled to an expenditure of about $43,000. We reported

the higher figure in the text, since, in comparison to rehab costs in other buildings, it appears the more accurate figure.

7. All the buildings studied entered DAMP programs in their early days. As programs developed, the procedures for obtaining Section 8 for tenants were improved. In later buildings, most eligible tenants were promptly certified.

5. RENTERS AND ABANDONMENT

1. The only exception occurred in a building with over 100 units. None of the co-ops were that large. City records confirm that the average co-op size is smaller than that of rental buildings. Here, size might have been a negative factor on par with absence of adequate technical assistance.

2. In the predominantly white building near Columbia University, Martin Kelly, a former manager, said one of his "great headaches" was the plumbing and heating systems.

"There was steam and hot water in various apartments like full force . . . in fact, I took over in January of 1981. [it] was one of the coldest stretches that we've ever had in New York; that was the freeze out. You can imagine trying to get a hold of a plumber during that unbelievable [period] and to get him to come to a building. No, I don't own the building, I'm just the court appointed manager to get a plumber up to that building to do repair work in the middle of January, 1981, in the coldest time the city has ever had. It was really very difficult. Again, I went down and sold somebody on coming up and we paid him very well too, but we just had a lot of . . . a tremendous amount of leakage from the steam system, and the hot water system."

3. All of the co-ops with predominantly Hispanic tenants had complex relationships with technical assistance groups and other institutions. Two also had experienced significant tenant conflict. One building on West 104th Street became a cooperative through the intervention of a local development corporation. This was the only building we studied that went from management by a community organization to cooperative ownership by its tenants. Another building on West 139th Street had been owned by a church. The church attempted to evict the tenants to pursue a gut rehabilitation development approach. This initiated a complex series of battles among local politicians and organizations as well as a private developer. UHAB staff played a critical role in helping the building's leaders reach their goal of cooperative ownership. In a third building, internal conflicts threatened the effectiveness of the tenants' association to the point that the city was about to revoke the tenant interim lease. Again, assistance from UHAB staff allowed a more effective and supported leadership to emerge.

4. It was clear from her discussion that she was referring to condominiums and cooperatives on the open market, and not the $250 required if tenants co-op city-owned buildings.

5. Findings from an interview in a third POMP building were so similar to these two buildings that we have not used quotes to further illustrate our points.

6. We have been told by people in DAMP that in more recent years, some private landlords have encouraged tenants' associations.

6. ORGANIZATIONS: A SUPPORTIVE INFRASTRUCTURE

1. Ronald Lawson, ed., with Mark Naison, *The Tenant Movement in New York City, 1904–1984.*

2. See Samuel M. Ehrenthal, "New York City's Labor Force." Ehrenthal also reported a high dropout rate (41 percent) in the city schools in the 1981–82 school year, high percentages who did not finish high school (in 1980, 29 percent of those 18 to 24 years of age; 40 percent of those 25 and over).

3. Even if Mayor Koch is successful in delivering 252,000 units of new, pre-served, and upgraded housing and 2,000 spaces for permanent or temporary housing for the homeless, it is not enough and it is late. Cuts in federal housing programs over the past five years have placed low-income people in a more precarious position than before. For all of these reasons, the New York based Citizens' Housing and Planning Council's 1985 report summarized the general consensus in New York City; there was a need for about 600,000 units, 200,000 new, and substantially rehabilitated, and 400,000 moderately rehabilitated units. In addition, 273,000 households eligible for but not receiving Section 8 rental assistance were paying over 35 percent of their income for rent. Also see Michael deCourcy Hinds, "252,000 Housing Units: Can Koch Do It?"

4. Robert Schur and Virginia Sherry, *The Neighborhood Housing Movement.*

5. In 1974, the Association of Neighborhood and Housing Development (ANHD), was started in response to foundations suggesting to community groups soliciting money, that they consolidate their requests. Existing neighborhood groups joined together, and over a ten-year period, the organization shifted its emphasis from advocacy to technical assistance to coalition politics, all intended to achieve gains for low-income tenants. At all times ANHD was a source of assistance to tenants, either providing less-expensive insurance, or fuel oil, or lobbying for protection of city programs and federal aid. This was most clearly seen in the struggle to save the $250 selling price per unit of co-oped housing when Mayor Koch wanted to sell buildings in the gentrifying Clinton area in Manhattan at market prices of $9,000 to $13,500. Although no one we interviewed mentioned ANHD specifically, it is clear that all tenants in city-owned buildings benefited in some ways from their activities.

6. A former organizer for UHAB was critical of its emphasis on helping co-ops deal with daily crises and the requirements of gaining control of and managing the building. In her opinion they seemed not to have time, nor a policy directed toward educating people in the meaning of cooperation, nor in the development of group solidarity and leadership. In a follow-up interview with Mrs. Baylor after their building went back into Central Management, she made similar remarks. She told us that if there was one message to convey about her building she hoped it would be a plea for the kind of in-depth education that struggling co-ops needed.

7. At least one study has pointed out that the boards whose areas included

people with higher education and skills were less in need of technical assistance than boards which lacked such people.

8. See, for example, Denise Griffin Fairchild, "Social Activism Among Working Black Mothers" (Ph.D. dissertation, UCLA, 1987). Fairchild sampled 370 black families using market and non-market child care agencies in the Los Angeles region. She concludes the black women do participate in civic organizations. Forty-five percent of her sample participated, including women who were single parents and those with low to moderate income, with a mean educational level of 13 years. Church participation was particularly high: "Black women were more inclined to participate in religious organizations (75%), as opposed to any other type of informal and formal organization" (p. 180). In line with our argument, Fairchild goes on to say: "Women tended to join groups that were aligned with their family responsibilities. While only one-third of the sample were able to engage in parent-child activities sponsored by their child care agency, close to half of that group did join. This compared to a 25% participation rate for other informal and formal groups and associations" (p. 180).

9. In tenant cooperatives, our introduction to leaders was through the auspices of Theresa Kilbane and Ed Moses, at the time two of UHAB's most highly regarded organizers. Tenants' enthusiasm for UHAB always appeared to be authentic, a genuine gratification that the organization had been there to assist them, particularly with the city's bookkeeping requirements.

10. See Judah Gribetz and Frank Grad, "Housing Code Enforcement: Sanctions and Remedies"; Nathan H. Mann, ed., "Receivership of Problem Buildings in New York City"; "Symposium: Code Enforcement: Issues and Answers for the '80s"; Jacqueline Leavitt, "Resident and Community Receivership Programs in New York City," pp. 97–107; David Listokin, Lisabeth Alleweit, and James J. Németh, *Housing Receivership and Self-Help Neighborhood Revitalization.*

11. Anthony DePalma, "New York Plays Reluctant Landlord." When interviewed by DePalma, Paul A. Crotty, the then Housing Preservation and Development Commissioner, said: "We'll be in the business of providing housing for low-income New Yorkers for the forseeable future. . . . It's not a business we like to be in, but there is no alternative."

DePalma comments: "Mr. Crotty is the first housing commissioner to acknowledge publicly what housing advocates have long considered an inescapable truth: most buildings in central management have no future but in city ownership. Previous administrations have maintained that despite the huge gap between revenues and operating costs for these buildings, someday they would be returned to the private sector."

The current thinking about expenditures in Central Management buildings has changed. DePalma writes: "The implications of the agency's permanent role in housing the poor already have been felt in adjustments to the enormous machinery required to run almost 40,000 dilapidated apartments. This year, the aged dwellings will cost the city $180 million, including $25 million for capital improvements that are part of a 10-year plan to pump $250 million into major systems replacements in the city's second-hand housing.

"Previously such improvements were made only when they were essential to keep a building open. By spending money to replace roofs, plumbing, windows and electrical systems, officials hope to reduce operating expenses that they concede are 150 percent higher than private industry standards."

In an interesting turn of events, Joseph Schuldiner, formerly the deputy commissioner for both Central and Alternative Management, has become the general manager of the New York City Housing Authority. DePalma writes:

"Housing advocates have suggested that the Office of Property Management is not the proper agency to permanently run in-rem housing and that another, independent agency dedicated to the task would be better. Their initial target was the New York Housing Authority, which has 50 years' experience in housing low-income people. But authority officials have backed off from the suggestion.

"Our style of management wouldn't work with in-rem housing," said Joseph Schuldiner. . . . He pointed out the contrast between the two systems. While the Housing Authority has four times as many apartments as central management, they are contained in only 3,000 buildings. And those buildings, all constructed by the authority itself, are clustered in just 300 sites, which favors a concentrated management style. . . .

"On the other hand, the 36,954 city-managed apartments are contained in some 4,180 buildings in 4,180 sites scattered all over the city. The Office of Property Management has no say over which buildings it takes, where they are located or who will live in them. "You almost need to have the antithesis of an authority for that," Mr. Schuldiner said. "It's dispersed control, not central."

12. For a discussion of the earliest informal cooperatives, see Robert Kolodny, assisted by Marjorie Gellerman, *Self Help in the Inner City.*

13. Joanne M. Martin and Elmer P. Martin, *The Helping Tradition in the Black Family and Community.*

14. See Kenneth Auletta, *The Streets Were Paved With Gold;* William K. Tabb, *The Long Default: New York City and the Urban Fiscal Crisis.*

15. Tenant leaders in the building near Columbia University appeared confident of their abilities to find other programs. Anne Marie, the white female leader, said: "We had a lot of knowledgeable people who, one of the presidents, the older president who's now vice-president, works for the city so he's up on a lot of the stuff. We got the manuals and we were really interested in trying to work out the best system. So if it wasn't TIL it probably would of been some other type of program. . . . We had a person who through another relative or something had a lawyer that helped us get the building."

Another tenant was involved with the local Morningside Tenants Federation. However, it should be emphasized that these tenants did not always seem better able to negotiate with the city; they were rife with dissension at one point just before buying the building and wondering if the city was going to sell to them. They were anxious about whether Columbia University was going to intervene or whether "someone's just gonna come up and slap us with $10,000 an apartment. We had a lot of grief, a lot of anticipating these problems."

16. The Center on Budget and Policy Priorities has documented the impact of proposed spending cuts from 1987 to 1992. In Fiscal Year 1988, one-third of the

President's proposed spending cuts were to come from programs for the poor. Among those that would be cut the most are: medicaid, student financial assistance, low-income energy assistance, low-income housing, Indian health programs. Fourteen other programs would be cut altogether, including temporary emergency food assistance, legal services, work incentive training programs, farm labor housing, very low-income housing repair grants, rural housing loan programs, and the community services block grant (the latter to be phased out over four years.)

17. One criticism of the Alternative Management programs concerns the amount of work tenants are left with after they have bought the building. Tenants in predominantly white buildings also faced this issue. Michael Stansky told us of the woes of the $10,000 roof. The tenants weren't sure they would go co-op, and after deciding to replace the roof, it was installed improperly. The tenants had developed a priority list, and the roof was not prominent.

"We plan to install new windows, not just because of the noise, but mostly for preserving heat, since we spend a lot of money on heat. We also plan to put in new bathrooms, especially new pipes and fixtures. A lot of the bathroom floors are in disrepair, with a lot of leaks, which is a big hazard. We also need to put in new wiring from the basement to the apartments so that tenants can rewire their apartments. The wiring in the basement is very shoddy. Other things that we have to do include fixing the drains in the basement, repaving the backyard and basement and completing the installment of new front doors. My door can easily be kicked in, and it's unnerving. We see these things as priorities. Beyond that, we need new air valves for the radiators so that the heat will flow more evenly in the apartments, as well as a hot water heater for the summer months so that we don't have to use the boiler."

They had applied for an Article 8A loan from the city which would cover the costs, but they were being "hassled" by bureaucrats.

"I walked into the office to ask about the loan, and the first words out of the guy's mouth were, "You people go to college, and you come here telling me you're low income." Well, how about the fact that I'm a musician, that there is a senior citizen, that there are people who are unemployed, that most of us are just getting by. I guess we were dressed too well to need any assistance. The city told us that they would help us get the loan because we didn't take any of their money under the TIL program. We're still hopeful but that might be a bit of a snag."

Stansky's thoughts about the use of a repaired roof echo those of Mrs. Michael in the building on Convent Avenue:

"If we don't get help with the loan, the improvements that we have in mind might take a longer period of time. We really want to get the roof fixed. I used to go up on the roof a lot. You could see the sunset; you could get a tan during the summer; you could just go up with some friends at night; you could make it look nice with plants. The roof might not get done for ten years. There are so many things we could do with a new roof."

18. See an early assessment of the need in Daniel Bayer, "Tenant and Community Ownership: A Proposed Policy" (New York: Task Force on City-Owned Property, 1982); and a later evaluation, Brian Sullivan, Robert Schur, Howard

Burchman and Meadows/Woll, "Analysis and Assessment of the Alternative Management Program for New York City's In Rem Properties."

7. GENDER AND RACE

1. Michael A. Stegman, with Doug Hillstrom, *Housing in New York: Study of a City, 1984,* pp. 219–236.

2. Robert Kolodny, assisted by Marjorie Gellerman, *Self Help in the Inner City.*

3. We drew from Carol Stack, *All Our Kin;* Carol Gilligan, *In A Different Voice: Psychological Theory and Women's Development;* Nel Noddings, *Caring: A Feminine Approach to Ethics and Moral Education;* Mary Field Belenky, Blythe McVicker Clinch, Nancy Rule Goldberger, and Jill Mattuck Tarule, *Women's Ways of Knowing: The Development of Self, Voice, and Mind.*

4. See Barbara Myerhoff, *Number Our Days.*

5. See for example Carol Stack, *All Our Kin;* Jacqueline Jones, *Labor of Love, Labor of Sorrow;* Bonnie Dill, "The Dialectics of Black Womanhood," *SIGNS: A Journal of Women and Culture* (Spring 1979), 4:543–555.

6. Of two cooperative buildings with white tenants, one had male leadership and the other, after first having an all-male board, then an all-women board, had a mixed board. Not enough is known of the first building to comment on gender issues. In the second building, according to Anne Marie, currently the treasurer, there were some differences in positions taken by each of the boards. When asked to explain this, she responded:

"The reason why I'm laughing is because with the all-male board we had a lot of personal problems. There was supposedly this, actually two sides as to how to run a building. Some people wanted to get management outside the building and some people, we should keep the management inside the building. . . . It's a long involved political kind of thing and it was just a, some people went into this meeting one day and suggested this plan. It was talked about and then voted down and the people who had suggested it, got up and walked out and vowed never to come back. And so, and these were all men that this happened between and they just didn't deal with the problems. So when we became the board members, there are just three of us . . . not only were we the board members but we also shared the management fee, which was just, was a third of seven percent. So we were slapped all of a sudden with this problem cause it still existed.

The three of us tried very hard to deal with it because we wanted everybody to get along and we wanted it to work out. We talked to this group of people, we met with them and we decided basically that they were causing more problems than it was worth so we tried to ignore it. . . . So we kept going to the old board and asking for advice and they were very nice because they realized what they had left us with. They always, a few of them always said they wanted to get off the board because when they came into the building they wanted to feel like they were coming home and not into this den of lions. So we were just able to handle them a little bit better I feel."

One of the frankest discussions around gender issues came from Monica, a woman of Hispanic origin in her thirties who was completing an undergraduate degree in psychology. She was an officer in a 49-unit building on West 106th Street. She related how Latin men "they tend to think that they are tough, and this goes, this goes. It's more like a dictatorship, you know. They think whatever they say has to go for some reason." She used the word persevering to distinguish between women and men who act "so strong and so macho." Women, she said: "don't intend to fight. We know that we can't punch anyone and if we punch a man we are going to lose because they are much stronger. But I think we are a lot more persevering than men. We tend to struggle more and keep at it. It may take us a long time but we are going to get there."

At the time of the interview, the president of the building was a man, but the other officers were women. When asked how the men felt about women being in control, she responded:

"The others will say [to the male president], "What is happening to you? Are you letting all the women make the decisions for you?" That type of thing. So sometimes the guy feels he doesn't know what to do. He thinks maybe they are just trying to get me upset. He really doesn't know what to do because sometimes he is pressured."

7. In one of the Hispanic buildings, Mr. Rameros, unlike Jack Fuller, had not moved in specifically to organize, and unlike Mr. Bridely and Mr. Williams, had not lived in the building for a long time. In October 1980, he moved into a building in the West 130s when he and his wife emigrated from Santo Domingo. He was aware of the building because a relative had lived there once but did not find out about the tenants' association until after he arrived. Two months after he moved in, Rameros was elected the new president. Since then, he suffered a work-related disability and the building activities clearly filled a gap in his life.

8. One of the black elderly women had been accepted into a senior citizen project but her grandson lived with her and would not be allowed into the building. She had turned the opportunity down. Similarly, one 74-year-old woman of Hispanic origin explained why she preferred her apartment to a public housing project.

"Well, before I was looking for three rooms for myself because I was living here alone, you know that. I made a couple of applications for moving to a city house or something like that, but they give me only one room. But I don't want one room. I wanted three rooms because I can't do nothing with one room. I have to find room here. My children come here, and they stay here on the weekends. I have my kid in Puerto Rico, and they come from there to visit me with their family and stay here with me. In one room, I can't put my children."

9. Ronald Lawson and Stephen E. Barton, "Sex Roles and Social Movements: A Case Study of the Tenant Movement in New York City," *SIGNS: A Journal of Women and Culture* (Winter 1980), 6:230–247.

10. The outpouring of attention to the building had a number of positive results. Non-leaders recognized in interviews, if not sufficiently in their contacts with the leaders, the commitment leaders had to the building. Sometimes their expectations for the future of the building and even their current evaluations seemed based as much on this perception as on the building's apparent physical condition. Con-

versely, renters sometimes complained about the conditions of buildings that were in the experience of interviewees among the better ones in the study. The immediate attention to crises and to small details may, however, have affected the overall level of physical conditions of buildings. The survey data of 131 respondents did reveal higher ratings of physical conditions in co-ops. Data on conditions identified three years before our study confirmed the finding that tenants were more likely to be satisfied in co-ops.

11. Brenda Doyle Farge, "Women, Leadership and Co-op Housing: Some Questions."

12. Gerda R. Wekerle and Joan Simon, "Housing Alternatives for Women: the Canadian Experience.

13. Ibid., p. 13.

14. Karen K. Russell, "Growing Up with Privilege and Prejudice."

15. Joanne M. Martin and Elmer P. Martin, *The Helping Tradition in the Black Family and Community.*

16. Jacqueline Jones, *Labor of Love, Labor of Sorrow,* p. 188; Jeanne L. Noble, *Beautiful, also are the souls of my black sisters;* Paula Giddings, *When and Where I Enter . . . : The Impact of Black Women on Race and Sex in America;* Joyce A. Ladner, "Teenage Pregnancy: The Implications for Black Americans"; Bettina Aptheker, *Women's Legacy: Essays on Race, Sex, and Class in American History.*

17. Bernice Johnson Reagon, "My Black Mothers and Sisters or On Beginning a Cultural Autobiography," pp. 82–83.

18. This issues crosses race and ethnicity lines. One of the buildings in our pilot study had become a cooperative prior to the formation of the Tenant Interim Lease program. It was a 6-story tenement on the Lower East Side of Manhattan. The only child of a white couple was not allowed to play in Sara Delano Roosevelt Park, across from the building where they lived. The park was a notorious drug center. The halls and stairwell, as well as the apartments of friends of his parents, was his "at home" play area.

19. Disposition of vacant buildings heated up during 1986–1987. A request for proposals was issued through the Housing Preservation and Development agency. Low-income housing advocates have argued that the proposed disposition will favor moderate income people at the expense of low income.

20. The selling price of limited equity cooperatives would prohibit prices as high as $65,000, which could only attract higher income people.

21. See, for example, Barbara B. Reagan, ed., *Census Bureau Conference on Issues in Federal Statistical Needs Relating to Women.*

8. GETTING OLD

1. Robert Kolodny, assisted by Marjorie Gellerman, *Self Help in the Inner City;* Ronald Lawson, *Owners of Last Resort: An Assessment of New York City Early Low Income Housing Cooperatives* (New York: New York City Department of Hous-

ing Preservation and Development, Office of Program and Management Analysis, 1983).

2. Kyriakos S. Markides and Charles H. Mindel, *Aging and Ethnicity* (Beverly Hills, Calif. Sage, 1987); Maurice Jackson and James L. Wood, "The Black Aged," in *Aging in America: Implications for the Black Aged,* No. 5 (Washington, D.C., National Council on Aging, 1976).

3. Jacquelyn J. Jackson, "The Plight of Older Black Women in the United States," *The Black Scholar* (April 1976), 7:47–55.

4. Karen C. Holden, Richard V. Burkhouser, and Daniel A. Myers, "Income Transitions at Older Stages of Life: The Dynamics of Poverty," *The Gerontologist* (1986), 26:292–297.

5. Jackson, "The Plight of Older Black Women in the United States," p. 48.

6. Jackson writes of organizational proliferation that accompanies what she considers artificial categories that dissect older black women, e.g., by race, sex, age, health and income levels, and location. She believes that the older black woman is bombarded by organizations which target blacks, the elderly, or women, or partisans of special interests such as better consumerism in health, welfare rights, or disease prevention and detection. Jackson urges joining more politically directed organizations such as the National Association for the Advancement of Colored People (NAACP), a "major organization which can speak and work effectively for the rights of blacks" (p. 55). In our last chapter, we address how activities around co-oping can be linked to greater power at the city and national level.

7. W. C. Swanson and C. L. Harter, "How do Elderly Blacks Cope in New Orleans?" *Aging and Human Development* (1971), 2:210–216.

8. For an essay on the connections between black women, children, and culture, see "Bernice Johnson Reagon, "My Black Mothers and Sisters or On Beginning a Cultural Autobiography," *Feminist Studies* (Spring 1982), 8:81–96.

9. Jackson and Wood.

10. See Nancy W. Sheehan, "Informal Support Among the Elderly in Public Senior Housing," *The Gerontologist* (1986), 26:171–175. In her study Sheehan found that it was necessary to distinguish between impaired elderly and healthier, more independent elderly. One reason why a frail elderly person may withdraw from social relationships is because of a perception that she is losing her sense of independence: Sheehan identified three ways in which the sense of independence is maintained—social distancing, denying the need, and obtaining support from elsewhere, i.e., families or social service agencies. Healthier and more independent elderly "also perceived the need to limit their involvement with frailer tenants, and did so in the following ways—"1) acknowledging the need to conserve their own energy and stamina, 2) limiting involvement to only mutually supportive relationships." Exceptions to this general pattern were found "in the emergence of a neighbor who is a 'high helper' of less fortunate neighbors" (p. 174). Sheehan generalized that:

"While there was little evidence of extensive informal support provided to the more impaired neighbors, most tenants insisted that they did provide their neighbors with a basic source of support. . . . In the words of Mrs. W., "We all watch out for one another." Tenants also expressed feelings of security knowing that someone was there should an emergency arise. Keeping track of one another may be a way of providing support to one's neighbors while minimizing the social costs involved in certain ongoing relationships" (p. 175).

We would characterize the tenant leaders we interviewed as "high helpers." But what also was evident in our interviews was that in the tenant co-ops in particular, the commonality of shared landlord abandonment created at the least the same type of "feelings of security knowing someone was there should an emergency arise." As the elderly tenants age in place, further research should look to issues about social relations among the frail elderly.

11. Anne Marie, in the building near Columbia University, spoke of the sense of security before and after co-oping. Her account was also reminiscent of the feelings of Ethel, the former dancer. Anne Marie felt that "getting into my door downstairs was the first step and then getting up into here was the second step." When asked about how she felt after the tenants co-oped, she answered with a mixture of feelings. "Recently since we bought and since the building's been much safer I felt, once I got through the front door I felt pretty safe." She continued, recalling the muggings of roommates by the mailboxes and on nearby streets. Probed further about why she thought buying the building led to more security, she responded in more social terms.

"Well, I don't know. I guess maybe it hasn't. It's just that as we as a group have gotten to know each other, all the tenants are pretty close, they're pretty protective. But there have been, there was a time when four apartments got robbed in the same day so there are things that happened. Not since we bought but I'm sure things will happen; you just have to be careful, just your bad luck. But we have a super that hangs out on the corner and the Triangle Moving Company is there and we have one senior citizen that lives in the basement. There's an apartment in the basement and he has a tendency to hang out cause he knows the neighborhood. So it gives it a feeling of security."

12. The deaths of older people provided an opportunity to tenant a building with younger ones. In the predominantly white building near Columbia University, the informal network of students, musicians, and visual artists led to available apartments being tenanted by people similar to themselves. In one case, a vacancy occurred because an elderly woman was taken forceably from her apartment by her daughter; in another the tragic murder of an old blind woman who ran a very small newspaper and magazine store across from the building resulted in a vacancy.

13. There are other examples of organizing around housing that began with children's needs, and then reached out to their parents. In Jersey City, New Jersey, Robert Rigby, the head of their housing authority, began to restore services to tenants by handing out paint supplies to children and adults on each floor. The tenants could decide on and create their own hall mural. Similarly, the Upper Park Avenue Association in New York City, UPACA, started out with a white community organizer and two black residents, women, who developed a play area for the children. In Newark, New Jersey, where Leavitt worked on a community organizing project, play streets were an organizing device. In St. Louis, at Cochran

Gardens, obtaining facilities for children was also used as a strategy to organize the parents. Also see Ruth A. Brandwein, "Women and Community Organization," in Diane S. Burden and Naomi Gottlieb, eds., (New York: Tavistock, 1987). *The Woman Client: Providing Human Services in a Changing World*, Brandwein draws attention to neighborhood organizing and the particular roles women as community organizers can play.

"Women practitioners are important in community organization because of the areas of organizing which they can address. In such sensitive areas as child sexual abuse, wife battering, and teenage pregnancy it is obvious that the client system may be more open in developing relationships with women workers. Moreover, women workers are more likely to have experience from the clients' viewpoints which gives them greater credibility in organizing the client system to advocate for new policies or services. In other less obvious areas, the gender of the worker may also be a key. Neighborhood organizing often begins around issues pertaining to children—safe street crossings, recreation and day care facilities, after-school activities, and toxic wastes in the community. Because of the increase in single-parent families and the unfortunate continuation of traditional roles in two-parent families, mothers have primary responsiblity for children. Women workers therefore can often play a key role in such organizing" (p. 120).

14. The way in which the young and old can work together and why it was important was exemplified by John Paynes, the young man and a new father, in Mrs. Michael's building.

"I think you always have to incorporate youth in anything that you do cause you're not going to be around. When I say you, the older person, the person's not going to be around for always and if you want to have something ongoing, if you want to build an insititution or what have you, you need youth. You know you have to start educating the youth. Educating the younger people to what is happening out here. Give them the tools to work with and let them go out there and do what they have to do. You know if there's a void between the elder and the young, ok, the elderly and the young, once the elderly spills off what's going to happen to the young? Where do they go from? My feeling is why should they have to repeat what those who are before them have done? Why shouldn't there be just a smooth continuity? Anyway, you can get that, a merging of the two working together so it be a smooth flow, alright. I'm younger than some of the people in here. Ok, let's communicate, get the thing to go and I learn from them so when they go on I'll be the eldest person, than I can pass on to those coming in then. I can pass it on to my son in there. You know that's the only thing, only way it's going to develop."

15. The conjunction of these issues leads to what we call the community-household which is described further in chapter 9. It is of interest to note Hilda K. Ross' article, "The Neighborhood Family: Community Mental Health for the Elderly," *The Gerontologist* (1983), 23:243–247. Ross explains why her model was called the Neighborhood Family:

"(1) to enlist individuals from an area which they themselves defined psychologically as well as geographically, as their neighborhood, and (2) for the bonding values and relationships implied by the term 'family.' The latter term was chosen advisedly to counter the defensive wariness and social isolation among older people, particularly those living alone who have migrated and/or have lost their friendship networks and kinship base. The premise was that such older people might adopt a surrogate family of 'brothers and sisters' to replace the ties of mutual succorance and concern remembered within the biological family. Organization within a specific neighborhood ensured easy accessibility of a resource center and meeting place, common environmental problems, realistic boundaries for community action and a psychological 'home base' for supportive and outreach activities" (p. 243).

9. THE COMMUNITY-HOUSEHOLD MODEL

1. Julian Rappaport, "Terms of Empowerment/Exemplars of Prevention: Toward a Theory for Community Psychology" (Department of Psychology, University of Illinois), p. 3. Based on address delivered at the Annual Meeting of the American Psychological Association, Washington, D.C., (August 1986). See also Robert Fichter, John F. C. Turner, and Peter Grenell, "The Meaning of Autonomy," in John F. C. Turner and Robert Fichter, eds., *Freedom to Build: Dweller Control of the Housing Process* (New York: Macmillan, 1972):

"When dwellers control the major decisions and are free to make their own contributions in the design, construction, or management of their housing, both this process and the environment produced stimulate individual and social well-being" (p. 241).

2. Rappaport, "Terms of Empowerment/Exemplars of Prevention," p. 15.

3. Ibid., p. 38.

4. Ibid., p. 39.

5. Harry C. Boyte, *Community Is Possible: Repairing America's Roots.*

6. Ibid., p. 137.

7. Ibid., p. 155.

8. Carol Gilligan, *In A Different Voice: Psychological Theory and Women's Development.*

9. Nel Noddings, *Caring: A Feminine Approach to Ethics and Moral Education.*

10. Mary Field Belenky, Blythe McVicker Clinch, Nancy Rule Goldberger, and Jill Mattuck Tarule, *Women's Ways of Knowing: The Development of Self, Voice, and Mind.*

11. Throughout the literature we have reviewed runs a common thread: poor people survive despite their lack of command of economic resources, often by substituting domestically produced goods and services for those provided by the economy. In this process women as significant carriers of domestic tradition play a primary part. Networks of support and exchange are organized from the household outward. Experiences of the 1930s and managing during the Depression years provide examples of coping with poverty. See E. Wight Bakke, *Citizens Without Work: A Study of the Effects of Unemployment Upon the Workers' Social Relations and Practices* (New Haven: Yale University Press, 1940); Eleanor Roosevelt, *It's Up to the Women* (New York: Frederick A. Stokes, 1935); Ruth Milkman, "Women's

Work and Economic Crises: Some Lessons of the Great Depression," *Review of Radical Political Economics* (Spring 1976), 8:81–85; Susan Ware, *Holding Their Own: American Women in the 1930s* (Boston: Twayne, 1982). Also see Martin D. Lowenthal, "The Social Economy in Urban Working-Class Communities," for a review of postwar literature showing how the poor cope with poverty. For an analysis of Canadian housing that is in this vein, see Roger G. Krohn, Berkeley Fleming, and Marilyn Manzer, *The Other Economy: The Internal Logic of Local Rental Housing* (Montreal: Martin, 1977).

12. See Herbert G. Gutman, *The Black Family in Slavery and Freedom,* pp. 455–456; Eleanor H. Norton, "Restoring the Traditional Black Family"; John E. Jacob, "An Overview of Black America in 1985"; David Swinton, "Economic Status of Blacks 1985"; Barbara Ehrenreich, "Two, Three, Many Households."

Jacobs and Swinton document that the presence of two-parent stability, for blacks or whites, does not exclude the simultaneous occurrence of unemployment, teenage pregnancy, and the formation of female-headed households. Over 40 percent of black households are now headed by females, a figure which has been rising steadily since 1960. In 1982, almost 25 percent of all black births were to teenage women, 87 percent were out of wedlock, and 90 to 94 percent of the teen mothers kept the children. Black teenagers, men and women, are not finding jobs. John A. Jacob, one of the authors in the National Urban League report on blacks, wrote: "The attrition of black males from various causes from conception through adulthood finally results in an insufficient number of men who are willing and able to provide support for women and children in a family setting." Given these circumstances, options for a "normal" two-parent household are limited.

Even were teenage pregnancy reduced, and males employed, the income disparity between whites and blacks is too high to assume males could adequately support families by themselves. The median family income of blacks in 1984, low at $15,432, reflected a rise of $800 from 1982, but this was only $250 more from 1983. In constant dollars it was actually $540 less than at the beginning of 1980 and the start of the Reagan administration. In constant dollars, black family income was almost $2,500 less than in 1970. Median black family income was worst in the Mid-West and the South, reaching a high in the West of $19,209 and $16,326 in the East. As Barbara Ehrenreich caustically points out, it would take three black men per nuclear family to make about $26,500, the median family income.

13. Carol Stack's work *All Our Kin* has presented one of the best documentaries of a positive view about black families. Stack challenged the view that black families were matriarchal from the perspectives of blacks themselves. Rather the poor employment conditions of black men relative to women and the regulations surrounding welfare eligibility made conventional marriages untenable. Instead, complex, changing domestic networks served the functions of households. Such networks could encompass nearly ten separate houses sheltering three times as many households whose composition fluctuated. However, within a domestic network, the same people shared each other's lives and contributed financial support and care to the total group. Men participated in this sharing, providing money when they could, and care for women and children as relationships permitted. The eco-

nomic conditions of black men combined with discrimination made it particularly difficult for them to provide housing for their families. When a man can do this, he can also assume the traditional role of head of the household. When he cannot, he tends to become a resident in a home headed by a woman, even if he heads a family within the dwelling.

The responsibility women have for domestic life translates into a system in which older female kin tend to be the more stable occupants of a home, welcoming in, sometimes evicting, and often welcoming back again children, nieces and nephews, newly formed households of relatives and friends, and newly separated men, women, and their children. Women's roles as mothers and housekeepers seems to give them a claim on housing that men only have when they are able to contribute economically or possibly in the very rare instances in which they own their own homes.

14. If the environment started from this alternative perspective, it would look quite different. In Toronto, Women in/and Planning and an executive committee kept track of and/or met with 25 groups which were then classified into 9 groups: employed women, full-time homemakers, women in transition, immigrant women who belong to support groups, native women, young women, elderly women, disabled women, and sole support mothers. Four major issues were discussed: place, community, getting around, and finding understanding and support. The women focused on the pervasiveness of problems such as isolation, caused by distances and specialization in existing cities and suburbs. Under a "wouldn't it be nice" section they wondered how there could be more integration between work and home; how zoning could be used to support greater integration of uses with a range of services such as day care, a transition house, or shelter or emergency facility, integrated subsidized and non-subsidized units, schools, libraries and other services, always closer together; more pedestrian zones, community centers which went beyond recreation centers but were places "where you can drop in and participate and leave when you want to and it was an extension of your home," or where you "could drop in without getting babysitters first, and without being mistaken for prostitutes." They wanted a community where movies houses were better distributed and "there was some place—not someone's apartment—where we could sit down and have a coffee or just a place that we could take over for a while."

15. We consciously use household as the basic social unit, as opposed to family, as the latter term is fraught with ideological tension. Household is also used in urban planning but most often as a way to enumerate living arrangements, and living units, or apartments. There is a large literature in anthropology and a newer one in women's studies and feminist theory that distinguishes between the household and the family. For an anthropological approach, see, for example, Michelle Z. Rosaldo and Louise Lamphere, eds., *Women, Culture and Society* (Stanford, Calif.: Stanford University Press, 1974); Robert McC. Netting, Richard R. Wilk, and Eric J. Arnould, *Households: Comparative and Historical Studies of the Domestic Group* (Berkeley: University of California Press, 1984); Also Jane Fishburne Collier and Sylvia Junko Yanagisako, eds., *Gender and Kinship: Essays Toward a Unified*

Analysis (Stanford, Calif.: Stanford University Press, 1987). For a basic book that combines an interdisciplinary approach, see Amy Swerdlow, Renate Bridenthal, Joan Kelly, and Phyllis Vine, *Household and Kin: Families in Flux* (Old Westbury, N.Y.: Feminist Press, 1981.

16. Daniel Zarza and Harriet Cohen, *Loisiada: Strategies for Neighborhood Revitalization.*

17. Ibid., p. 92.

18. Dolores Hayden, "The American Sense of Place and the Politics of Space" (Paper presented at symposium, American Architecture: Tradition and Innovation, Columbia University, April 21–22, 1983).

19. Carol Felstein and Sydelle Knepper, "Housing Need and Housing Production in New York City" (Report prepared for Pratt Institute Center for Community and Environmental Development, November 1985), p. 30.

20. Ibid., p. 30.

21. Recently services have been provided to homeless families.

22. For a study that included how inner city elderly people in New York City relate to nonkin, see Marjorie H. Cantor, "Life Space and Social Support." There were 1,552 respondents interviewed in their homes for Cantor's study. Her observations of neighborhoods reflected a period in the city's history when abandonment had not yet taken its toll. She defined three levels of support: children, close friends or intimates, and neighbors. One of her conclusions was that the most important category of neighboring activities is emergency assistance or crisis intervention. She wrote:

"Two-thirds of those who knew neighbors well state that neighbors help them when they are ill, and that they help neighbors in turn. In addition, about 22 percent of the neighbors accompany respondents to the doctor or clinic, while almost one-fifth of the elderly escorted neighbors to medical services." [It should be noted that in these comparisons the same people are not necessarily involved.] (pp. 52–53)

Her findings also included the fact that friendship existed between the elderly and younger neighbors. The form it took was either sitting and talking, or visiting. A smaller but significant group had even closer relationships. She found that "28 percent eat together, 25 percent shop together, and 18 percent go to church or synagogue together."

23. In the co-op near Columbia University, various feelings about children were expressed by Anne Marie, the white female leader. In thinking of the future, she revealed a different and higher expectation about what was possible. She mused about wanting to have a family but thought the apartment was too small to have more than one child. (In commenting on the history of the building, she wondered who lived there "because the rooms are so tiny, especially the bedrooms.") She thought that maybe she would have a small house or another apartment somewhere else and sublet her current one. She was caught between thinking that she had worked so hard that she didn't want to simply give the apartment up but also thinking, "Well God, I might be here for the rest of my life. What my mother always says about her house out on Long Island. When she bought it, she never dreamed

that she'd live in it for thirty, forty years." In the same building, Joanne, the struggling black single parent, with two children in a smaller-sized apartment, also envisioned the possibility of moving but there was a difference.

"What this apartment means to me, I'll tell you. Having this apartment means security. Okay when I got this apartment, just getting the space before one 'corporates it was like half a roof over my head. But knowing that I have it and knowing that it's going to be mine, it's security. It's a place that my children, you understand, will always have it because I've already told them that if I have to I will find someplace else. When they are old enough, I would leave and they could have it, it's a home for them. It's security for them."

Martin Kelly, a young white man who was a former manager in the same building, offered a point of view that bore resemblances to both women's answers.

"As soon as I had a second child and they had to have separate beds. I would . . . unless the economy takes a turn for the worse, I would move out. But I definitely look at that place for insurance. I'm telling you. You could raise two children in there by the standards that people raise children up until like the 1950s: two in a room, two or three in a room. You can do it. That's what they were built for."

24. Barbara Bess Brown, "Territoriality," in Daniel Stokols and Irwin Altman, eds., *Handbook of Environmental Psychology*, Vol. 1, pp. 505–532; Frances M. Carp, "Environment and Aging," ibid., pp. 329–360; Stephanie Riger and Paul J. Lavrakas, "Community Ties: Patterns of Attachment and Social Interaction in Urban Neighborhoods"; Graham D. Rowles, "Growing Old 'Inside': Aging and Attachment to Place in an Appalachian Community"; Susan Saegert and Gary Winkel, "The Home: A Critical Problem for Changing Sex Roles"; Susan Saegert, "The Role of Housing in the Experience of Dwelling."

25. D. Geoffrey Hayward, "Psychological Concepts of Home Among Urban Middle Class Families with Young Children" (Ph.D. dissertation, City University of New York, The Graduate Center, Environmental Psychology Program, 1977); Charles J. Holohan, "Environmental Effects on Outdoor Social Behavior in a Low-Income Urban Neighborhood: A Naturalistic Investigation," *Journal of Applied Social Psychology* (1976), 6:48–63; Saegert and Winkel, "The Home: A Critical Problem for Changing Sex Roles."

26. Frances M. Carp, "Environment and Aging"; Kathleen Gerson, C. Ann Steuve, and Claude S. Fischer, "Attachment to Place"; Stephanie Riger and Paul J. Lavrakas, "Community Ties: Patterns of Attachment and Social Interaction in Urban Neighborhoods"; Alvin L. Schorr, (1963) *Slums and Social Insecurity;* Michael D. Young and Peter Willmott, *Family and Kinship in East London* (Glencoe, Ill.: Free Press, 1957).

27. Marjorie H. Cantor, "The Informal Support System"; Halford H. Fairchild and M. Belinda Tucker, "Black Residential Mobility: Trends and Characteristics"; Linton C. Freeman and Morris H. Sunshine, *Patterns of Residential Segregation.*

28. M. Powell Lawton, "The Elderly in Context: Perspectives from Environmental Psychology and Gerontology"; Graham D. Rowles, *Prisoners of Space? Exploring the Geographical Experience of Older People* (Boulder, Colo.: Westview Press, 1978).

29. Studies regarding the importance of proximity to services are reviewed in Carp, "Environment and Aging."

30. Barbara Bess Brown, "Territoriality, Street Form and Residential Burglary: A Social and Environmental Analysis" (Ph.D. dissertation, University of Utah, 1983); Robert B. Taylor, "Toward an Environmental Psychology of Disorder: Delinquency, Crime, and Fear of Crime," in Daniel Stokols and Irwin Altman, eds., *Handbook of Environmental Psychology*, pp. 951–986.

31. Sandra J. Newman and Michael S. Owen, "Residential Displacement: Extent, Nature, and Effects."

32. Relevant studies are reviewed in Carp, "Environment and Aging"; Daniel Stokols and Sally A. Shumaker, "The Psychological Context of Residential Mobility and Well-Being"; Daniel Stokols, Sally A. Shumaker and John Martinez, "Residential Mobility and Personal Well-Being" provides recent data clarifying these relationships.

33. See W. Dennis Keating, "Housing/CD Linkages: A Tested Strategy"; W. Dennis Keating, "Linking Downtown Development to Broader Community Goals: An Analysis of Linkage Policy in Three Cities," *Journal of the American Planning Association* (Spring 1986), 52:133–141.

10. STRUCTURING THE COMMUNITY-HOUSEHOLD MODEL

1. Peter Marcuse, "The Ideologies of Ownership and Property Rights," in Richard Plunz, ed., *Housing Form and Public Policy in the United States* (New York: Praeger, 1980).

2. William G. Grigsby and Louis Rosenburg, *Urban Housing Policy* (New York: APS, 1975).

3. See Barbara Solomon, "Alternative Social Services and the Black Woman," in Naomi Gottlieb, ed., *Alternative Social Services for Women*, pp. 333–345 (New York: Columbia University Press, 1980).

4. Richard S. Scobie, *Problem Tenants in Public Housing: Who, Where, and Why Are They?* (New York: Praeger, 1975), p. 68. Scobie, who has written what may be the definitive book on "problem tenants" in public housing, describes a range of responses by public agencies to the services issue. The Syracuse housing authority established a new staff position, "coordinator of social services," to organize social and recreational services in public housing. The welfare agency in Washington, D.C., located field offices in housing projects in order to decentralize caseworkers. Cincinnati resorted to a community organization approach in efforts to bring services to the projects. The education department in Gary, Indiana, offered home-economics training. In Columbus, Missouri, the Department of Agriculture sent extension agents to teach tenants the use of appliances. Boston created a multiservice center in one development and brought together an interdisciplinary team of a community organizer, home economist, family caseworkers, and area youth worker with group work training.

5. Francis X. Russo and George Willis, *Human Services in America* (Englewood Cliffs, N.J.: Prentice-Hall, 1986), p. 186.

6. Portions of this appeared in Jacqueline Leavitt, "The House of Ruth," *The Nation* (April 1988), 246:472–474.

7. Women United for a Better Chicago, *Women and Safe Shelter: Creating and Recreating Community* (resource directory for women seeking safe and affordable shelter/housing, University of Illinois at Chicago Circle, Chicago, n.d.), p. 119.

8. See Deborah Belle, "Social Ties and Social Support," in Deborah Belle, ed., *Lives in Stress: Women and Depression,* pp. 133–134.

Her findings were based on interviews with 43 women and their children. Belle reinforces Carol Stack's argument that it doesn't have to be those who are "free from drain" themselves to act as natural caregivers. Belle writes:

"It is the mothers who are least "free from drain" who must band together for their own survival and that of their children. The woman who lends her neighbor a pint of milk also needs that pint of milk, and the woman who tends her neighbor's children for an afternoon expends energy and attention on these children that she may well need for her own young ones. A woman provides such aid because in return she can then request such assistance when she needs it badly. Yet the costs of such giving should not be underestimated" (p. 142).

From our interviews, we conclude that mutual aid is more complicated than dividing the respondents into groups based on whether or not they are least free from drain. Particularly where older leaders were concerned, they were past the period of most demands regarding child-rearing. By banding together into shared leadership, they were able to go beyond their own experiences and make collective gains in their living environment.

We did not administer psychological tests or attempt to evaluate whether people we interviewed were depressed or not, other than in cases where the information was volunteered. This occurred with one black woman, a non-leader, with a life history of mental disorders, hospitalization, and depression; a second black woman told us she was going to therapy and it was clear that she was struggling with two small children by herself. That inadequate living conditions can compound individual stress seems self-evident. Christine H. Carrington, in "Depression in Black Women: A Theoretical Appraisal," in La Frances Rodgers-Rose, ed., *The Black Woman,* pp. 265–271, writes that black women, like white women, are socialized to nurture others around them. But the black woman "is still the lowest-paid worker, held in least esteem, and holds the least power on the economic-social hierarchical ladder" (p. 267). Carrington's work provides an important avenue of research that can combine an analysis of individual feelings with collective actions.

See also Denise G. Fairchild, "Social Activism Among Working Black Mothers" (Ph.D. dissertation, UCLA, 1987). Fairchild reviewed the literature and raised concern that there is so little known about role strain as it affects and is affected by civic and social roles. One of the findings of her study of 370 black women was that "social networks were positively related to participation." She found, however, that "they worked primarily to mediate the negative effects of family and job strain as it impacted social participation. Another important distinction was that extrafamilial support was most useful in offsetting affective aspects of family functioning, while household support worked directly to improve behavioral indices of family functioning. In other words, friends were more likely to provide moral or psychological support than they were to help out with child care, housekeeping, or other family duties. Household composition, especially in terms of numbers and ages of residents, was most critical for relieving family work load" (p. 181).

Our research would confirm this finding but there were also cases where family functioning services were mutually exchanged.

9. See Cheryl Townsend Gilkes, "'Holding Back the Ocean with a Broom': Black Women and Community Work," in La Frances Rodgers-Rose, ed., *The Black Woman*, pp. 217–231. Gilkes' study is based on 25 interviews with black women in the black community of Hamptonville (a pseudonym). Gilkes identifies the occupation that black women have as "community person." She writes:

"As one explores the situation of Black women known for their hard work, one discovers a division of labor within the community and a system of routine activities organized around coping with and eliminating the problems of oppression. One discovers that the problems existing within Hamptonville are so complex and differentiated that it takes a group of specialists working full-time to meet community needs" (p. 220).

These women have made, in Gilkes' words, "the step from the arena of 'private troubles' to the arena of 'public issues.' Once they are 'out there' and have shown some skill in solving problems shared by other members of the community, people seek them out." For them as for Mrs. Knotts, the telephone doesn't stop ringing. Gilkes quotes several of the leaders who describe the phone calls at all hours of the day and night:

"The telephone becomes a physical symbol of the license they have received from the local community whose demands for their skills exceed the abilities of the women to handle the demands. It is the variety and the number of these problems as well as the complex politics surrounding their solutions that produce these women's feeling that they are 'holding back the ocean with a broom'" (p. 222).

Gilkes then describes the mandate, which in our formulation of the community-household model would be for the leader or activist who speaks for more than the building. Corroborating the results of our own research, Gilkes finds that the woman leaders can find encouragement from the people that they are helping—while nevertheless being annoyed with what they see as "crisis-oriented and divisive behavior"—and "stand out as a group separate from the men engaged in community work."

"Housing, violence, employment, health, and legal problems are critical issues in Hamptonville's Black community. They have, as the women can see, their greatest impact on the youth of the community. Their roles as wives, mothers, aunts, and neighbors give them a special day-to-day insight into the community situation. The community generally agrees with them and defers to the women's expertise, treating them like the professionals they claim they are *not*" (p. 227).

10. A similar experience happened to Warren, the white leader of a building in Clinton, an area adjacent to Manhattan's theater district. He told us:

"It took almost two months to sit there and learn to do bookkeeping. I would come home from work and I would sit down and I would do this and it was learning the entire system of accounting from scratch. I bought accounting made simple and all those little guidebooks and how does a balance sheet, what does it look like, what does it mean, what do you do, what's an asset, what's a liability, where do the debits go, where do the credits go, and I put everything down and. . . . [I] hadn't taken the UHAB course, we weren't part of the TIL [program]. We were trying to get relieved of this 7A administration so we could become a TIL building."

11. Tied in with the restructuring of rents is the problem that some share-holders have understanding that they are responsible for repairs. Warren also faced difficulties when rents were being restructured. In one small 8-unit building David, a Hispanic leader, explained purchasing caused problems and led to an actual fist fight. He explained to us that raising rents is in the interest of the building, but "it's taken personally." There was not enough money for repairs, a situation that was aggravated by the delays in Section 8 rental assistance. This was the only building in which we interviewed where women were referred to as lacking basic educational skills and therefore unable to participate in management. In this very building, nevertheless, the president was a woman. In another building, it became apparent to the technical assistance person from UHAB that the tenant leader was learning basic skills through her activities as board president.

12. Ricardo, a Hispanic male leader, describes how rents affected decisions in his building, in the Manhattan Valley section of Manhattan, below 110th Street and between Broadway and Central Park West, to co-op.

"When we started some paid $89, another one $120, highest is about $180. So when we had our first meeting, people [who] came and they tried to impress the tenants. They said, well if you value your own building, the first thing you have to do is increase your rents. I remember when everybody tried to get rid of her, but what are they going to do. I was there and I had an idea. I said, wait a minute, let me ask you something. If we bought the building we would have to increase the rents, so what about if the Manhattan Managing Agency takes over the build-ing, are you going to increase the rents? They said yes, we will have to do that. I said well, since you are going to do each building like that, we will do it by ourselves. We will do our own raise. The tenants were very happy and they said how come you can think so fast and I said somebody told me about it."

Asked about how the tenants would respond to someone having trouble paying rent, Ricardo said:

"Like one of the tenants he has some problems and he said that he could not pay the rent for one month. He told us this in advance and let us know to the board members of the association what was going to happen that month because he has that kind of problem. It was okay with us because we knew in advance that he could not pay the rent for that month. He agreed to pay two months together the following month. This happened just one time and is over now.

So if it should happen, the best thing is to call the other tenants and the directors and let them know what is happening. Because if you don't pay your rent and then you don't say anything, maybe they can give us another idea. Because if that should happen, nobody can be perfect."

Warren's building in the Clinton section of Manhattan is primarily inhabited with people who make their living in the theater. He offered further insight into this issue. He described the rationale for *not* raising the rent of an elderly lady on the first floor who has a heart condition and yet chased away "a couple of thugs."

"First of all these people suffered through a great deal of hardship in the old days when the landlord didn't provide this that and the other thing, and they stayed and they kept it, and they kept it from getting broken into and they chased people out off the building. . . . So fair is fair, and it doesn't cost you anything more than that, it's not thousands of dollars, it's a couple of dollars. That's what it boils down to because you're spreading it amongst seventeen apartments."

He had this to say about a late rent policy:

"Well in a short-term thing we are very stringent about our rents. . . . We have a great infrastructure of fines, penalties, and assorted, you know, you get taken to the dungeon and why not. If we're in a position where we can afford not to pay our rent until maybe the 15th of the month a check is given to the treasurer and he is asked if he would mind holding onto it until it would be covered, and it's covered, and there's no big harrassment about it. It just happens. But on the long thing like where there's somebody who's out of work and go on unemployment or whatever, 160 dollars is not that bad, but when you mount that against everything else, yeah."

Warren went on to say that in ways other than the rent people helped such as the example he gave us of his roommate cooking for everyone. He said, "There's a constant kind of low level environment, like almost like a microcosm family, if you will." Two people on the first floor keep their doors open all the time and people are constantly stopping by saying hello and what's going on.

What has seemed to be more difficult to resolve stems from the lack of a deep reserve fund for emergencies. A fire had broken out in the building and severely damaged one apartment. In Warren's words:

"One of our people put out money, out-of-pocket, to repair the damages to his apartment. It is the consensus of the board that since he did this without requesting permission from the board to do it, without getting the proper contractor bids for the work, we cannot recognize the work. Therefore the only thing left, the only thing we can do and still be legal and be human about it is to give him an abatement of his rent till such time as we will either accept the work that he's done as making the apartment habitable. . . . He wanted the money now; he laid three thousand out-of-pocket and he needs the money. You know the guy has to go out and, he's a pianist, he has to go out and run a concert tour and he's gonna go out with fifty cents in his pocket and a subway token."

The board in the building was rethinking its contingency fund; there was bound to be a rent increase according to Warren. This was the only building where a leader told us of people moving in intentionally to make a profit, but in balance, the tenants were trying to sort through the issues to find a "logical humanitarian approach."

13. Michelle Neugebauer, "The Problem Tenant in Public Housing—A Preliminary Perspective" (Paper for a housing course at Columbia University, Graduate School of Architecture and Urban Planning, December 1981), p. 28. Also see,

Neugebauer, "Integrating Human Services Into New York's In-Rem Housing Program."

14. See Robert Kolodny, *Multi-Family Housing: Treating the Existing Stock.*

15. Harry C. Boyte, *Community Is Possible,* p. 101.

16. Ibid., p. 103. This type of bartering, using sweat equity, is found among people forming cooperatives in New York City.

17. Ibid., p. 103.

18. Robert Kolodny, *Multi-Family Housing: Treating the Existing Stock,* p. 70.

19. Terry L. Haywoode, "College for Neighborhood Women: Innovation and Growth," in Charlotte Bunch and Sandra Pollack, eds., *Learning Our Way,* p. 53.

20. Ibid., pp. 52–53.

21. Ibid., p. 55.

22. Ronnie Feit and Jan Peterson, (position paper on community development, NCNW, Brooklyn, New York, 1984); "National Women's Leadership and Community Development Program," NCNW, Brooklyn, N.Y., n.d.

23. National Congress of Neighborhood Women, "Preliminary Conference Report: Housing Options for Women" (Brooklyn, N.Y., October 9–12, 1987).

24. Rosemary Jackson, "Reclaiming Our Neighborhoods" (Paper presented at a conference at UCLA, Graduate School of Architecture and Urban Planning, May 14–15, 1988).

25. This perspective is also found in André Gorz' *Strategy for Labor: A Radical Proposal,* trans. Martin A. Nicolaus and Victoria Ortiz (Boston: Beacon, 1968), p. 7, n.2.

26. Urban Homesteading Assistance Board, *A Guide for Tenants Who Manage Their Own Buildings,* p. 13; Urban Homesteading Assistance Board, *Becoming A Cooperative.*

27. Common Space, "Cooperative Housing for Families" (Minneapolis: Common Space, n.d.).

28. Ibid., p. 10.

29. Milton Parc, "Milton Parc, A Co-operative Neighbourhood" (Montreal: Milton Parc, 1983), p. 6. Also see Christine Cousineau, "Milton Park: Housing Ownership and Community Control."

30. Ibid., p. 6.

31. Ibid., p. 6.

32. Ibid., p. 8.

33. Howard F. Andrews and Helen J. Breslauer, "Reflections on the Housing Process: Implications from a Case Study of Cooperative Housing," in *Cooperative Housing: A Case Study of Decision-Making in Design and User Satisfaction,* 4 vol. (Toronto: Centre for Urban and Community Studies, University of Toronto, 1976), pp. 17–31.

34. Ibid., p. 18.

35. Women United for a Better Chicago, "Women and Safe Shelter," p. 142.

36. We would like to acknowledge Elliot Sclar's bringing this concept to our attention in an article by Martin D. Lowenthal, "The Social Economy in Urban Working-Class Communities," pp. 447–469.

Building a sense of community can occur in rental properties with strong tenant management and a commitment to this. For example, Voice of the People Uptown is a case study of cooperative management in Chicago, Illinois. See Women United for a Better Chicago, "Women and Safe Shelter: Creating and Recreating Community." Voice of the People Uptown is an integrated community, 35 percent black, 23 percent Hispanic, 22 percent Asian, 6 percent American Indian, and 14 percent white.

"A tremendous challenge to Voice of the People in Uptown, Inc. in addition to the creation of low-income housing is to simultaneously create community among its low-income tenants. It's not just a matter of filling buildings with tenants as Dovie [the tenant organizer] points out: 'I was screened three times! That shows you how hard it is to get in.' Voice is a community of numerous languages, colors and cultural backgrounds trying to cooperate in their common struggle to overcome the social barriers they all confront in one way or another. Sharing safe, sanitary shelter is only the beginning" (p. 141).

37. William Brill and Associates have developed a training program for crisis intervention in public housing for tenants and staff, U.S. Department of Housing and Urban Development, Office of Policy Development and Research, November 1980.

38. Elise Boulding poses the question in general terms: "How and where do women learn?" (*The Underside of History: A View of Women Through Time,* pp. 25–27). What is useful is to look more closely at what she calls the social space where learning takes place. Boulding diagrams the relative importance of different social spaces—family, neighborhood/community, public ceremonial life and mass media, school or informal learning sites, ritual learning sites, work sites, and peer group—as women pass through childhood, adolescence, and adulthood. Although we agree in general with the concept of social learning in social spaces, we think relative weight and importance vary by marital status, ethnicity, race, numbers of children, and type of work.

39. Lewis Mumford, *The Urban Prospect,* pp. 18–19. Mumford wrote that housing development should encompass "the virtues of both a village and a kindergarten" and that "real human communities must preserve social as well as visual variety."

40. Gerda R. Wekerle and Suzanne MacKenzie, "Reshaping the Neighborhood of the Future As We Age in Place," p. 82.

41. Richard Kinch, "Strengthening Families Through Informal Support Systems" (Racine, Wis.: The Johnson Foundation, 1979), p. 8. Also see Russo and Willis. Complementing our community-households is their suggestion that neighborhoods are mediating structures between personal lives and "megastructures of American society such as big government, big labor, and big corporations" (p. 216). They write:

"Neighborhood support systems, therefore, are not limited to providing informal and personal supports. Neighborhood groups may be organized for community development or advocacy, with agendas that include projects such as gardening, preventing illness, controlling crime, creating jobs, conserving energy, and rehabilitating housing. . . . Although some [of these] groups have worked directly to improve the physical adequacy of housing in urban neighborhoods through means such as construction, rehabilitation, and tenant advocacy, they have also illustrated how their efforts can be linked with attempts to improve the larger physical and social environments of neighborhood residents. They also show how mediating structures such as voluntary neighborhood associations can improve the lives of individual urban residents by working cooperatively with the formal, governmentally sponsored systems of human services that exist in the United States" (p. 217).

42. UNESCO, "Training of 'Barefoot' Architects" (Bangkok: UNESCO Regional Office for Education in Asia and the Pacific, 1983), p. 2.

43. Ibid., p. 3.

44. Ibid., p. 5.

45. Ibid., p. 23.

46. Ann Withorn, "For Better and For Worse: Social Relations Among Women in the Welfare State," *Radical America* (1984), 18:37–47.

47. Carrington ("Depression in the Black Woman: A Theoretical Appraisal," in La Frances Rodgers-Rose, ed., *The Black Woman*) makes the point that with women who see that society treats them like losers knowledge is needed about both internal and external pressures. In so doing, Carrington presents an important research agenda:

"The most pervasive external factor operating on Black women is racism. We must understand not only the contemporary functioning of racism on Black women but also the historical functioning of racism. Specifically, we would need to know how racism interferes with the ability of Black women to earn a living, get an education, and help raise their children. Further, we would need to be able to separate those conditions which affect the psychological well-being of Black women; conditions which, on the surface, may not appear to be a consequence of racism but whose root causes are indeed racism. Likewise, we must begin to identify those factors that impinge on Black women which are the consequences of sexism. We need to know what the similarities are in the depressive states of Black and white women. Are there variations in the cause of depression between middle- and working-class Black women? Are some social classes more prone to depression than others?" (p. 270).

Carrington also includes questions about interpersonal relations among black women and with black men. Some of the questions she raises are: ". . . what types of interpersonal relations between Black women and men account for increases in depression among Black women. Are there differences in the depressive states of Black women who have mates and those who do not?" (p. 270).

48. Brill, "Crisis Intervention Training Curriculum for Public Housing Tenants and Staff," p. 16.

49. NCNW, *Guidelines for Women's Leadership Support Groups* (Brooklyn: NCNW, n.d.).

50. Brill, p. 20.

51. Ibid., p. 22.

52. NCNW, *Guidelines for Women's Leadership Support Groups.*

53. A complimentary set of questions may be found in Jacqueline Leavitt, "Fem-

inist Advocacy Planning in the 1980s," in Barry Checkoway, ed., *Strategic Perspectives on Planning Practice,* pp. 184–185 (Lexington, Mass.: D. C. Heath, 1986).
1. Does this reform [that is, plan] materially improve the lives of women, and if so, which women, and how many?
2. Does it build an individual woman's self-respect, strength, and confidence?
3. Does it give women a sense of power, strength, and imagination as a group and help build structures for further changes?
4. Does it educate women politically, enhancing their ability to criticize and challenge the system in the future?
5. Does it weaken patriarchal control of society's institutions and help women gain power over them?"
54. Ruth A. Brandwein, "Women and Community Organization," in Dianne S. Burden and Naomi Gottlieb, eds., *The Woman Client: Providing Human Services in a Changing World,* pp. 111–125 (New York: Tavistock, 1987).
55. Dolores Hayden, *The Grand Domestic Revolution: A History of Feminist Designs for American Homes, Neighborhoods, and Cities* (Cambridge, Mass.: MIT Press, 1981).
56. Brandwein, "Women and Community Organization," p. 112.
57. Susan Saegert, "The Androgenous City," in Gary Gappert and Richard V. Knight, eds., *Cities in the 21st Century,* pp. 196–212 (Beverly Hills, Calif.: Sage, 1982).
58. Brandwein, "Women and Community Organization," pp. 116–118.
59. Ibid., pp. 116–118.
60. Lisa Leghorn and Katherine Parker, *Woman's Worth: Sexual Economics and the World of Women* (Boston: Routledge & Kegan Paul, 1981).
61. Ibid., p. 287.
62. Dolores Hayden, *Redesigning the American Dream: The Future of Housing, Work, and Family Life;* Jacqueline Leavitt, "Two Prototypical Designs for Single Parents: The Congregate House and the New American House," in Karen A. Franck and Sherry Ahrentzen, eds., *New Households, New Housing* (New York: Van Nostrand Reinhold, 1989); Jacqueline Leavitt, "Rethinking Housing with the Homeless in Mind," in *Assisting the Homeless: State and Local Responses in an Era of Limited Resources* (Paper from a policy conference sponsored by the Advisory Commission on Intergovernmental Relations, Washington, D.C., 1988); Jos Boys, Frances Bradshaw, Jane Drake, Benedicte Foo, Sue Francis, Barbara McFarlane, and Marion Roberts, *Making Space: Women and the Man-Made Environment* (London: Pluto Press, 1984); Eugenie L. Birch, ed., *The Unsheltered Woman: Women and Housing in the Eighties* (New Brunswick, N.J.: Center for Urban Policy Research, 1985).
63. Marjorie H. Cantor, "Life Space and Social Support," in Thomas O. Byerts, Sandra C. Howell, and Leon A. Pastalan, eds., *Environmental Context of Aging: Life-styles, Environmental Quality, and Living Arrangements,* p. 38 (New York: Garland STPM Press, 1979).
64. Wekerle and MacKenzie, "Housing Alternatives for Women: The Canadian Experience," pp. 6, 9–72.

65. M. Powell Lawton, *Environment and Aging.*

66. Jacqueline Leavitt and Susan Saegert, "An Ideal American House."

67. Anne Vernez Moudon, "Platting Versus Planning: Housing at the Household Scale," *Landscape* (1986), 29:30–38.

68. Ibid., p. 34.

69. Dolores Hayden, "What Would a Non-Sexist City Be Like? Speculations on Housing, Urban Design, and Human Work."

70. Patrick H. Hare and Gail A. Price, "Home-Based Services: Expanding Social Services Without Expanding Public Facilities or Public Bureaucracies"; "Services Begin at Home."

71. Hilda K. Ross, "The Neighborhood Family: Community Mental Health for the Elderly."

72. Clara Fox, "A Vertical Neighborhood in an Urban Renewal Community: Report of the Goddard Tower Cooperative."

73. Vernez Moudon, "Platting Versus Planning: Housing at the Household Scale," p. 35.

74. Ibid., p. 38.

75. Cecilia Henning, *The Social Services as "Network Organizers"* (Stockholm: Swedish Building Council, 1987).

76. Leon Festinger, Stanley Schacter, Kurt Back, *Social Pressures in Informal Groups: A Study of Human Factors in Housing* (Stanford, Calif.: Stanford University Press, 1963).

11. COMMUNITY-HOUSEHOLDS IN SOCIETY

1. The Low Income Housing Information Service, Washington, D.C., 1988. The Service reports that the estimated figure for housing assistance programs for 1988 is $10.5 billion; proposed for 1989 is $9.2 billion. Different sources cite other figures; for example, David W. Myers in "The Affordability Gap: Millions Not Able to Buy a First Home," *Los Angeles Times,* May 15, 1988, Real Estate section, uses a $25 billion figure for 1981 and $7.1 billion for 1977.

2. In attempting to understand the place of households in the world economy, Immanuel Wallerstein has succinctly summarized the forces that face working-class households:

"The endless accumulation of capital is the defining characteristic and *raison d'etre* of this system. Over time, this endless accumulation pushes towards the commodification of everything, the absolute increase of world production, and a complex and sophisticated social division of labor. The objective of accumulation presupposes a system of polarizing distribution in which the majority of the world population serve as a labor force producing surplus-value, which is somehow distributed among the remaining minority of the world population."

"From the point of view of the accumulators of capital, what problems are posed by the ways in which this world labor force is produced and reproduced? I think the accumulators can be seen to have three main concerns:

"(1) They benefit by having a labor force whose use is variable in time. That is to say, individual entrepreneurs will want to have expenditures only directly related to production and therefore will not wish to pay a rental fee for future option on unused labor time. On the other hand, when they wish to produce, they also wish to have persons willing to work. The variation in time may be decade to decade, year to year, week to week, or even hour to hour.

"(2) They will benefit by having a labor force whose use is varible in space. That is to say, individual entrepreneurs will wish to locate or relocate their enterprises according to some considerations of costs (the costs of transport, the historical costs of labor power, and so on) without being unduly constrained by the existing geographical distribution of the world's labor force. The variation in space can be continent to continent, rural to urban or one particular immediate locus to another.

"(3) They will benefit by having the cost-level of the labor force as low as possible. That is to say, individual entrepreneurs will want their direct costs (in the form of wages, of indirect monetary payments, and of payments in kind) to be minimized, at least over some middle run" (pp. 17–18). Immanuel Wallerstein, "Household Structures and Labor-Force Formation in the Capitalist World-Economy," in Joan Smith, Immanuel Wallerstein, and Hans-Dieter Evers, eds., *Households and the World-Economy,* vol. 3 (Beverly Hills, Calif.: Sage, 1984).

3. For a recent analysis of the contradictory needs of capital accumulation as they relate to individuals, households, and communities, see Neal Smith and Peter Williams, eds., *Gentrification of the City;* David Bartlet, David Elesh, Ira Goldstein, George Leon, and William Yancy, "Islands in the Stream: Neighborhoods and the Political Economy of the City," in Irwin Altman and Abraham Wandersman, eds., *Neighborhood and Community Environment,* pp. 163–190, (New York: Plenum Press, 1987); Michael Peter Smith and Joe R. Feagin, eds. *The Capitalist City: Global Restructuring and Community Politics* (London: Basil Blackwell, 1987).

4. This can be seen in the designations of historic and special districts. See for example, Wayne Saitta, "Will Hell's Kitchen Serve Brunch? Zoning as a Tenant Protection Strategy Against Displacement," master's thesis, New York University, New York, June 1981.

5. Lisa W. Foderaro, "Harlem's Hedge Against Gentrification: Many Residents Finding Key Is Home Ownership," *The New York Times,* August 16, 1987, Real Estate section.

6. Thomas J. Lueck, "Japanese Interest in Harlem, Megaprojects Create Hope— And Fear," *The New York Times,* April 17, 1988, News of the Week in Review. Lueck was reporting on a range of proposals:

"Public officials and builders talk optimistically of plans for new apartment towers, theaters, recording studios, hotels, stores, offices and a trade center along a broad swath of the neighborhood, bounded roughly by the Hudson and East Rivers, and 110th and 155th Streets."

Residents should harbor some fears, since the reporter makes no differentiation between neighborhoods in Harlem that will be differentially impacted by such projects.

7. We have already described in the text and footnotes how the cooperatives provide jobs and a social life for older and retired people. There are other instances as well among the whites and Hispanics whom we interviewed. Warren, in the building in the Clinton section of Manhattan, spoke of ways in which residents formed a support group for a tenant when he was between jobs, offering meals and social acceptance. Warren also related the ways in which he uses skills learned in managing the building in his present job:

"This has been the experience of a lifetime. Not only learning about the hands on, the accounting, the managing of it, the paying of the bills, the taxes, the this and the that and the other thing, but the dealing with the people. The constant interaction of personalities and how to get people to do what you want them to do, you know. That's the kind of thing, and how to be calm and collected in the face of irrational arguments and totally irrational. I mean this business when we went from the $60 a month to the 160, you had to hear some of the arguments that were raised as to why the rents should all be lowered to $60 a month."

Ricardo, the Hispanic male leader of one of the few community management buildings that became a cooperative, offered some insight into the benefits he has gained from co-oping. His small 8-unit building includes several storefront businesses that help defray operating expenses. A tailor by profession, at the same time, he has been able to open a shop in the building.

8. These same positive effects were found among people in the co-op near Columbia University we have characterized as housing predominantly white, voluntary poor, residents. Michael Stansky, the current manager, reflected on life in the co-op and highlights the concentric rings of social networks in a 25-unit building. What the tenants in that building are feeling is in a way a reverse image of the more elderly black tenants, men and women. Where they looked back, relating how their neighboring occurred and how this was mobilized to fight abandonment, the younger people are looking ahead, anticipating the stages in life they would be going through:

"Now that we've co-oped, we look at each other like we're going to know each other for maybe the rest of our lives, and our kids might grow up together. Therefore, people who ordinarily might not have much to do with each other find themselves interacting together. I threw a party and invited about eight people from the building. There are certain people that you don't hit it off with, but by and large, most people are really friendly. We want to be a little community. We want to put a laundry room in, and we've read that some co-ops take that and make it into a little day-care center. We may at least get a couch or two in so that people could get together, the groups could get together and really change the nature of things. This is the age of isolation or anxiety, but I feel that I have a lot of friends in this building, and I don't have to be lonely. There are three apartments of people that I really consider good friends, and there are another three people that I could call on and talk to, and another three beyond that of people who speak to me in the hallway. It's really great."

In another interview, the building was Warren's social life. When asked about friends or relatives in the neighborhood, he replied that he was basically a loner, that his friends were the other cooperators and his co-workers.

9. Robert Kolodny, assisted by Marjorie Gellerman, *Self Help in the Inner City:* Ronald Lawson, *Owners of Last Resort: An Assessment of New York City Early Low Income Housing Cooperatives* (New York: New York City Department of Housing Preservation and Development, Office of Program and Management Analysis, 1983).

10. One promising avenue is the national demonstration by LISC (Local Initiatives Support Corporation), an offshoot of the Ford Foundation. LISC is linking corporations and community based groups, using new federal income tax credits, to produce rehabilitated units. See Anthony DePalma, "Tax Credits Produce Housing for the Poor," *The New York Times,* January 17, 1988, Real Estate section; for an overview see Arthur C. Nelson and Michael A. Stegman, "Tax Reform and Planners," *Journal of the American Planning Association* (Summer 1987), 53: 299–302.

11. A case in point is Ricardo's building in the Manhattan Valley section. At first, the community management group bought the building because the tenants couldn't agree enough. When the tenants realized that the community group would raise rents, and that the lease was for only two to three years (whereas they erroneously believed the tenant lease was for 99 years), the tenants decided to raise their own rents.

12. Allan David Heskin and Dewey Bandy, "The Dialectics of Community Planning," University of California at Los Angeles, School of Architecture and Urban Planning Working Paper, 1986; Allan David Heskin, "People's Justice: Decision Making in a Federation of Limited Equity Cooperatives," paper presented at the national American Planning Association Conference, Montreal, Canada, April 1985.

13. Information about this organization and those mentioned in the following section was obtained from presentations at "Mutual Housing Comes to New York: A Conference on a New Form of Housing Ownership and Development," organized by UHAB and funded by the Fund for The City of New York, January 1988.

14. Neighborhood Housing Services of America, Baltimore Office, has prepared *A Discussion Document for Formation of a Mutual Housing Association* (Baltimore: Neighborhood Housing Services of America, September 1981). It describes the elements of a MHA and the benefits and responsibilities of residents.

15. The Association of Neighborhood and Housing Development (ANHD) has over the past decade offered some of these services. At various times ANHD has connected individual groups and coalitions to political issues. UHAB has a similar history.

16. The Commission on the Year 2000, *New York Ascendant* (New York: New York City, June 1987). Chapter 7 is on housing.

17. Manhattan Borough President, "Comments on *New York Ascendant.*"

18. From the presentation of Mark Goldblatt, Executive Director of the Cooperative Housing Foundation of Canada, "Mutual Housing Comes to New York: A Conference on a New Form of Housing Ownership and Development" (New York, January 1988). For an analysis of the way in which co-op housing in Canada has provided grounds for class struggle, see Ruth Fincher and Susan Ruddick, "Transformation Possibilities Within the Capitalist State: Cooperative Housing and

Decentralized Health Care in Quebec," *International Journal of Urban and Regional Research* (March 1983), 7:44–71.

19. Howard F. Andrews and Helen J. Breslauer, "Reflections on the Housing Process: Implications from a Case Study of Cooperative Housing" (Report prepared for the Ministry of State for Urban Affairs, Centre for Urban and Community Studies, University of Toronto, February 1976), p. 50. See pp. 41–57 for a complete discussion of the authors' implications.

20. Ibid., pp. 53, 52.

21. John Mollenkopf, "New York: The Great Anomaly." *PS* (Summer 1986), 19(3):591–599. This issue of *PS* is a special issue on minority power in city politics.

22. Allan David Heskin and Robert Heffner, "Learning about Bilingual, Multicultural Organizing," Institute for Social Science Research, UCLA, Working Papers, 2 and 7 (Los Angeles, 1986).

23. Women United for a Better Chicago, *Women and Safe Shelter: Creating and Recreating Community* (Resource directory for women seeking safe and affordable shelter/housing, University of Illinois at Chicago Circle, Chicago, n.d.), p. 142.

24. See materials, "Low Income Housing Information Service," 1012 14th Street, Washington, D.C. 20005, a service of the National Low Income Housing Coalition.

25. Bruce Kappel, *The Prairie Housing Cooperative: A Case Study of a Cooperative, a Community, and a Cultural Event, 1982–1985* (Report for the Canadian National Institute on Mental Retardation, Toronto, July 1985); English materials on Stolplyckan and Lambohöv, Linköping, received from Marion Berger, in authors' files.

26. Richard P. Appelbaum, Chester Hartman, and Carole Norris brought together a group of housing people who met over a three-year period to draft a "Progressive Housing Program for America," July 1987. The group is also known as the Washington, D.C. based Institute for Policy Studies Working Group. Richard P. Appelbaum, Emily Achtenberg, Chester Hartman, Peter Marcuse, and Michael Stone had primary responsibility for putting the program into written form. Peter Drier, Jacqueline Leavitt, Christine Minnehan, and Carole Norris provided or edited drafts of specific sections. Also involved were John D. Atlas, Arthur Collings, Robert Goodman, Daniel Lindheim, Michael Rawson, Florence Roisman, and Joel Rubenzahl. The program "begins with the assumption that *every person is entitled to adequate housing in a decent neighborhood at an affordable price, with secure tenure, and meeting the special housing needs of women, minorities, and others traditionally disadvantaged in the housing market" (emphasis in original; p. 25).*

The program defined "social ownership" as housing "operated solely for resident and community benefit, subject to resident control and [which] cannot be resold for a profit. No one form of social ownership is to be favored over another, so long as the ownership arrangement is designed to further social housing goals, rather than private profits" (p. 25). The program also stated that residents will be involved in day-to-day decisions, through "non-profit management companies, mutual management associations, direct tenant management, or other forms of social management encouraged by the program" (p. 25).

27. Rhetaugh Graves Dumas, "Dilemmas of Black Females in Leadership," in

La Frances Rodgers-Rose, *The Black Woman*, ed., 203–215. Dumas proposes the "hydraulic systems principle of male-female relationships," where "black males can rise only to the degree that black women are held down. Finding themselves [the women] unable to submit to their dissatisfactions when survival in a hostile and increasingly violent environment held primacy and when a sense of community and togetherness seemed so essential, ambitious black females with leadership abilities concentrated their efforts on relieving the suffering imposed by illiteracy, poverty, and disease" (p. 204).

Among the women we interviewed, the congruence of their age and their desire to attain better living environments led to a situation where they often outnumber the men and thus their leadership abilities did not always rise in competition with men. However, it was clear that in Mr. Williams' building and Mr. Grayson's that Williams' wife and Grayson's friend, Mrs. Baylor, were supportive of the men's leadership.

28. Ibid., 204.
29. Ibid., 205.
30. Dumas sees a problem for black women leaders because:

"[Their leadership] is derived from her relationships in the *informal* system—her willingness to put her *person* at the disposal of those around her. And it can be maintained only as long as she is willing or able to provide what is demanded of her.

"The demands very often go beyond the responsibilities of her formal position. For example, the black woman in leadership is expected to comfort the weary and oppressed, intercede on behalf of those who feel abused, champion the cause for equality and justice—often as a lone crusader. She is expected to compensate for the deficits of other members of her group—speaking up for those who are unable or unwilling to speak for themselves, making demands on behalf of the weak or frightened, doing more than her assigned tasks. Expected to be mother confessor, she counsels and advises her superiors and peers as well as her subordinates, often on matters unrelated to the tasks at hand" (p. 207).

The women and men we interviewed are not usually accorded any status, for either formal or informal work, in the society. This record of what they do is intended not to glorify but to unveil their enormous amount of work that is often unrewarded and unrecognized. We agree with Cheryl Townsend Gilkes, who in "'Holding Back the Ocean With a Broom,'" in Rodgers-Rose, ed., *The Black Woman*, pp. 217–231, provides an alternative way of viewing the work that black women do in the community. Gilkes makes the argument for viewing community work as an occupation, drawing from Emmett C. Hughes' classic work on occupations. Gilkes writes:

"I hope to demonstrate that Black women, through their work in the community, aid the community in its response to the problems of surviving in a racist society while attempting to change that same society. They provide an interlocking network that binds together groups of competing interests and ideologies. I hope to show that an occupational analysis more than a social movement analysis of Black women's work provides a key to understanding the potential stress and strain which exists within Black communities as they deal with the routine problems of oppression" (p. 218).

However, we also think that a social movement analysis can connect the struggles of the people we interviewed to the larger society.

31. Gerda R. Wekerle, *Women's Housing Projects in Eight Canadian Cities* (Report to the Canada Mortgage and Housing Corporation, 1987, CR File No.:6858/W7:1).

32. See Jacqueline Leavitt, "Housing Acts and Architects," *Progressive Architecture* (October 1988), 69:9.

33. The CRA is one of two major agencies in Los Angeles involved in housing; the other is the Housing Authority. The CRA has the power to designate redevelopment areas where new development is taxed and the difference between the old tax assessment and the new accrues in a fund that can be used to refinance and subsidize low-income housing. This discussion draws from minutes of meetings and position papers of Housing L.A. and newspaper clippings—materials which are in the authors' files.

34. The idea that there is a people component to planning was a part of 1960's programs. To begin with, President Johnson endorsed the rebuilding of the slums as a coordinated set of programs, not just "brick and mortar." A task force report had called for a program for cities to cover a large area with a series of mandates, which, had they been accomplished, would have been a major advance in restructuring power relations between the rich and poor, bureaucratic agencies, administrative regulations. The recommended program anticipated private-public partnerships by two decades, and would have produced results in two years and assured funding for five years. The program that emerged was far more modest in its implementation. Model Cities was influenced by the preceding anti-poverty programs of the Office of Economic Opportunity, and in particular its Community Action Program. The intent of Model Cities was to coordinate a variety of resources and develop innovative programs, specifically tied to the physical environment—housing, infrastructure and transportation—bringing in social welfare, job creation, health care, and education programs for the population living in designated areas.

Underfunded, uneven in their application, politically untenable, and unable to match the structural changes in the economy, these programs were not likely to bring about major social changes. What was remarkable was that some people benefited through paid jobs, improved housing and services, and the programs provided a basis for leadership development among blacks. There was a certain amount of mobility that occurred as confining boundaries of ghettos around the country burst open, either as a result of riots and rebellions, or because indigenous leaders traveled to Washington, D.C., or even downtown city halls—a new experience for many—to ask for more funding. As disappointment with the War on Poverty and Model Cities set in, another approach toward alleviating conditions of the poor was being developed through Community Development Corporations (CDCs). Charles Hampden-Turner has interpreted the CDC's rise to the failure of the War on Poverty to give poor people control over the structure of development. Geoffrey Faux, an early theoretician of the CDC movement, has distinguished it from a variety of different agencies, beginning with Community Action and Model Cities agencies, which were not controlled by representatives of impoverished areas and which did not themselves engage directly in economic development programs; from municipal economic development agencies, which may have supported and provided technical assistance to ghetto development, but which did not implement programs and were not controlled by representatives of impoverished areas; and from local private nonprofit agencies established to help minority entrepreneurs. See Charles Hampden-Turner, *From Poverty to Dignity: A Strategy for Poor Americans* (Garden City, N.Y.: Anchor, Doubleday, 1974); Peter Marris and Martin Rein, *Dilemmas of Social Reform: Poverty and Community Action in the United States,* 2d ed. (Chicago: University of Chicago Press, 1982).

35. Hampden-Turner, *From Poverty to Dignity: A Strategy for Poor Americans,* pp. 116–117, 119.

36. Ibid., p. 118.

37. Ibid., p. 118.

38. Ibid., pp. 118–119.

39. Ibid., p. 125.

40. Ibid., p. 128.

41. A similar point is made by a nonprofit developer, Becky Johnson, whose work in New England is around creating land trusts and cooperatives. She has observed that cooperatives are more empowering for women than are other structures. (Becky Johnson, "Housing Design and Development for Women" [Presentation at a conference, "The Women and Planning: Theory, Practice, and Teaching" Massachusetts Institute of Technology, Boston, 10–11, March 1988]).

42. Mrs. T. J. Bowlker, "Woman's Home-Making Function Applied to the Municipality," *American City* (June 1912), 6:863–869.

43. Betty Friedan, *The Feminine Mystique* (New York: Norton, 1963).

44. In the preface to *Woman's Work: The Housewife, Past and Present* (New York: Vintage Books, 1976), Ann Oakley writes:

"First of all, this is a book about *women.* It is not a book about marriage or the family, and it does not aim to look at the situations of men and women equally. In current social imagery "housewife" is a term often used casually to mean "woman," "wife," or even "mother." In this book, the term "housewife" refers only to women's unpaid work role in the home (emphasis in original).

"A vast number of books have been written about men and their work; by contrast, the work of women has received very little serious sociological or historical attention. Their unpaid work in the home has scarcely been studied at all. This book is an attempt partially to redress this balance. Its perspective is feminist: it challenges the set of conventional values which label work a masculine activity and assign women to the home."

45. Joann Vanek, "Time Spent in Housework," *Scientific American* (November 1974), 231:116–20.

46. Eva Kaluzynska, "Wiping the Floor with Theory—A Survey of Writings on Housework," *Feminist Review* (1980), 6:27–54.

47. Ruth Schwartz Cowan, *More Work for Mother: The Ironies of Household Technology from the Open Hearth to the Microwave* (New York: Basic Books, 1983).

48. Susan Strasser, *Never Done: A History of American Housework* (New York:

Pantheon Books, 1982). Strasser nicely summarizes the relationship between housework and the economy:

"No static conception of the function of housework in the economy will provide the theoretical basis for a clear historical picture. The colonial household was colonial society, as one historian, calling it 'the little commonwealth,' points out; it served the functions of home, factory, school, and welfare institution. One by one, private industry and government have assumed those functions, moving the work of the household from the private realm to the public. Before industrialization, most housework produced goods and services used within the household: women spun and wove cloth and sewed it into clothes, grew food and prepared it for eating or storage, made soap and candles, and washed clothes for other family members, who shared those tasks and—according to the sexual division of labor—worked in the fields and as small craftsmen. As increasing numbers of men and single women went to work in factories during the nineteenth century, housewives served their society by reproducing the labor force, both in the literal sense of conceiving, bearing, and caring for children and in the broader one of preparing workers to go to work daily. At the end of the century, as households began to consume the products of American society, as the economy expanded and factories produced a wide variety of consumer goods on a mass scale, housewives began to serve the economy by organizing consumption for the individual households" (p. 5; underlining in original).

49. See for example, Michelle Barrett, *Women's Oppression Today: Problems in Marxist Feminist Analysis* (London: Verso Editions and New Left Books, 1980); Johanna Brenner and Maria Ramas, "Rethinking Women's Oppression," *New Left Review* (1984), 144:33–71.

50. Kaluzynska, "Wiping the Floor with Theory—A Survey of Writings on Housework," p. 37.

51. Juanita Krebs, *Sex in the Marketplace: American Women at Work* (Baltimore: Johns Hopkins University Press, 1971).

52. This is also reflected in Ann Petry's novel, *The Street,* when Lutie is forced to take a job as a live-in domestic in Lyme, Connecticut. Her husband and child are left in New York City; Lutie sends them money and only quits when her father writes her that her husband has been living with another woman.

53. Lisa Leghorn and Katherine Parker, *Woman's Worth: Sexual Economics and the World of Women* (Boston: Routledge & Kegan Paul, 1981), p. 170.

54. Suzie Fleming, "Housework for Sale," *Centerpiece* (March 1986), 3:8.

55. Suzie Fleming, "Eleanor Rathbone: Spokeswoman for a Movement," introductory essay to *The Disinherited Family* by Eleanor Rathbone (Bristol, England: Falling Wall Press, 1986; original publication, 1924), pp. 9–120.

56. Ibid., 12.

57. Leghorn and Parker, *Woman's Worth: Sexual Economics and the World of Women,* p. 304.

58. Ray E. Pahl, *Divisions of Labour* (Oxford: Basil Blackwell, 1984), p. 84.

59. William M. Nicholls and William A. Dyson, *The Informal Economy: Where People Are the Bottom Line* (Ottawa: Carrier Institute of the Family, 1983).

60. David P. Ross and Peter J. Usher, *From the Roots Up: Economic Development As If Community Mattered* (Croton-on-Hudson, N.Y.: Bootstrap Press, 1986).

61. Roger Starr, "Introduction," in Ira S. Robbins, with Gus Tyler, *Reminiscences of a Housing Advocate* (New York: Citizen's Housing and Planning Council of New York, 1984), p. 7.

62. See Kaluzynska, "Wiping the Floor with Theory—A Survey of Writings on Housework." For the opposing view, see Fleming, "Housework for Sale," where she makes the arguments in a review of Ellen Malos, ed., *The Politics of Housework* (London: Alison and Busby, 1980).

63. Hilary Rose, "In Practice Supported, in Theory Denied: An Account of an Invisible Urban Movement," *International Journal of Urban and Regional Research* (October 1978), 2:521–537.

64. Temma Kaplan, "Female Consciousness and Collective Action: The Case of Barcelona, 1910–1918," *SIGNS: Journal of Women in Culture and Society* (Spring 1982), 7:545–566.

65. See, for example, John Friedmann and Mauricio Salguero, "The Barrio Economy and Collective Self-Empowerment in Latin America: A Framework and Agenda for Research," in Michael Peter Smith, ed., *Power, Community and the City: Comparative Urban and Community Research,* vol. 1 (New Brunswick, N.J.: Transaction Books, 1988). Friedmann and Salguero's research on Latin America reflects a direction that can be usefully applied to the United States, particularly when informed by feminist thinking and gender research. In this regard, see Caroline O. N. Moser and Linda Peake, eds., *Women, Human Settlements, and Housing* (London: Tavistock, 1987).

REFERENCES

Anderson, Jervis. *Harlem, the Great Black Way, 1900–1950.* London: Orbis, 1982.

Appelbaum, Richard, Chester Hartman, Carol Norris, et al. "National Comprehensive Housing Program." National Task Force on Housing Policy, February 1985.

Aptheker, Bettina. *Women's Legacy: Essays on Race, Sex, and Class in American History.* Amherst: University of Massachusetts Press, 1982.

Auletta, Kenneth. *The Streets Were Paved With Gold.* New York: Vintage Books, 1980.

Belenky, Mary Field, Blythe McVicker Clinch, Nancy Rule Goldberger, and Jill Mattuck Tarule. *Women's Ways of Knowing: The Development of Self, Voice, and Mind.* New York: Basic Books, 1986.

Belle, Deborah, ed. *Lives in Stress: Women and Depression.* Beverly Hills, Calif.: Sage, 1982.

Bonnett, Aubrey W. "Volunteerism Among West Indian Immigrants." In Vernon Boggs, Gerald Handel, and Sylvia Fava, eds., *The Apple Sliced: Sociological Studies of New York City,* pp. 118–130. New York: Praeger, 1984.

Boulding, Elise. *The Underside of History: A View of Women Through Time.* Boulder, Colo: Westview Press, 1976.

Boyte, Harry C. *Community Is Possible: Repairing America's Roots.* New York: Harper and Row, 1984.

Burghardt, Steve. *The Other Side of Organizing: Resolving the Personal Dilemmas and Political Demands of Daily Practice.* Cambridge, Mass.: Schenkman, 1982.

Burns, Leland S. and Leo Grebler. *The Future of Housing Markets: A New Appraisal.* New York. Plenum Press, 1986.

Cantor, Marjorie H. "Life Space and Social Support." In Thomas O. Byerts, Sandra C. Howell, and Leon C. Pastalan, eds., *Environmental Context of Aging: Lifestyles, Environmental Quality, and Living Arrangements,* pp. 33–63. New York: Garland STPM Press, 1979.

Cantor, Marjorie, H. "The Informal Support System." In Edgar F. Borgatta and Neil G. McClusky, eds., *Aging and Society,* pp. 131–144. Beverly Hills, Calif.: Sage, 1980.

Capeci, D. J., Jr. "The Harlem Riot of 1943." Ph.D. dissertation, University of California at Riverside, 1970.

Carp, Frances M. "Environment and Aging." In Daniel Stokols and Irwin Altman, eds., *Handbook of Environmental Psychology,* 1:329–360. New York: Wiley, 1987.

Co-operative Housing Federation of Toronto. "Group Dynamics Workshops." Co-operative Housing Foundation of Canada, Toronto, June 1984.

Cousineau, Christine. "Milton Park: Housing Ownership and Community Control." M.A. thesis, MIT, 1980.

Cunningham, Roger A. "The New Implied Statutory Warranties of Habitability in Residential Leases: From Contract to Status." *Urban Law Annual* (1979), 16:3–154.

deCourcy Hinds, Michael. "252,000 Housing Units: Can Koch Do It?" *The New York Times,* June 22, 1986, sec. 8.

DePalma, Anthony. "New York Plays Reluctant Landlord," *The New York Times,* December 14, 1986, sec. 8.

Ehrenreich, Barbara. "Two, Three, Many Households." *Mother Jones.* 9 (1986): 8–9.

Ehrenthal, Samuel M. "New York City's Labor Force." *City Almanac* (December 1983), 17:1–12.

Engler, May and Roberta R. Spohn. "The Elderly in New York City: Demographic Characteristics." In Eugenie L. Birch, ed., *The Unsheltered Woman: Women and Housing in the Eighties,* pp. 53–67. New Brunswick, N.J.: Center for Urban Policy Research, 1985.

Fairchild, Halford H. and M. Belinda Tucker. "Black Residential Mobility: Trends and Characteristics." *Journal of Social Issues* (1982), 38:51–74.

Farge, Brenda Doyle. "Women, Leadership and Co-op Housing: Some Questions." *Women and Environments* (Winter 1986), 8:13–15.

Fox, Clara. "A Vertical Neighborhood in an Urban Renewal Community: Report of the Goddard Tower Cooperative." New York: Goddard-Riverside Community Center, 1969.

Freedman, Samuel G. "Harlem and the Speculators: Big Profits but Little Renewal," *The New York Times,* December 9, 1986.

Freeman, Linton C. and Morris H. Sunshine. *Patterns of Residential Segregation.* Cambridge, Mass. Schenkman, 1970.

Gerson, Kathleen, C. Ann Steuve, and Claude S. Fischer. "Attachment to Place." In Claude S. Fischer, ed., *Networks and Places: Social Relations in the Urban Setting,* pp. 139–161. New York: Free Press, 1987.

Giddings, Paula. *When and Where I Enter . . . .: The Impact of Black Women on Race and Sex in America.* New York: William Morrow, 1984.

Gilligan, Carol. *In A Different Voice: Psychological Theory and Women's Development.* Cambridge, Mass.: Harvard University Press, 1982.

Gribetz, Judah and Frank P. Grad. "Housing Code Enforcement: Sanctions and Remedies." *Columbia Law Review* (1966), 66:1254–1290.

Gutman, Herbert G. *The Black Family in Slavery and Freedom, 1750–1925.* New York: Vintage Books, 1976.

Guy, Rosa. *Bird At My Window.* Philadelphia. Lippincott, 1966.

Hare, Patrick H. and Gail A. Price. "Home-Based Services: Expanding Social Services Without Expanding Public Facilities or Public Bureaucracies," Staff Working Paper, 1985.

Hare, Patrick, H. and Gail A. Price. "Services Begin at Home." *Planning* (September 1985), 51:24–25.

Hayden, Dolores. *Redesigning the American Dream: The Future of Housing, Work, and Family Life.* New York: Norton, 1984.

Hayden, Dolores. "What Would a Non-Sexist City Be Like? Speculations on Housing, Urban Design, and Human Work." In Rachel G. Bratt, Chester Hartman, and Ann Meyerson, eds., *Critical Perspectives on Housing,* pp. 230–246. Philadelphia: Temple University Press, 1986.

Hayward, D. Geoffrey. "Psychological Concepts of Home Among Urban Middle-Class Families with Young Children." Ph.D. dissertation, The City University of New York, The Graduate Center, Environmental Psychology Program, 1977.

Haywoode, Terry, L. "College for Neighborhood Women: Innovation and Growth." In *Learning Our Way: Essays in Feminist Education.* Charlotte Bunch and Sandra Pollack, eds. Trumansburg, N.Y.: Crossing Press, 1983.

Heskin, Allan David. "People's Justice: Decision Making in a Federation of Limited Equity Cooperatives." Paper Delivered at the American Planning Association, Montreal, Canada, 1985.

Huggins, Nathan Irvin. *Harlem Renaissance.* New York: Oxford University Press, 1971.

Jacob, John E. "An Overview of Black America in 1985." In J. D. Williams, ed. *The State of Black America, 1986,* pp. ii–xi. New York: National Urban League, 1986.

Jones, Jacqueline. *Labor of Love, Labor of Sorrow.* New York: Basic Books, 1985.

Keating, W. Dennis. "Housing/ CD Linkages: A Tested Strategy." *Journal of Housing* (1986), 43:101–103, 138.

Kolodny, Robert. *Multi-family Housing: Treating the Existing Stock.* Washington, D.C.: National Association of Housing and Redevelopment Officials, 1981.

Kolodny, Robert, assisted by Marjorie Gellerman. *Self Help in the Inner City: A Study of Lower Income Cooperative Housing Conversion in New York.* New York: United Neighborhood Houses of New York, 1973.

Ladner, Joyce A. "Teenage Pregnancy: The Implications for Black Americans." In J. D. Williams, ed., *The State of Black America 1986,* pp. 65–84 New York: National Urban League, 1986.

Lawson, Ronald, ed., with Mark Naison. *The Tenant Movement in New York City, 1904–1984.* New Brunswick, N.J.: Rutgers University Press, 1986.

Lawton, M. Powell. "The Elderly in Context. Perspectives from Environmental Psychology and Gerontology." *Environment and Behavior* (1985), 17:501–519.

Lawton, M. Powell. *Environment and Aging.* Monterey, Calif.: Brooks-Cole, 1980.

Leavitt, Jacqueline. "A Neighborhood Housing Strategy for Community Board 9." Project of the Board 9 studio, Division of Urban Planning, Columbia University, Graduate School of Architecture and Urban Planning, 1978.

Leavitt, Jacqueline. "Resident and Community Receivership Programs in New York City." In Richard Plunz, ed., *Housing Form and Public Policy.* New York. Praeger, 1983.

Leavitt, Jacqueline and Susan Saegert. "An Ideal American House." *MS.* (July 1985), 14:81–82.

Leavitt, Jacqueline and Susan Saegert. *The Tenants Report: A Study of DAMP Buildings After Sale.* Report prepared for the New York City Department of Housing Preservation and Development, 1985.

Listokin, David, Lisabeth Alleweit, and James J. Németh. *Housing Receivership and Self-Help Neighborhood Revitalization.* New Brunswick, N.J.: Center for Urban Policy Research, 1985.

Lowenthal, Martin D. "The Social Economy in Urban Working-Class Communities." In Gary Gappert and Harold Rose, eds., *Social Economy of Cities,* pp. 447–469. Beverly Hills, Calif.: Sage, 1975.

Mann, Nathan H., ed. "Receivership of Problem Buildings in New York City and Its Potential for Decent Housing for the Poor." *Columbia Journal of Law and Social Problems* (Spring 1973), 5:309–362.

Marcus, Clare Cooper and Wendy Sarkissian. *Housing As If People Mattered: Site Design Guidelines for Medium-Density Family Housing.* Berkeley: University of California Press, 1986.

Marcuse, Peter. "Abandonment, Gentrification, and Displacement: The Linkages in New York City." In Neal Smith, and Peter Williams, eds., *Gentrification of the City,* pp. 153–177. Boston: Allen and Unwin, 1966.

Marcuse, Peter. *Housing Abandonment: Does Rent Control Make a Difference?* Conference on Alternative State and Local Policies, Washington, D.C., 1981.

Marris, Peter and Martin Rein. *Dilemmas of Social Reform: Poverty and Community Action in the United States.* 2d ed. Chicago: University of Chicago Press, 1987.

Martin, Joanne M. and Elmer P. Martin. *The Helping Tradition in the Black Family and Community.* Silver Springs, Md.: National Association of Social Workers, 1985.

Mumford, Lewis. *The Urban Prospect.* New York: Harcourt, Brace & World, 1968.

Myerhoff, Barbara. *Number Our Days.* New York: Touchstone, 1978.

Neugebauer, Michelle. "Integrating Human Services Into New York's In-Rem Housing Programs." M.A. thesis, Columbia University, 1984.

Newman, Sandra J. and Michael S. Owen. "Residential Displacement: Extent, Nature, and Effects." *Journal of Social Issues* (1982), 38:135–148.

Noble, Jeanne L. *Beautiful, also are the souls of my black sisters: A history of black women in America.* Englewood Cliffs, N.J.: Prentice-Hall, 1978.

Noddings, Nel. *Caring: A Feminine Approach to Ethics and Moral Education.* Berkeley: Calif.: University of California Press, 1984.

Norton, Eleanor Holmes. "Restoring the Traditional Black Family." *The New York Times Magazine,* June 2, 1985.

Osofsky, Gilbert. *Harlem: The Making of a Ghetto: Negro New York, 1890–1930.* 2d ed. New York: Harper Torchbooks, 1971.

Perry, Margaret. *Silence to the Drums: A Survey of the Literature of the Harlem Renaissance.* Westport, Conn.:Greenwood, Press, 1976.

Petry, Ann. *The Street,* Boston: Houghton Mifflin, 1946. Reprint. Boston: Beacon Press, 1985.

Rae, Ruth A. "The Facade is Fake: Perceptions of the Occupied Look Program." Paper prepared for second-year Ph.D. Environmental Psychology Program, City University of New York, Graduate Center, August 6, 1968, draft.

Rainwater, Lee. *Behind Ghetto Walls: Black Family Life in a Federal Slum.* Chicago: Aldine, 1970.

Reagan, Barbara B., ed. *Census Bureau Conference on Issues in Federal Statistical Needs Relating to Women.* Current Population Reports, Special Studies, Series P-23, No. 83, December 1979.

Reagon, Bernice Johnson. "My Black Mothers and Sisters or On Beginning a Cultural Autobiography." *Feminist Studies* (Spring 1982), 8:82–96.

Riger, Stephanie and Paul J. Lavrakas. "Community Ties: Patterns of Attachment and Social Interaction in Urban Neighborhoods." *American Journal of Community Psychology* (1981), 9:55–66.

Robbins, Ira S., with Gus Tyler. *Reminiscences of a Housing Advocate.* New York: Citizens' Housing and Planning Council, 1984.

Rogers-Rose, La Frances, ed. *The Black Woman.* Beverly Hills, Calif.: Sage, 1980.

Rosahn, Beatrice G. *Housing Management—Its History and Relation to Present-Day Housing Problems.* New York: National Municipal League, 1935.

Ross, Hilda K. "The Neighborhood Family: Community Mental Health for the Elderly." *The Gerontologist* (1983), 23:243–247.

Rowles, Graham D. "Growing Old 'Inside': Aging and Attachment to Place in an Appalachian Community." In Nancy Datan and Nancy Lohmann, eds., *Transitions of Aging,* pp. 153–172. New York: Academic Press, 1980.

Russell, Karen K. "Growing Up with Privilege and Prejudice." *The New York Times Magazine,* June 14, 1987.

Saegert, Susan. "The Role of Housing in the Experience of Dwelling." In Irwin Altman and Carol Werner, eds., *Home Environments*. Vol. 8, *Human Behavior and Environments*, pp. 287–309. New York: Plenum Press, 1986.

Saegert, Susan, Theodore Liebman, and R. Alan Melting. "Working Women: The Denver Experience." In Eugenie L. Birch, ed. *The Unsheltered Woman: Women and Housing in the 80's*, pp. 83–99. New Brunswick, N.J.: Center for Urban Policy Research, 1985.

Saegert, Susan and Gary Winkel. "The Home: A Critical Problem for Changing Sex Roles." In Gerda Wekerle, Rebecca Peterson, and David Morley, eds., *New Space for Women*, pp. 41–63. Boulder, Colo.: Westview Press, 1980.

Sanchez, Sonia. *Homegirls & Handgrenades*. New York: Thunder's Mouth Press, 1984.

Schaffer, Richard and Neil Smith. "The Gentrification of Harlem?" *Annals of the Association of American Geographers* (1986), 76:347–365.

Schniedewind, Nancy. "Feminist Values: Guidelines for A Teaching Methodology in Women's Studies." In Charlotte Bunch and Sandra Pollack, eds., *Learning Our Way: Essays in Feminist Education*, pp. 261–271. Trumansburg, N.Y.: Crossing Press, 1983.

Schoener, Allon. *Harlem On My Mind: Cultural Capital of Black America, 1900–1968*. New York: Metropolitan Museum of Art, 1978.

Schorr, Alvin L. *Slums and Social Insecurity: An Appraisal of the Effectiveness of Housing Policies in Helping To Eliminate Poverty in the United States*. Washington, D.C.: U.S. Department of Health, Education, and Welfare, 1963.

Schur, Robert and Virginia Sherry. *The Neighborhood Housing Movement*. New York: Association of Neighborhood Housing Developers, 1977.

Smith, Neal and Peter Williams, eds. *Gentrification of the City*. Boston: Allen and Unwin, 1986.

Stack, Carol. *All Our Kin*. New York: Harper and Row, 1974.

Stegman, Michael. *Housing in New York: Study of a City, 1982*. New York: Department of Housing Preservation and Development, 1982.

Stegman, Michael, with Doug Hillstrom. *Housing in New York: Study of a City, 1984*. New York: Department of Housing Preservation and Development, 1985.

Stokols, Daniel and Irwin Altman, eds. *Handbook of Environmental Psychology*. Vol. 1. New York: Wiley, 1987.

Stokols, Daniel and Sally A. Shumaker. "The Psychological Context of Residential Mobility and Well-Being." *Journal of Social Issues* (1982), 38:149–171.

Stokols, Daniel, Sally A. Shumaker, and John Martinez. "Residential Mobility and Personal Well-Being." *Journal of Environmental Psychology* (1983), 3:4–19.

Sullivan, Brian, Robert Schur, Howard Burchman, and Meadows/Woll. "Analysis and Assessment of the Alternative Management Programs for New York City's In Rem Properties." U.S. Department of Housing and Urban Development, Washington, D.C., 1982.

Swinton, David. "Economic Status of Blacks 1985." In J. D. Williams, ed., *The State of Black America 1986*, pp. 1–21. New York: National Urban League, 1986.

"Symposium: Code Enforcement: Issues and Answers for the '80s." *University of Detroit Journal of Urban Law* (Spring 1983), vol. 60.

Tabb, William K. *The Long Default: New York City and the Urban Fiscal Crisis.* New York: Monthly Review Press, 1982.

UNESCO. "Training of 'Barefoot' Architects." UNESCO Regional Office for Education in Asia and the Pacific, Bangkok, 1983.

United States Department of Housing and Urban Development. Office of Policy Development and Research. *Project Self-Sufficiency: Guidebook.* Washington, D.C.: GPO, 1985.

Urban Homesteading Assistance Board. *Becoming A Cooperative.* New York: Urban Homesteading Assistance Board, 1984.

Urban Homesteading Assistance Board. *A Guide for Tenants Who Manage Their Own Buildings.* New York: Urban Homesteading Assistance Board, 1984.

Vernez Moudon, Anne. "Platting versus Planning: Housing at the Household Scale." *Landscape* (1986), 29:30–38.

Wade-Gayles, Gloria. *No Crystal Stair: Visions of Race and Sex in Black Women's Fiction.* New York: Pilgrim Press, 1984.

Wekerle, Gerda R. and Suzanne MacKenzie. "Reshaping the Neighbourhood of the Future As We Age in Place." *Canadian Women Studies* (Spring 1985), 6:69–72.

Wekerle, Gerda R. and Joan Simon. "Housing Alternatives for Women: The Canadian Experience." *Urban Resources* (Winter 1986), 3:9–14.

Women Plan Toronto. "Shared Experiences and Dreams." Toronto, Canada, 1986.

Wood, Elizabeth. "The Public and Mrs. McGee." New York: Citizens' Housing and Planning Council of New York, 1956.

Zarza, Daniel and Harriet Cohen. *Loisiada: Strategies for Neighborhood Revitalization.* Report prepared for the U.S. Department of Housing and Urban Development, December 18, 1979.

INDEX